D1032747

Dryden and the Conservative Myth

A Reading of *Absalom and Achitophel*

Dryden and the Conservative Myth

A Reading of *Absalom and Achitophel*

by BERNARD N. SCHILLING

New Haven and London, Yale University Press, 1961

Publication of this book has been aided
by grants from the foundation
established in memory of
Amasa Stone Mather of the
Class of 1907, Yale College, and the
Louis Stern Memorial Fund.

FOR SUSAN

Acknowledgments

My work has been done entirely in four libraries: Rush Rhees Library of the University of Rochester, the Folger Shakespeare Library, Sterling Memorial Library at Yale, and the Library of the British Museum. I am greatly obliged to Mr. John Russell, Mr. Raymond Maier, Miss Vera Tweddell, Miss Marian Allen, and their associates in Rush Rhees Library for excellent service over many years. Mr. Louis B. Wright of the Folger Shakespeare Library was good enough to provide a fellowship which enabled me to continue my work at a vital stage. I wish to thank him and his excellent staff for their assistance. I have made the greatest demands upon Sterling Memorial Library at Yale, beginning with my years as a graduate student. The courtesy and helpfulness always available there have been indispensable. A year spent largely in the North Library of the British Museum enabled me to bring my work to conclusion. I wish to thank Mr. Dennis Rhodes and his colleagues for excellent service under trying conditions.

Mr. Lewis Curtis first pointed out to me the possibilities of my subject, and I must thank him for his valuable instruction as well as his personal kindness. Mr. James Osborn and Mr. Eugene Waith were good enough to offer early encouragement. Mr. H. T. Swedenberg, Jr. of the University of California at Los Angeles, Mr. M. E. Prior of Northwestern University, and Mr. James L. Clifford of Columbia University all read the manuscript and gave a number of invaluable suggestions for its improvement. At the University of Rochester, Mr. R. J. Kaufmann, Mr. J. W. Johnson, Mr. Hayden White, and David Hadas were diligent in reading and offering informed criticism of my work. I am also obliged to my former students, Dr. Judith Scherer Herz, Dr. Leo Rockas, David Osborne, and Louis Dickens, for many helpful observations.

Mr. Frederick B. Hilles was kind enough to bring my manuscript to the attention of Yale University Press. Mr. Louis Martz showed how the work could be greatly reduced in size while strengthening its central argument.

For assistance with the manuscript, my thanks are due to Mrs. Carl Wren, Miss Ruth Harper, and Harry Rusche. I am obliged to Mr. David Horne for attention to various editorial problems. Let me finally acknowledge the generosity of Houghton, Mifflin and Co. in granting permission to reprint the text of "Absalom and Achitophel" from George Noyes' splendid edition of *The Poetical Works of John Dryden*.

B. N. S.

Rochester, New York
February 1961

Contents

Introduction

Mr. Hugh Trevor-Roper has isolated the besetting weakness of academic writing—unwillingness to take a risk. Yet one of the offices of academic writing is to speak from fortified positions and to wait until strong certainty is established before concluding anything. Its main excuse for existing at all is to protect generalization. If the academic writer does not know before he speaks, no one else is likely to.

The following essay will both accept and avoid risk. On one side it will stay within the enormous mass of familiar notions about the age of Dryden, combining them and using their weight to support another reading of the deadliest poem in English, as Walter Raleigh has said. The risk comes in moving away from the security of the particular, in freeing a brilliant poem of exclusive reliance on the historical circumstances around its composition. Hence the title *Dryden and the Conservative Myth: A Reading of Absalom and Achitophel*. M. H. Abrams considers any poet as entitled to a predication, something that is "given" him, his myth. If we ask what Dryden has, what he can assume to have accumulated in the minds of his readers, we find that he can rely on a complex of ideas, feelings, attitudes of mind—a whole way of looking at things that people were going to accept without consciously deciding whether these things were true or not.

The term "myth" has become so useful in literary study that it can defend or illustrate almost any position one chooses. Myth takes the form of stories of Gods or heroes, anonymously composed folk tales, fictions that are bodies of truth, in themselves, and vehicles for a poet's rendering of truth, his explanation of human destiny; or apart from anything supernatural or embodied in a story, myth may be any common background of familiar reference, a shared consciousness of certain things whose origin is no longer clear. Myths then are always in the process of being made, efforts to suit human needs as life goes on. Representing accumulated wisdom, they work to hold society together, achieving social control against the restless working of strong individual intelligence. They come out of gathered feelings, not true or false but something cherished in order to justify the way things are. In modern times politics, political convictions, or ideals have replaced ancient myths, but the same processes are at work as of old. An element of wishful thinking seems present, and we believe things to be so because they serve our needs: we both know and hope that our myths are right. They give us a program to follow, one that we assume to be ideal, one that brings together the associations of many minds over long periods of time.

In applying these various notions to Dryden and the reading of *Absalom and Achitophel,* let us say first that like all good poets Dryden thinks mythically as well as rationally, if Frederick Prescott's distinction is workable. Dryden works from an inherited set of symbols and responses to them that make up a general interpretation of life. This might be called a mythology of order, a set of connected myths, drawing on the literary tradition from Rome through the Renaissance, on the Bible as read in the 17th century, on the political and religious experiences of the mid-century civil war, and on the assumptions of rule and control that dominate neoclassical literary theory. Dryden wishes to be at one with his society, and so combines various mythical elements with his own views, his own character and temper, to make something that everyone who matters will see at once to be true, partly from what he already knows or believes, partly from the poet's manner of presenting it in his poem. Writing mythically, poetically, Dryden draws close to his readers by relying on a shared consciousness, especially from the Bible and common political experience. He could be sure that these elements would work for him poetically, carrying the largest possible number of

involved meanings and associations to the reader, uniting inherited religious, social, and political symbols.

Now the whole view of things which Dryden represents is
governed by the principle of order—order which is the control
of energy. This commonplace in the history of ideas applies
to a universe held together by divine control; order governs
society, which must yield to strong authority from above; it
governs art as well, whose theory in Dryden's time is alive with
the language of curbing, checking, reining, bridling, shack-
ling—and similar terms that show how order is to be obtained
by the authoritative control of individual energy. In pursuing
the belief in order, Dryden does not think of himself as soar-
ing aloft into the realm of spirit or the ideal. For all his poetic
use of mythical materials, he believes that he speaks for what
is here and now, for what is at once necessary and happily
quite possible and real in everyday life. He displays ideas that
may govern men as political and social units, showing them
how to remain inside the realm of health and order.

The accumulated myth in whose terms he chooses to speak
is typically sustained by neoclassical artistic theory. This body
of theory had also gathered over a long period of time and
came to represent existing belief or conviction that was not
always clearly defined. Deriving in part from ancient and
other foreign authority, neoclassicism grew into pious hope
and belief, stating what ought to govern practice in the arts—
something that should always be striven for and kept in view,
rather than something that was always carried out in practice.
But to ask whether the rules actually did check, curb, or restrain the artist is not the question for us contemplating the
myth of which neoclassicism is a part. It is enough to know
what the desired virtue was and why it should obtain; so we
draw support more from what is said than from what is done.
If practice does not come near the professed ideal in Dryden's
age at all times, we need only recall that it never has done so
in any age. The fact remains that order, the control of energy,
was the principle thought to be right in human endeavor, and
actual practice was supposed to come as near to it as possible.

As for *Absalom and Achitophel*, the poem before us, it emerges as a statement of what order in society has to mean, and in
its own form it comes near to practicing its theory: it is under
control from beginning to end.

Criticism has emphasized the triple relationship among the
poet himself, the literary tradition of which he is a part, and
his contemporary world. The study of Dryden must consider
his own temper, his reliance on the past, and his kinship with
late 17th-century England. Hobbes had approved of the heathen poets in whose work none of those "indiscretions" were
to be found "that tended to subversion or disturbance of the
commonwealths wherein they lived." The same applies to
Dryden, the classical figure of literary conservatism. Its most
characteristic voice reflects the age and shares its temper, responding to its influence and expressing its needs in a happy
union of man and hour. If conservatism, like classicism in
Oliver Elton's phrase, is the triumph of obedience, Dryden
seems to have obeyed naturally. He seems free, with no sense
of straining toward what was required by neoclassical authority in art, by the demands of political and religious order. If he
is a critic, no matter in what form he happens to be writing, he
seems able to move freely amid all the possible positions open
to him—to test them all and see what may be said for each
while in the end making the strongest case for authority.

It is said that conservative ages are defensive, and that conservatism as such is harder to analyze than radicalism. It
maintains what is already achieved, blends with ordinary assumptions, with the way things are, feeling no special need to
explain or to justify what is taken for granted as true. Only
when it seems threatened, as in the late 17th century or a
hundred years later in Burke's time, does conservatism seem
compelled to state its principles or declare its own meaning.
As in Dryden's time it then grows vigilant and suspicious,
strikes out in criticism and satire against what seems to threat-
en social harmony in the form of belligerent energy, especially
when shown by brilliant or untractable individuals. Conservatism does not allow its enemies a defensible position; estab-

lished authority alone can be right. As Mr. Tillyard says of Clarendon, he lacked sympathy for his opponents and could not see that they might have been inspired by their own principles of freedom, truth, and justice. They created disorder and therefore had to be wrong. So the chief commandments of Dryden's age are those beginning "Thou shalt not" from the Old Testament, there being so many things needing to be prevented. The "Thou shalt not" commandments refer to what the human race is most prone to do excessively or dangerously; they set a tone of negative prohibition as against the radical urge to act. The language of encouragement toward fresh action is not the language of fear that feels compelled to warn, threaten, or prohibit.

If a heavy weight of control in precept and theory oppresses the age of Dryden, events would seem to have justified a share of it. The age had enough of danger and upheaval to arouse its vigilance, especially near the time of *Absalom and Achitophel.* The conservative mythology that had been so long in accumulating and representing what should be, did not always govern what was actually done, thus showing the need for its constant reassertion. Neoclassical theory could not prevent some undisciplined poems from being written, nor did authoritarian political theory prevent actual upheaval in the state. For all their rhetorical flavor and studied effect, the questions of John Spencer in "England's Distractions to be England's Directions" (1658) have some justification:

> ... is this a time to be raising of unnecessary disputes, to be wrangling in controversies about points of Church-government, when God knows whether we shall have any government either in Church or State at all, when there is *Hannibal ad portas,* a generation of men crying out, No government, no church, no ministers, no sacrament. . . . Is this a time to divide: Is such a time as this, a time to trouble England with new opinions?

Yet however justified at times, the expression of energetic alarm itself might turn out to be part of the literary tradition

blending in with the writer and his age. A marked habit had
established itself at least by Juvenal's time, of drawing up lists
of epithets or synonymous terms often of abuse or denunciation. Poor, plodding Gulliver never quite knew what his creator was using him to make fun of; when he solemnly lists all
the things wrong with the 17th century, he is Swift's means of
ridiculing the violent exaggeration of similar lists drawn up
by the frightened, the angry, the zealous, or the merely pedan-
tic. By itself the accumulation of terms in John Webster's comment on scholastic theology might be convincing: "what is it
else but a confused chaos, of needless, frivolous, fruitless, triv-
ial, vain, curious, impertinent, knotty, ungodly, irreligious,
thorny, and hell-hatched disputes, altercations, doubts, questions and endless janglings, multiplied and spawned forth
even to monstrosity and nauseousness?" In a single paragraph
Samuel Parker inveighs against folly, indiscretion, passion,
forwardness, rage, fierceness, combustions, fury, tumults, seditions, flames, disturbances, commotions, discords, heats,
and controversies. And yet like so much else in the conservative myth, these impassioned catalogues may be only a device,
recognized and expected by those familiar with the arts of
persuasion. One has the sense of a repository or stock of
standard terms and devices on which a writer would draw,
using them to get an effect preordained and expected. Thomas
Blount in his *Academy of Eloquence* gives this impression. In
illustrating the rhetorical term "amplification," he distinguishes a number of types, the third of which is mere "accumulation" or piling up of synonyms for praise or accusation.
Conveniently for us and naturally for an age that feared it
most, he chooses for example "to amplifie a sedition; tumults,
mutinies, uproars, desperate conspiracies, wicked confedera-
cies, furious commotions, trayterous rebellions, associations
in villany, distractions from allegiance, bloody garboyls, in-
testine massacres of citizens." Is he being comic deliberately
when he closes the passage with "But this example is somewhat too swelling"?

In drawing upon this kind of practice one falls into a kind

of imitation, for much of the same quality results from piling up generalizations out of old and conventional sources, as if to say with Buckingham that unlike women, laws are none the worse for being old. In Dryden's age neoclassical theory dealt in what ought to be, in what was supposed to be so. And now with our own criticism and interpretation, we continue groping for what should be the case until it becomes, too, a kind of myth from having been said so often, being composed of common notions and assumptions. The use of old-fashioned writers like Raleigh, Saintsbury, and Gosse and the repetition of their primitive views contribute toward the effect of something unexamined as a cherished inheritance, of things that ought to be so whether a fresh and energetic review would expose them or not. In detail, therefore, no effort is made to give a fresh reading to the ancient neoclassical positions: they are on the contrary deliberately offered as if they were the only possible views and hence beyond dispute.

Let this passive statement of neoclassical commonplaces stand as imitation of Dryden's own rhetoric, which strives to write from the collective literary sense of his day and so gain a mythical sanction. So also it is hoped that the following essay will support its own argument by a certain tightness and control in expression. The general theme of order that is achieved by the control of energy will gain from something that is never allowed to break out of a carefully defined set of limits, if this sense is given by the manner of expressing the dominant notions of energy under control.

Nevertheless the reader will become aware of repetition, especially of certain materials that seem to force themselves back into the discussion. But the materials used are harmonically related, being meant to assist and not to confuse or oppress the reader. A wide exploration of Dryden's age will lead one toward a recurrent set of ideas, or return one to certain positions. Far from being inadvertent, these repetitions suggest that the reader is compelled to end in the same places, no matter where he has begun. The early chapters, then, establish the terms more fully explored or applied later on. The per-

vasive terminology of rule and control, references to the multitude, the loyal few, and similarly important themes come
early to the reader's attention. In particular the dominant
figures of speech begin early and are mentioned at intervals
throughout; the architectural figure is allowed to reappear frequently with the hope that it will seem to apply with unde-
niable force to our reading when it occurs in the poem itself.

We shall come to the end of what we can learn about a
given work through studying what preceded or accompanied
its creation, and will at last be attracted by Dryden's poetic
language, the figures and comparisons by which he, like all
poets, reaches out to extend his meaning. His comparisons
ought to reveal what is in his mind, what kind of material he
chooses when he desires to speak most poetically. Dryden, let
us not forget, thought of himself as being first and last a poet,
a man wishing to be judged as a poet and resting his case with
posterity on his quality as a poet. Dryden's images are functional, as Nichol Smith remarks, growing naturally from what
he is saying. They reflect his vision of the world, a vision that
precedes the language in which he chooses to express it.

No modern student of letters would deal with a serious
poem without considering its imagery, yet we no sooner address the subject than we retreat behind numerous cautions
and reservations. If we try to eliminate everything possibly
contradictory to our point, the effect may be to cancel out
the entire argument. Nevertheless we must beware of a fall
into intemperate Spurgeonism, and keep in mind for example
the useful warnings of Rosamund Tuve's *Elizabethan and
Metaphysical Imagery*. We must not consider images in isola-
tion from the poem as a whole, from the author's other work,
or from the figurative language common in his age. We must
not rely too much on counting images arithmetically, and we
must consider the function of an image, knowing that what it
is used for affects what it is poetically. Men live so much by
comparison that analogies and resemblances among things
may be only what anyone might see. Demetrius discussing
style urges this form of analogy available to anyone's imagina-

tion: a general, a pilot, a charioteer all resemble one another as being in command and so offer a useful and appropriate comparison but one that tells nothing in particular about the mind of a given poet. So also images may be drawn from traditional lore, from proverbial or other wise sayings, from a wide inheritance of common knowledge shading into a more literary or learned storehouse established by preceding poets. Then, too, literary decorum may join a certain form of expression with certain themes or subjects, so that the imagery in a given poem by Dryden may turn out to be like that used in all such poems written in or about his time. He may draw on a sort of poetical counter or follow general practice as in using medical images for satiric effect.

In Dryden's period especially, literary, political, and religious discourse all draw heavily on a set of comparisons that sustain the principle of order and the control of energy. Judicial, military, and architectural figures, the language of bridling, reining, or in Longinus' phrase curbing a steed: figures of piloting or navigating to suggest necessary leadership—these and related terms recur with such frequency and in such similar contexts that they too assume a kind of mythical force. Figurative language, then, returns us to our guiding notion of myth which itself may grow into a kind of extended metaphor. It seems well agreed that if a certain image recurs often enough, it may become a symbol, part of a symbolic or mythical system; we shall find that the dominant images of *Absalom and Achitophel* have so established themselves and are central to the conservative myth. Indeed it may not be too fanciful to think of the poetic metaphors that Dryden shares with his generation as having the effect of ritual, a part of the regular ceremony by which a myth is repeated and renewed. Dryden's medical and architectural figures derive much of their force from their common usage, suggesting something inherited and used over long periods of time, and thus drawing together a series of familiar lessons into a persuasive mythology. Again, if they have the effect of a kind of ritual, so must the staging of Achitophel's tempta-

tion be the ritual that carries the myth of the false rebel leader
so recently given its classical form in *Paradise Lost*. Finally,
the speech of King David is the ceremony that reassures a
common human need for life and well-being, invoking the
assurance of a divine authority, final and unquestioned. Knowing the myth beforehand, we recognize in the king's ritual
utterance the comforting assemblage of faith, morality, and
long-established governing custom.

By now the reader may have begun to ask why a single
poem needs so great a preliminary effort, whether in fact
Absalom and Achitophel will sustain the weight it is called
on to bear. If the poem does not yield meanings large enough
to justify such preparation, the reader may join Mr. Moody
Prior, a most learned and acute student of letters, in asking,
"is not the worship greater than the God?" Do we, in trying
to recapture the fullness of this poem, commit the mortal sin
of exegesis and make our own poem in its place?

The only true answer comes after the poem is read in the
light of its myth. Without such assistance, we cannot account
satisfactorily for the poem as it is, yet we may well go beyond
the point at which more inquiry will be repaid by fresh insights into the poem. The danger in all such readings is that
they become themselves too poetic, enlarging, intensifying
materials so as to develop a meaning greater than the poem
will hold. Thus by worship of our own creation, we make a
new poem.

Whether the "worship" surpasses the God for the reader
will depend somewhat on his response to Dryden's use of his
myth as here reviewed. Myth for Dryden is a fiction, a ration-
alized prejudice contrived to suit himself, to justify what he
will believe; thus like most conservatives, he does not allow
the opponents of order the benefit of doubt. Yet he shows a
defensible belief in the regulative myth, a force actively working to bind together English society at a time when it needed
such renewed cohesion, to "restore" the Restoration mood of
1660. Dryden fuses these attitudes largely by instinct and loyalty. He is not a great philosophic historian compelled by

learning and profound analysis to write his poem, and so long
as we do not claim this, our "worship" is not greater than the
God. We believe that far more lies behind this poem and is
needed to understand it than previous readings have allowed.

As we prepare to read a poem which though topical and
allusive has become a great classic, we may persuade ourselves
that we have found a way to answer the long-established objections to *Absalom and Achitophel.* Indeed we may turn
them into virtues or at least elements functional to the poem's
design. We may profitably see *Absalom and Achitophel* as a
"big" poem, just the right poem for Dryden to write in place
of his dreamed epic, giving him his best chance for poetic
fulfillment and demanding of us that we establish a set of
terms large enough as fiction and allegory to meet the poem's
widest dimensions while accounting for its chief ingredients
in a more satisfactory way.

In 1730 Matthew Tindal argued against receiving religion
on grounds of authority in his *Christianity as Old as the Creation.* It is an odd jumble, he says, "to prove the truth of a
book by the truth of the doctrines it contains, and at the same
time conclude those doctrines to be true, because contained
in that book." This cannot be avoided in reading *Absalom
and Achitophel.* We determine from the poem what to look
for in the ideas surrounding it. We look for these things and
find them abundantly present to prove that the poem is indeed
saying what our reading has suggested. The poem is used to
confirm an interpretation of itself, or to make things found
outside of it seem to have meanings that will confirm the
poem's meaning. We find true what is necessary in order to
make the poem mean what we say it means. We now have no
course but to let the supporting evidence stand for what it is
worth. If the poem's ingredients existed before it was composed, and if the poem dramatizes and systematizes them, the
poem both derives power from them and adds to their force.

The point is clearer when we recall the standard procedures
of satire. Things as they are combine good and evil, and the
satirist constructs his fictions upon these opposites, extending

both good and evil beyond their ordinary human bounds. Men are both better and worse than they think they are, as capable of falling back into Yahoo as rising into Houyhnhnm. The satirist's ideal is a fiction upon the actual good in man, just as his view of vice and folly is a fiction upon the actual weakness in man. Each side of satire, then, is what it must be for the sake of the other, satiric vice as much a literary invention as the satirist's own virtue: duncehood and hypocrisy are just as mythical as the goodness and consistency which give the satirist the right and duty to expose them. Insofar as these notions are just, a satirist may not need particular examples of vice or folly in his immediate world to call forth a corrective message. Literary good and evil can be recreated at any time from their standard qualities, so that a set of conventional fictions will serve to condemn the particular wrongs in any given age. These wrongs are likely to correspond to the imagined dangers always presented in satire, which in turn have been derived from their steady recurrence in human affairs.

For Dryden in *Absalom and Achitophel,* if David is idealized far beyond the virtues of Charles II, so also is Achitophel extended far beyond such evil as Shaftesbury himself was capable of. Achitophel is bound to be what he appears in the poem, just as David must be the virtuous king with all the right qualities. Dryden's treatment of the good must be intensified so as to show the ideal to be desired; so also his version of evil must be enlarged to make clear what should be avoided. Both seem equidistant from life as it is, life which moves from one side to the other as it can, or must. We see Dryden, then, working within certain fictions that he is not free to alter; his false politician and ideal king resemble characters in the heroic plays who show a standard set of qualities. Not only does he show his skill in making it seem as if these qualities actually belonged to the particular individuals referred to, but he uses his ready-made fictions to justify the view he takes of rebellion. Thus for him the goodness of David and the evil of Achitophel show the only view of revolution possible to a prudent man, as in the 19th century the fictions of justice and love govern the view taken of the French Revolution by Carlyle and Dickens. For Dryden, revolution will recur unless everyone resembles the Loyal Few in revering the king; for Carlyle and Dickens, revolution is inevitable unless justice and love replace selfishness in the ruling aristocracy.

We must be encouraged, then, to see the poem in relationships that account for its materials and structure. We gain something even from seeing it within the frame of Dryden's own career. His contempt for popular approval had to meet his need of writing for the commercial stage, where he had always to do what he professed to despise, to write below his instinct and court a favor he did not respect. He desired fame but hated to seek it at the popular level, and the resulting tension in him must have increased as the years went by and he saw no chance to write what he thought proper to him. But now with *Absalom and Achitophel* Dryden had his chance; at last the age demanded something in harmony with his own nature and convictions, enabling him to use the conservative myth at the ideal, the personal, and the historical levels—to fuse the three relationships of poem, man, and age.

Standard objections to the poem as repeated from Dr. Johnson down to C. S. Lewis, not to speak of more recent distrust of Dryden's reasoning, may well yield, however, to a mythical reading. We have long heard that the poem was badly constructed, that the allegory was too long-drawn out, that there was too little imagery or description, that no complete action was possible because the conflict presented had not been concluded historically, that the disproportion between the rebel forces and the weak friends of the king was unpleasant, and that the ending seems like an abrupt anticlimax, with the enchanted castle vanishing into thin air. To this standard diatribe, C. S. Lewis would seem to have contributed the blow from which no recovery is possible. *Absalom and Achitophel* is simply botched: "The work is not merely maimed, it is diseased at the heart." But let us start afresh and read the poem as we find it, to see whether we cannot justify its being the way it is and saying what it says—whether, in fact, its ap-

parent disproportion is not proper to its aim. At the same
time we shall have to admit some unevenness in our reading,
since like all considerations from a certain point of view, this
one will not account for everything in the poem. In the service
of a single way of looking at things, there will be some loss
of thoroughness and accuracy; some passages, like the elegy
on Barzillai's son, will seem hastily read when they are made
to serve only the poem's myth. And yet our terms have to
begin large enough to take in a "big" poem, and we may at
least suggest lines to follow that will lead more deeply into
the poem than is possible with the readings now available to
us.

For we must agree with the almost lyrical praise of Sir John
Pollock, that "the flashes of Dryden's insight illumine more
than the light shed by many records." The distance that *Absalom and Achitophel* carries us in its moral allegory beyond
a contemporary historical reference is the measure of its greatness. Dryden sets up a parallel between ideas and events, with
one interpreting the other; his myth is so applied as to establish itself as a rational, coherent view of life, going far beyond
the mere loyalty to the Kings Charles and James that Dryden
was supposed only to be capable of—a loyalty dragged down
by the quality of its object. On the contrary, we see now that
with its mythical sanction Dryden's loyalty was beyond con-
tamination by its object, by whatever happened to embody
it in passing. His poem gains like other moral allegories from
its superiority to immediate historical reference. Is not *Gulliver's Travels* a far richer experience when it abandons high
heels and low heels or the mechanics of England's shutting
out the rain and sun from Ireland, in order to face the great
human dilemmas of Voyage IV? *Candide,* too, gains when its
frame of reference grows away from particular events like
the Lisbon earthquake, and allows for a sober way of looking
at things. How much better is the *Penguin Island* of Anatole
France when it ceases to be troubled by the Pyrot-Dreyfus
analogy and looks toward the insoluble conflicts of modern
life! How powerfully Norman Douglas writes of the nature of

all tyranny in *South Wind* when he absorbs its qualities within the monstrous behavior of the good Duke Albert! Even the feebler recent effort in the genre of satiric allegory made by John Steinbeck in *The Short Reign of Pippin IV* gets what effect it is capable of during the general ironic application of its earlier chapters. In its larger presentation of good and evil, too, Dryden's *Absalom and Achitophel* will show why, for all its topicality, it remains the classic of its kind in English.

PART ONE

The Myth and the Temper of Dryden

CHAPTER 1

The Divinity of Order

In the year 1662 a bill for the uniformity of public prayers was supported by Sir Edward Turnor in these words: "We hope the God of order and unity will conform the hearts of all the people in this nation, to serve him in this order and uniformity." These terms suggest that God had established one order for the universe and all its parts, that the actions of all created things were directed by a system of laws, that not only nature but man throughout the whole of his political and social life was subject to an authority from which there was no appeal. The method established by Descartes had shown in the very processes of human thought a kind of mathematical clearness and regularity; systematic thinkers imitated the mathematicians and seemed bent on making their subjects into branches of mathematics, wherein all problems have solutions.

Against this universal principle of order stood the energy of individual men. The dualism of order against energy was typical of the late 17th century, that tended to see things in opposing units which had then to be harmonized or directed so as to live side by side. The necessary third element, to bring energy into order, was control. Order demanded the control of energy in the service of worthy ends, throughout the main areas of human activity. In art, the words *wit, genius, imagination, fancy* suggest the kind of personal gifts demand-

ing government by rule. In religion all forms of unique inspiration, in politics the urge of private ambition must yield
to law and custom; no one is to imagine that the settled order
should give way for his sake. Energy out of control would
bring division to the church, rebellion to the state, and formless wild heaps of wit to literature. The past age had shown
that these results must follow, as witness the Puritans in religion, civil war in the state, metaphysical extravagance in
poetry, and excessive eloquence in prose.

The whole of human society in this view exists for conservative purposes. Society aims to bring individuals under conformity, to get peace instead of original contention and disorder. The existence of society shows that it was intended to
seek a peaceful condition under recognized authority. Any
force tending to disrupt or to change radically the existing
harmony has to be wrong. Any man who goes his own way,
who is selfishly ambitious—headstrong, bold, or turbulent
of wit—is a common enemy. A form of self-assertion like eloquence, any release of great imaginative energy, has to be
questioned or suppressed in the general interest. And if the
institutions such as the church, set up for harmonious common life, fall into the very divisions they are supposed to
prevent, men will go elsewhere, even into the by-paths of
odious superstition and idolatry in Rome, where they have
heard "there was more unity, order, and reverence to authority."

The order in the world applies to works of art whose laws
resemble the laws of nature and of life. In literary theory that
was supposed to govern practice, this meant time-honored
authority and the "rules." Among endless repetitions of this
and related ideas, let us try one from John Dennis' *The
Grounds of Criticism in Poetry* (1704):

> . . . poetry is either an art, or whimsy and fanaticism. If
> it is an art, it follows that it must propose an end to itself,
> and afterwards lay down proper means for the attaining
> that end: For this is undeniable, that there are proper

means for the attaining of every end, and those proper means in poetry we call the rules. Again, if the end of poetry be to instruct and reform the world, that is, to bring mankind from irregularity, extravagance, and confusion, to rule and order, how this should be done by a thing that is in itself irregular and extravagant, is difficult to be conceived. Besides, the work of every reasonable creature must derive its beauty from regularity; for reason is rule and order, and nothing can be irregular either in our conceptions or our actions, any further than it swerves from rule, that is, from reason.

As the beauty of the universe, itself a kind of noble poem, proceeds from its regularity, so do the artistic aims of pleasure and instruction depend on rules. The line of thought is simple: An artist aims to instruct and to please. To do so he must imitate Nature, preferably by imitating the authors who have most successfully followed Nature in the past: to imitate them is to imitate Nature. As Dryden himself says, there have to be rules for imitating Nature rightly, "otherwise there may be an end, and no means conducing to it." The rules then are precepts set up for the various forms or kinds, each having its own principles of guidance. From ancient times the rules have been derived, especially by Aristotle and Horace, from the practice of the best writers who have gone before. The forms in which these have succeeded best are the best forms, epic and tragedy, and represent the highest of literary aspirations.

Neoclassical criticism tries to find out what made the ancient classics great, so that modern literature can learn how to achieve greatness. The sacred names of Homer and Virgil, Aristotle and Horace govern all discussions of the epic. The Greeks and Romans were seen as the equivalent of Nature and Truth, as well as the means of achieving lasting merit; indeed their power seemed at times to paralyze devotion. The Earl of Mulgrave fears that Homer and Virgil have left nothing for lesser men to attempt:

Homer and Virgil: with what awful sound
Each of those names the trembling air does wound!

But it was Aristotle who had left scarcely anything for succeeding ages to do. His rules were Nature and good sense in
summary—the last word in control of wit. In a critic like
Thomas Rymer anything wrong was simply due to ignorance
of Aristotle. One could believe that reason ruled, "mais
qu'Aristote gouverne."

We may say that literature lends itself better to ancient
authority and a close orthodoxy than science does, and so will
throw off authority much later than 17th-century science. Yet
a high priest of science like Thomas Sprat, praising the new
thinkers who freed human understanding from "the slavery
of dead men's names," nonetheless appeals to ancient authority, which also revered the authors of natural discoveries. He
is so careful to do them justice that he cites the ancients' own
practice to support his argument, as if he could not even defend his questioning of them in modern terms without showing that in fact they had done the same thing before him.
Sprat's effort to get free of the ancients had still to be justified
by referring to their own previous example of free inquiry.

Again, the ancient writers taught the lessons of morality
and obedience which poetry was called upon to convey. Sir
Richard Blackmore shows how the age had finally escaped
from all chance of error in the role of poetry: "To give men
right and just conceptions of religion and virtue, to aid their
reason in restraining their exorbitant appetites and impetuous
passions, and to bring their lives under the rules and guidance
of true wisdom, and thereby to promote the public good of
mankind, is undoubtedly the end of all poetry." Dennis is
sure that "writing regularly, is writing morally, decently,
justly, naturally, reasonably" so that poetry becomes a means
of popular restraint and edification. One of Rymer's objections to *Othello* is just this, that the play unsettles the mind
and causes discontent, instead of charming into peaceful obedience by harmonious lessons. Davenant has found the people

more unquiet than in former ages so that the four aids of
government—religion, arms, policy, and law—cannot hold
them in check. Poetry will persuade men to obey without
grievance with its "harmonious and delightful insinuations."
The numerous demands that poetry should instruct are seldom explicit as to its lessons, beyond the standard requirements of the age for morality, conformity, and order. One is
taught things acceptable to men of sense and reason, a feeling of obligation to accepted ways in a settled society, of having to keep ordinary human behavior within limits that it
would otherwise prefer to ignore. And the pleasure given by
poetry was there only to ensure the right lessons. This principle extends amusingly even to playing cards. Designed to
make command of Latin and English easier, a scheme offers
various games in which cards make up words, sayings, or
short speeches all of which are profitable and moral, avoiding
anything profane and substituting wholesome improvement
for the waste of time and money in card games played for a
stake. But in the end, the ancient masters Homer and Virgil
turn out to be the ideal means toward the right end of instruction. As Dryden himself says, he takes over Homer's moral
lesson in *The Conquest of Granada,* and admires the conviction of his beloved Virgil, that a nation is made happy by respect and obedience toward its monarch.

In this oracular authority of the ancients and the rules derived from their practice the free intelligence seems cramped.
There is always a tendency, Mr. Eliot says, "to legislate rather
than to inquire," which shows again in trying to form an English academy or national body of taste and literary standards.
English itself seemed weak and barbarous, unable to carry a
true poet into assured fame. Then, too, the general need of
control over individual excess called for a literary standard
to which all would have to conform and by which all might
be judged—a kind of law for words and phrases, as John
Evelyn says, to refine the crude or fulsome in literary performance.

Literature seems under a kind of assignment from society

to aid in the general problem of order which is the control
of energy. Like the aristocracy in 18th-century England, literature is told off as a branch of the moral and educational
institutions of society. Its theory is alive with the terminology
of rule and government in which there is at work the force
seen by Mr. Empson in all Augustan style, "the digesting and
controlling mind." Since there is a right way of doing everything, a monotonous terminology is applied with such relentless thoroughness that a rule becomes available for the most
minute literary activity, down to the last syllable of every
word. We hear of judgment, learning, proportion, regularity,
exactness, wisdom, discretion, moderation, economy, connection and dependence of parts; of unity, probability, harmony,
and symmetry; of decorum of manners on the stage and the
adoption of appropriate style and content for each poetic
kind; of the need for hard work, vigilance, pains, long study,
and practice as insisted by Horace and Ben Jonson; of the
need to subdue, forbear, retrench, submit, and command to
an almost military degree. Amid all this characteristic terminology, the word "design" perhaps carries best the essential
meaning. The familiar parallels of poetry and painting, or
of poetry and other arts requiring formal planning or disposi-
tion of parts, invite the use of such a term as "design" for the
regulation of thought toward a given end. To be sure, the
term would apply to any careful scheme. In actions against
the established order, "design" carries a heavy sense of scheming, diabolical villainy, as in Clarendon's view of the Puritan
rebellion, Sprat's narrative of the Rye House Plot, or any of
the numerous accounts of Shaftesbury's contention against
Charles II. Swift's hero Partridge in his almanacs gives "design" a variety of opprobrious epithets, and we learn that to
build up or destroy, in rebellion or successful art, one must
follow a well-laid plan under deliberate control. Rapin insists upon design for every sort of verse, and in his "Epistle
Dedicatory" to an *Essay Towards a Real Character* (1668)
John Wilkins uses the term seven times for his work as a
whole. In H. Prideaux's *Letter to the Deists* (1697) "design"

is used, in one stretch of six pages, at least ten times in various applications.

Reference to Rapin and Prideaux recalls the enormous influence of the French school on neoclassical English criticism. Even if France merely confirmed what England would do of itself or had already begun in essence, the ready translation and acceptance in England of French principles did much to establish the neoclassical scriptures. Boileau's *The Art of Poetry* (1683) is heavy with admonition, negative warnings, and caution. With a kind of austere preaching it reviews the standard precepts, and observes its own compromise by allowing a "brave disorder" amid all of its prescription and classification. M. Hédelin's *The Whole Art of the Stage* (1684) expressly sets out to tell anyone who undertakes to be a poet what he has to do. He prescribes a thorough reading of all accepted authorities, ancient and modern; then a command of the established great works themselves, after which the artist is told how to meet every problem likely to arise, down to the precise number of verses allowed for each division of his play. Le Bossu's treatise on epic poetry, which Dryden used after its appearance in 1675, analyzes Homer and Virgil and deduces a minute series of principles for future guidance. The moral and social lessons of great epics emerge in examples of virtue and right conduct; we must know the limitations of all things and keep within them. Precepts guide the poet to the right solution of every problem. As the fable has its essential parts to be dealt with in certain ways, so also the action and subject matter. This is made up of episodes, of which one must know the nature, union, and qualities. Of epic action in general there are four qualities: unity, integrity, importance, and duration. Unity in turn has three essential elements, and an episode likewise can be irregular in three ways. As to the manners of an epic, again four things are to be observed: the manners must be good, suitable, likely, and even. Under unity of character, advice is reduced to five headings, while for elocution three things are expedient.

These and similar governing formulas might extend to

every sort of literary activity, including criticism, so that
bounds and limits were set for those whose business it was to
set bounds and limits. Rymer's *Essay Concerning Critical and
Curious Learning* (1698) defines the critic's function with
great care. And for the use of religious materials in poetry
John Dennis lays down no less than nine rules. If a writer is
troubled by versification or rhyme, *The Art of English Poetry*
by Edward Bysshe (1702) will assist him with a dictionary of
rhymes that excludes words under ten separate headings. How
so much rule and method might afflict the individual mind is
suggested by John Webster's remarks on languages. That
which is gotten by rule and method

> . . . doth exceedingly rack and excruciate the intellectual
> memory . . . forced at the same time, not only to find words
> agreeable to the present matter discoursed of, and to put
> them into a good rhetorical order, but must at the same
> instant of speaking collect all the numerous rules, of num-
> ber, case, gender, declension, conjugation, and the like, as
> into one center, where so many rays are united, and yet
> not confounded, which must needs be very perplexing
> and gravaminous to memorative faculty.

Are not the regulations of neoclassical theory certain to be
"gravaminous" to a poet's imagination, his wit, fancy, invention, "genius," or any other faculty that must exist in him to
make him a poet, that must demand a chance to go its own way
or to be what it can be? The persistent language of governing,
curbing, bridling, or chaining for "poetical fury" should not
mislead us. The true province of the poet, essential to his
nature or his success as an artist, remains a special divine gift.
If it was a danger in practical affairs which had to remain im-
personal and civil, in poetry it kept a high place. Wit and
fancy are exuberant, and Thomas Pope Blount invokes the
orthodox panoply of their government from Rapin, Rymer,
Dryden, Mulgrave, Charles Cotton, and Cowley; yet his very
insistence shows how strong is the role of a poet's special gift.
Closer inspection of the rules shows them rather means than

ends, part of a confederation aimed at a high result. Sir William Temple's language seems austere in his essay "Of Poetry":

> But, though invention be the mother of poetry, yet this child is, like all others, born naked, and must be nourished with care, clothed with exactness and elegance, educated with industry, instructed with art, improved by application, corrected with severity, and accomplished with labour and with time, before it arrives at any great perfection or growth.

Yet "perfection" and "growth" are the end, and the rules are less a form of suppression than a means of enlargement and freedom. The pontifical Rymer himself admits that wholesome laws do not remove human liberty. If the nature of a poet's gift is such as to demand restraint by other faculties, he is not to feel impeded. Law then assures the security of freedom, and man finds his most complete and characteristic expression under its control; the rules offer the only condition under which man is able to express himself to his best advantage.

Yet all phases of artistic expression came steadily under laws appropriate to each. Prose and verse alike met the law designed in various ways to suit them to the needs of the age. The reform of prose style brings under control qualities that otherwise should not be trusted to follow their own course. Again the terms suggest a prose sought for steady didactic purposes. We hear of the need for clearness, brevity, appropriateness, plainness, purity, naturalness, economy, conciseness, antithesis and point, aphorism and sententiae. Some of these words are synonymous, some shade into each other in meaning, some develop contradictions in time. A great variety of causes, which are likewise not mutually exclusive, have been offered for the many detailed changes in prose. Anti-Ciceronianism, Senecan example; political pamphlets and popular journalism; religious attitudes like Puritanism, Deism, Quakerism, or Stoicism; the demands of science, mathematics,

Cartesianism and allied influences sustained by the Royal
Society; the influence of the court and the conversational
ideal of urbane London life—all had their role to play, even
though some were results rather than causes or apply only to
limited areas of usage.

But it would seem that literature is always in search of a
direct and natural utterance, and whenever a new movement
of any sort is declared, it seeks a return to "nature." Mr. Eliot
has said that "every revolution in poetry is apt to be, and sometimes to announce itself as, a return to common speech." Certainly the 17th-century need for a direct and natural utterance
in prose, a functional, economical style free of affectation or
excessive ornament, is as old as the conscious discussion of
what literary practice is or ought to be. Quintilian pleads for
direct and natural speech, making us see that literature is always groping for the best way to say things clearly, and that in
periods of the greatest complexity and ornateness there is a
foundation of simplicity and naturalness. In the English movement there is much talk of going back to a style that had once
been dominant, or of bringing to the surface again a mode of
utterance that had continued since the days of King Alfred.
Sprat himself in the now classical statement of the Royal Society's ideal, desires to "return back to the primitive purity,
and shortness" wherein things and words were equal in number. Like so many "new" things, the prose of Dryden's age
was only a return to something old. Its characteristics are
among Ben Jonson's anticipations of the neoclassical gospel.
Language should follow a middle course; round, composed,
elegant, and accurate words enable us to "speak what we can
the nearest way" and let sunshine into obscure places: "Pure
and neat language I love, yet plaine and customary." Apart
from the literary tradition seen in Walton, Bunyan, Hobbes,
and others, plenty of direct, functional prose was on hand,
much of it in the form of pamphlets running into the tens of
thousands between 1640 and 1660—four or five each day.
Later on, the Tory propagandist Roger L'Estrange was an
effective and enormously prolific writer at this level.

Whether it sought to revive older inheritance temporarily obscured by individual writers of genius, or whether it absorbed a journalistic influence or was affected by the many other voices calling for its reform, English prose seemed bent on realizing an ideal of useful simplicity. To escape from the old Ciceronian love of words instead of things had long ago been recommended. Seneca had preferred signs over words of "discourse," and early in the 17th century Sir John Beaumont had urged strong figures "consisting less in words, and more in things." Various schemes for drawing up a universal language or "character" emerge, the most elaborate of which by John Wilkins recalls Swift's machine in *Gulliver's Travels,* Book III, by which the "Academy of Projectors" would simplify the writing of books. To carry out his proposal for "the expression of our conceptions by marks, which should signify things, and not words," Wilkins arrives at a "more easy and convenient language," as he calls it. His table of letters and symbols is fifteen columns wide and thirty-one columns high, until, as the satiric medical image will show, the means taken to avoid confusion are more involved than the trouble they aim to cure. Yet things over words became part of a demand by scientists in particular for a style that would suit the needs of fresh experiment in the practical, material world as it is. Reform may have applied only to serviceable expository prose while allowing greater freedom to poetry; still, a medium was demanded for the work of doers, experimenters, and plain laborious observers, in Sprat's words. If, after Bacon, men are to rely more on experience, nature, and the senses than on uncertain intellectual faculties with their dangerous general rules; if the heavy weight of old authority is to give way and let the mind go where real evidence might lead it; if after the recent agonies and disputes of the civil war men are happier with the king's return and long to seek after "the peaceable, the fruitful, the nourishing knowledge," then they must draw up their results and share them with others in terms precise and clear. Language is a form of necessary evil, and if it could serve its new uses to their satisfaction, scientists were willing to leave education to itself with the universities free to go on as before serving a larger, more literary need.

The general demand that literature be instructive now joins with the need to convey practical knowledge clearly. Roscommon has laid it down that "truth shines brightest through the plainest dress," and since the truth is simple and natural without being so perplexed and difficult as men seem to think, it calls for a didactic style "pure, perspicuous, succinct, unaffected, and grave." The art to be gained consists in expressing thought clearly in the fewest possible words, words likewise intelligible to everyone. This affects the preacher whose aim is to edify his auditors and who must avoid "hard words," just as the popular journalist must choose a few plain words. Roger L'Estrange writes to be "read by all, and understood by all; for my business extends to all." But here as elsewhere in exploring ideas, we find things turning into their opposites. If one writes too briefly and concisely, before long one becomes obscure; in the effort to speak so economically as to be understood by everyone, a writer may end by being intelligible only to an alert, selected few. Even in prayer, as John Wilkins urges, "let thy words be few," because economy here suggests devotion.

The poet meanwhile is allowed to be free in order to be inspired, but he too must bring his energy within the strict requirements of language and form in the heroic couplet. If, as Ezra Pound has said, poetry deserves to be or ought to be as well written as prose, we should expect also that "a poet's lines should be correct and few." Dennis was sure that "every expression that is false English in prose is barbarous and absurd in verse too," and certainly the language needed, if one is to be brief and clear and didactic, is the right language for the couplet, as much as for the Royal Society. Yet the age tended to be conscious of the difference between prose and poetry even when using them for similar purposes, and a form like the couplet would seem more clearly to be poetry. Standard characteristics of the form had long been established by Ben Jonson with some two hundred poems in the couplet,

and the celebrated rocking-horse of Waller's rhymes was preferred as a model to the greater negligence and freedom of
Donne's couplet usage.

The right poetic form then for what the late 17th century
had to say was even more ready to its use than a functional
prose; as Ruth Wallerstein says, "the new expression and the
new metrical form have an organic imaginative harmony with
the substance they embody." Hence the use of couplet verse
for the characteristic genres of the age. It was the ideal medium for getting down to business, as Saintsbury said, for
argument, criticism, definition, portraiture, for the wisdom
of common sense, for summary and conclusion, saying the
last thing in a series or drawing up the results of thought and
experience for general benefit. The couplet is best for comment on things as they are, keeping within the prevailing
order of its time, as its own form prescribed a carefully
bounded area. The couplet does not invite the seeing of visions for the future, the inciting or declaring of revolutions,
the expression of hope for things not yet established. A lean,
athletic form that has to make all its resources count, the
couplet controls because the poet is already controlled and
disciplined in what he chooses to say.

The Augustans, then, worked habitually in a pattern whose
rhetoric bestowed and suggested intellectual order. The couplet is easy to control because of all verse forms its mechanics
are the clearest; it can achieve an ideal of "correctness," since
what it requires for being "correct" can be so easily laid down.
Saintsbury thought it the most mechanical and metallic of
the forms known to prosody; it is the most clearly arranged
into parts, superficially easy to write in, because its recurring
machinery seems to start all over again every two lines. Rhyme
in general was a troublesome and modern bondage to Milton,
and while Yvor Winters can find the couplet so flexible "because a bell is rung at the end of every second line," its constant demand for rhyme has inspired most of the charges of
autocracy against it. While the comments on rhyme contemporary with its usage are abundant, they often seem less

troubled by its constraint than later views. Daniel defends
rhyme as a proper stay for the mind, and Butler sees it as
useful to verse as a rudder to a ship. Both Dryden and Sir
Robert Howard see rhyme as a wholesome check on a too
luxurious fancy, and for an age that makes such an overwhelming choice in favor of the couplet, the form could
hardly have seemed so fiercely oppressive. Yet one may accumulate a whole thesaurus of familiar nouns and epithets to
describe the controlling force of rhyme and the couplet's other
restraining features. One hears of a curb, chain, bridle, cramp,
check, stocks, rein, of a chastener, an encroachment—all exerting a galling, Procrustean, tyrannous domination, keeping
inspired poetry at bay and forcing verse into hateful, uniform
battalions. Nonetheless, rhyme was most welcome to an age
needing it for epigram and aphorism, and the couplet as it
went on was glad to draw on Virgil's supply of words ideal for
the rhyme position. After Boileau, satire used stressed syllables
and end rhymes to transfix the names of unhappy victims, and
ideas generally gained emphasis from placing strong words
in rhyming positions. Skillful use of rhyme supported the
couplet's great rhetorical variety; things could be made to
seem inevitable and to agree with one another because they
rhymed; an air of certainty and finality might follow, statements might seem more convincing, as if already proved,
merely because they ended with such finality.

But rhyme was only the plainest of the couplet's immense
resources. Rhyme was not the only means of pause, although
it emphasized the real secret of the couplet's intimacy with the
age—its pervasive dualism. Nothing is more commonly observed of man, the world, and human life therein than the
mass of antipathies or contrarieties of which all is made. All
things, says the wise Peter Charron, have two handles and
visages; the world to Roger L'Estrange is composed of dis-
agreements, hot and cold, heavy and light; even dissimulation,
says Trimmer Halifax, is like most other qualities in having
two sides, one necessary and the other dangerous. Human life
for Mr. Empson too is a juggling with contradictory impulses,

first one and then the other dominant. The dualism of Restoration England established some of the classic divisions in human affairs that continue to this day. In politics Puritan and Cavalier gave way to Whigs and Tories, the government itself after 1688 to checks and balances; in religion the Clarendon Code had deepened the clash between orthodox and dissenting groups, as in their sentiments toward God men were warned neither to despair nor to presume. Literary discussion turned upon ancients and moderns, the ancients falling into Greece and Rome, Homer and Virgil, Aristotle and Horace, Cicero and Seneca. The terminology of pleasure and instruction, reason and passion, wit and judgment, beauties and defects keeps to the prevailing dualism, and satire becomes involved with virtue and vice, fools and knaves. Popularity of the dialogue form suggests again that there are two sides to all questions, with every view having to face some objection.

From a habit of thought that set up oppositions or balancing equalities, things grew into a process of being or becoming their opposites, and no one could think of accepting what was said or done at its face value. Everything seemed to carry within itself the means of its own transformation, as Marx was to argue later to herald a revolution. Thus dualism if continued might remain fixed in opposition; an element might turn into that which it was trying to avoid; as when a brief prose style trying to be clear becomes obscure through concentration; or a balancing equality might emerge into peaceful coexistence, moving toward unity.

The couplet seems the ideal form to carry this endless duality. Before its two lines move to agreement with each other, it may have paused repeatedly, balanced and contrasted, set up antitheses and parallelisms, inverted and divided, established metaphysical clashes and reconciled them, explored dilemmas and paradoxes, posed word against word, line or half line against its equal, placed thought against thought. The management of this dualism gives a poet desiring it a powerful control, as he explores the five pauses in every two lines that may act as units of antithesis: at the end of each couplet, at the end of each of its two lines and within each line. The caesura as recommended by Puttenham may indeed serve to correct the poet's licentiousness, or to give him an absolute command over his thought. End-stopped lines with pauses near the middle, especially after an accented syllable, give a new importance to adjectives on either side of the caesura. These can be made parallel or antithetical, with alliteration used to bring out their joint, double effect. Antithesis may be placed in the two rhyme words with alliteration added to point up the device, instead of or in addition to exploiting the two adjectives on either side of the caesura. The process of dividing and working in twos may thus proceed down to individual letters on either side of a pause.

Many of these devices of couplet verse suited the needs of heroic plays whose very titles and subtitles consisting of two names suggest the degree to which the plays themselves become a discussion of issues, especially conflicts between love and honor or duty. The speeches lose any personal emotion as they seem merely to debate the issues; the characters debate first with each other and then discuss within themselves as to which is the dominant force, lest anything be too hastily assumed or affirmed. The endings of heroic plays at first tended to be happy, as if the couplet form enabled them to explore all possible differences while ensuring that peace would come at last, and that human beings would find more to unite and compose their lives than to disorder them. The ideal of settling into a medium composure had a long history, and couplet verse with its special resources gave support to this ideal.

Its qualities in turn were an aid to satire, the literary genre which met the more general need of the age for correction. Satire was instructive, of the nature of moral philosophy, ideal for criticism and for the double role of pleasure and instruction, concerned to hold men responsible to a high standard of honor and reasonable behavior, supporting the need for law and order:

> For law and satire from one fountain flow:
> Were men not vicious there would be no law.

Satire restrains men by making them ridiculous, says Marvell to the painter. A satirist has to speak out against what is wrong as it appears to his superior insight and as justified by his own virtue. He is the only force able to compel a high level of achievement in art; so also he alone may fully rebuke moral and social evils. These are so prevalent in the world that like Juvenal he finds it difficult not to write satire. A man who thus supports the Muses and the Gods and in turn corrects the inadequacy of their justice in the world must be himself a wise and grave man, as Puttenham says, one perhaps influenced in his own temper by the gloom and frigidity of the planet Saturn. Feeling so responsible himself, as he aims to hold other men responsible, the satirist must define his right to speak, his own possession of the virtues he seeks to defend. This ethical right is much argued by Juvenal, and later by Boileau in considerable detail. Horace in particular with ingratiating blandness establishes his satiric character on the four-fold assertion that he is himself blameless, that he writes well, that he attacks only those who deserve it, and that in fact Caesar approves of him.

While satire might take almost any literary means toward its goal, in late 17th-century England it took up an already strong native satiric tradition and developed its many forms in the absence of great drama or lyric poetry. Dominance of heroic plays and their groping toward epic qualities, with ideal types of love and honor and human beings above the common level, would check the drive of satire toward things that are actually wrong in people as they are. When satire is free to seek its full expression—however various its literary combinations or allegorical its medium—it has to follow Horace's demand for terseness in keeping with its role, wisely managing its strength, remaining serious without being passionate, as Saintsbury says, disdainful without losing temper.

Its language would therefore sustain the neoclassical ideal, clear and under command, with its imagery becoming homely or violent as the argument demanded. The most characteristic figures were medical, curative of disease, since the satirist is concerned with illness and must act as physician or surgeon. No man, we are told, "can be said to write well, unless he can find fault well. For faults, like diseases, when perfectly discovered, are half cured." The renaissance metaphor of the barber-surgeon, the doctor of physick applying the instruments and remedies of curative science, holds for the satirist well into Dryden's time.

The natural objects of his attention are everywhere to see, especially bad men of any kind. "Nemo malus felix," cries Juvenal; no bad man is happy, and one of the offices of satire must be to distinguish between good and bad in art and morals. The satirist attacks bad writing, however popular; vanity, foppery, whatever is foolish, extravagant, or dishonorable, especially the knavery, artifice, and impertinence that imposes on all good men and disturbs the general peace of society. The standard satiric themes are explicitly laid down by Horace and Juvenal, and echo through Jonson and Boileau into the 18th-century masters. Extremes of any kind or falling prey to one's passions; miserly pursuit of money, gross materialism or luxury and extravagant living; unrestrained ambition, pride, or selfishness; fickleness or restless discontent; ingratitude, libertinism, or personal immorality; obsequious currying of favor, "licking of the dust" before the rich and powerful while refusing to judge honorable men on their merits—all these properly concern the satirist, but above all he must lay bare every form of pretense.

Satire constantly shows a language of exposure, as if naturally aimed at whatever is ungenuine or unable to live up to what it professes. To show what is false, to bring all cheats and imposters out of the dark, to throw the dry light of Cartesianism, as Basil Willey says, on failure to practice what is maintained in theory—such will be the high service of satire to mankind. To Dryden's age all the world seemed bent on appearing something other than it was, aided by the demands of a stratified society wherein only a certain element counts; men are tempted to seem what they are not in order to draw nearer to what actually counts in the world. In turn, such behavior invites satire to expose what is not genuinely high, good, cultivated, rich, or talented, and we get the ignorant doctors, the moral hypocrites, the *Précieuses ridicules* of Molière. Seen in this light, satire protects the established order from invasion by anyone not to its manner born; they must fear it most, as Dacier says, who fain would seem what they are not, from writers whose books are a mass of deceit, to selfish and ambitious men seeking their own benefit at the expense of general peace and welfare.

Northrop Frye has said that "the use an age makes of satire thus depends on its own problems," and it would seem that satire might recommend changes in thought and practice toward revolutionary ends instead of supporting the established order. Certainly Marvell could write satire in favor of Puritan or republican sentiments as well as Samuel Butler in favor of the opposite. Yet these differences would only be relative, since the satirist's criticism will refer to some form of permanent order or value. The task of satire is easier when it writes from approval of present society, since deviations from common standards are more obvious. Walter Raleigh doubts whether it is even possible for satire to advocate novelty; in Saintsbury's view this applies with special force to verse satire—itself so heavily controlled by its own forms of order and authority. When such verse is written by poets close to the court itself, by those most secure in the general opinion and most envied, it will readily make fun by satire and epigram of those who deviate from standards so clear; thus Rochester can be praised for ridicule of vices that endanger public bodies and the general peace. Laughter is most readily indulged from secure positions, from superiority and assurance; it is often argued that the Augustan literary mode, when most serious, best expresses itself in laughter. Horace had long ago recommended telling truth while one laughs, and as

Dryden says, there is a sharp, well-mannered way of laughing at folly which is easiest for one in high place, representing the accepted standard of his world. The clearer this standard is, the sillier does anyone seem who departs from it. No sensible man laughs, as Dennis says, at what is general and expected, and the men of irony, for Anthony Collins, are ranged on the side of orthodoxy, of organized religion and law. Swift allows even the King of Brobdingnag to see virtue in the church underneath its blot of corruptions, its theory and first perfection being admirable and hence a proper object of the satirist's loyalty. Even Dryden himself seems to have aroused the suspicion of Apollo by questioning the Test Act and other religious disabilities. On Parnassus, the Gods "and the whole house were mightily concerned to find that any member among them should go about to oppose or alter the known and established laws of government."

The long history of satiric inquiry into what is wrong, weak, and foolish in human behavior would seem to recommend virtue and wisdom, not changes in particular institutions or social arrangements. The sensible man adheres to the common forms; he does not make himself the object of satiric laughter by being foolish, eccentric, or peculiar—or worse still, by being violent in pushing some scheme of his own, by being overenthusiastic or self-assertive with some notion peculiar to himself. Men ought to be sure of controlling themselves before tampering with institutions, and if they fail to observe the central lines of behavior their energy will be reproved by satiric laughter. Neither the discernment behind it, its general attitude, or the ironic clashes of its expression will be popular. The amendment of vices by correction is work for the few who have the capacity and are in a position to do it; it will not flourish in a general society of equals. Most men do not ask what is wrong with them, either as members of mankind in general or as persons living in a particular time and place. They will not be comfortable in the face of irony which forces them back to what is real, which defeats their illusions, recalls them from error or false hope back to what is actual

and possible. The ironist must rely on a small circle to understand him, and his art as a satirist depends on getting entire
moral agreement from his loyal few. Good and sensible men
form a company that must stand above the objects of satiric
exposure; this company is itself immune, in its own judgment,
and must represent the virtues opposite to the vices being
exposed. No wonder Dryden agrees "that satire is a poem of
a difficult nature in itself, and is not written to vulgar readers."

But the satiric mode is not alone in stating the primacy of
the few, of the limited number of those in the conservative
myth who know and can. On all sides we shall meet, before it
is so dramatically shown in Dryden himself, the wide contrast
between the many and the few, the majority and the remnant
of Matthew Arnold's *Numbers*. Long after Plato, Charron
had seen the vulgar multitude as the mother of ignorance, in-
constancy, and folly, the chief agent of error and its continu-
ance. They have not wit or judgment to produce an idea that
is not ridiculous; to attempt subtle explanations or the sharing of anything abstruse with them is a casting of pearls
among swine. Higher education for these would be a danger,
since it would lead to illusions of grandeur and provide them
with something that in their ordinary stupidity and folly they
would lack the capacity to use sensibly. Such an inconsiderate
rabble is easily misled, a prey to discontented spirits, since
the majority cannot tell what they really desire or what is good
for them. Horace has warned that the Roman throng could
not have any taste or reliable artistic judgment; nor can the
populace have a true concept of the general welfare, including
their own. Hobbes disdains the seditious blockheads who are
more fond of change than of their peace or profit; in their
foolish rage they are capable of more mischief than the worst
of tyrants. In their pursuit of new-fangled opinions they seem
"as changeable, unconstant, and variable as the weather . . .
weary of present things, desirous of change and alteration."
One day the multitude cries Hosanna, the next, cries to cru-
cify him, such is their giddy-headed clamor. Their fickleness

suggests the influence of the moon, if their subordinate or derivative position with respect to royal authority, the sun, did not call up the comparison. In his almanac for 1688, *Annus Mirabilis,* the great John Partridge refers to the moon as signifying the people in general and those of London especially. Along with changeableness, the moon might signify the people in their madness, a theme repeated with endless variations. We hear of the mad common people, the furious, the unbridled, the raving multitude, the distracted and ungrateful mob, and steadily of the most odious symbol applied to their nature—the many-headed beast.

The word "mob" for the lower classes of society seems to have become common in the agitated period around 1680, presumably derived from the Latin "mobile vulgus." The "masses" is of more modern use, but the usual standard terms recur; the people, the multitude, the crowd, the mob, the rout, the rabble. These references are at least at the human level, and indicate nothing worse than human individuals in bulk, however mindless or uncontrollable. But allusion to the strong-headed beast, to the creature with many heads but no mind, the "swinish" mass of mankind suggests something monstrous, abnormal, or loathsome, changing the usual feelings of suspicion or mistrust into physical revulsion. Dryden himself in *Absalom and Achitophel* employs the "people" as a political term, and rarely with the combined disdain from above and the offended delicacy of Sir Thomas Browne, for whom the multitude is the great enemy of reason, virtue, and religion. It is a "numerous piece of monstrosity" that taken individually seems made of men, but taken together forms "but one great beast, and a monstrosity more prodigious than Hydra."

If such is the nature of the large majority, there is no choice but to return for guidance in human affairs generally, or for leadership in the creation of art and its appreciation, to the saving remnant, the few. Both criticism and original work are by and for a limited number. The usual terms come to mind, as we read endless repetitions of men of sense, learning, and moderation; wise, grave, and sober men as Meric Casaubon demands, or modest, sober, and staid, in Charron's words. The higher literary forms demanding the virtues of decorum and propriety, their appeal will rise above the vulgar level. Having to avoid all buffoonery, familiarity, and rude or clownish phraseology, poetry will look to men of high station—as Boileau says, a high-born audience, "commonly persons of the best quality" in Hobbes' phrase. The sense of a gentleman writer appealing to a group of similarly inclined friends emerges in Roscommon's summary:

> For none have been with admiration read,
> But who, beside their learning, were well-bred.

Thus sense, learning, and moderation are likely to be qualities of those who have the leisure and resources to develop them. Such men can never be amused or instructed save by others like themselves. They would not care about a large popular appeal even if they considered most men able or willing to respond to their refinement. They would agree with Horace's quotation from Arbuscula, who had been hissed by her audience: "nam satis est equitem mihi plaudere." Rochester, too, is content if the knights alone will applaud him. Among "the few who know" he lists eight of his contemporaries by name:

> I loath the rabble; 'tis enough for me
> If Sedley, Shadwell, Shephard, Wycherley;
> Godolphin, Butler, Buckhurst, Buckingham,
> And some few more whom I omit to name,
> Approve my sense: I count their censure fame.

Criticism in particular was bound to address the trained judgment of expert men, to seek enlightened taste and opinion. This is likely to be true of serious critical activity at any time. If the aim of criticism is to see things as they really are, and to make clearer the distinctions so easily blurred between good and bad, its writers will speak mainly to other minds like their own. And if as in neoclassicism so much of its expression employs the weapons of wit and irony, it must with Ben Jonson realize that the subtler forms of laughter are not available to the many. These forms tend to bring things to a standard, as Anthony Collins says, "to fix the decency and propriety of writing, to teach men how to write to the satisfaction of the ingenious, polite, and sensible part of mankind."

Yet for all this support of the few against the many, some confusion and uncertainty remains. Dennis seems to maintain this doctrine of the few only for the age of the writer, who then may appeal to a larger audience in later ages. Dennis might easily show "that they who in all ages have appeared at once good poets and good critics have writ to a few persons . . . but he who writes to the knowing few at present, writes to the race of mankind in all succeeding ages." This would seem to clash with the ideal of clearness and simplicity for purposes of instruction. If, as Roscommon and others cry, "the multitude is always in the wrong" and the appeal has to be to rare discrimination, why the struggle for a clear, unmistakable meaning, for the simplest possible language and form in both prose and poetry? Why not indulge a cult of obscurity, as charged against certain pre-Restoration poets? Like Hobbes, Davenant, for example, appeals to a select, high-born audience for poetry. Yet he disagrees that people should be kept in ignorance, and seems to desire a mass audience for poetry. He gets round the difficulty lamely, by saying that although poetry is to persuade the masses to the right virtues, this will be done through those in high places who follow the moral lessons of poetry and make them of wider effect by giving good example to the multitude. This is at least preferable to the verbose and parenthetical Henry Reynolds; he finds that his beloved ancients chose to express themselves in such enigmas and fables as would conceal their more profound meanings from "unworthy minds."

Is the inner meaning of the best literature and criticism reserved for a small number, then, as unavoidable in the nature of things, or is it kept so exclusive deliberately? Is it simply an unfortunate result of the way literature is, and most men are, that the best things can appeal only to a few? Further pursuit of the line of reasoning at work here seems only to deepen a sense of dualism, of desiring contradictory things, or giving different reasons for maintaining both. Even the meaning of the term "multitude" in discussions of the literary audience becomes blurred, since it may include anyone of low standards and bad judgment, however well-born. The audience of the few are supposed to be of high station as alone having a chance to be cultivated. Yet there are those in high social position who cannot appreciate excellence in poetry. If this is so, they belong to the "multitude," which in turn might contain persons whose literary responses would be excellent if invoked or given a chance. But the over-all number would still be small, even if the point were conceded that high place in life alone does not enable one to read good poetry.

But neoclassicism will have exclusiveness and appeal to the few. First, it assumes that most men have no judgment and cannot tell good writing from bad. But most men here, "the multitude," include what Ben Jonson, Browne, and Shadwell clearly point out, a rabble of high-born persons as well. When literature cultivates the virtues of polish and unified composition, the result automatically excludes most readers and confines itself to the men of sense, learning, and moderation. Are the virtues of neoclassical literature cherished, then, in order to exclude most readers, or does it merely become apparent after an excellent work is created that it can appeal only to a few? In any case, literature must have certain qualities which cannot be changed in order to take in a larger audience; yet part of its ideal calls for clearness and simplicity, the better to convey its lessons. Thus neoclassical literature seems narrow, then wide in appeal, but more deliberately narrow, as if trying to keep itself refined so that those who should not judge because they supposedly can not, will have no chance to try. Like so many bodies of theory, neoclassicism seems to make a virtue of something that will be true anyway. It finds exclusiveness desirable, yet this is already assured by the fact that

most men are by nature limited; the age is likewise organized
so that few persons will have the chance to cultivate the literary graces, either as writers or readers. Since those who matter prefer to keep things as they are and to hold society to its
established forms, they seem to develop a theory to justify
this. The theory of exclusiveness justifies what has to be, in
view of human weakness, justifies what is going to be kept as
it is in the prevailing order. The resulting dualism is typical,
and clearness may be sought as if it had no clash with the aims
of subtlety and refinement. If clearness enlarges the audience
and exclusiveness narrows it, both are going to be pursued
just the same. But the theory of literary exclusiveness does not
confine the audience of men of sense, learning, and moderation to those in high places. This is done through a social and
political application. In fact there will be only a few readers,
since only a few will have a chance to get the equipment needed to respond to literature, however clear and simple. No matter that *Absalom and Achitophel* quickly saw four editions
and provoked many replies. When Dryden applies the doctrine of the few to the loyal followers of the king in *Absalom
and Achitophel,* he shows us nothing but men of high station
in life. They are grave and sober men, of wealth and position,
cultivators of the arts and of learning, with no hint of unre-
fined taste or bad judgment, with no thought of asserting
themselves against order, whose loyalty to the king seems the
natural result of high birth and culture. Here there is no
sign as in literary theory that the "multitude" might contain
men of high place who were still crude and ignorant in their
literary judgments. The well-born who are misled into con-
spiring against the king, who break out of control by the established order, do so for other reasons, as called for by the
conservative myth. For Dryden the loyal few are beyond adverse criticism, in all respects what they should be, at once the
symbols and custodians of the divinity of order.

CHAPTER 2

Danger

From our view of the divinity of order in all of its wide-ranging influence, we might suppose that Dryden's world lay under
a heavy yoke, so exhausted and depressed by rule that individual energy had no chance whatever to declare itself. Every
impulse met by some prohibition, every affirmative note can-
celed by some opposite force must have given the individual
a hopeless sense of confinement, of being driven toward some
common center where he was held by the might of corporateness. Perhaps such an explicit body of law and order suggests
that it was needed, that in fact it was to hold in check something always present against whose dangerous outbreak the
force of order had to be vigilant. So much control implies
danger to be feared.

Now a rule that lays down strict procedure and works out
a complex theory always threatens to become an end in itself,
so that after a certain point, the more detailed the law, the less
likely are men to obey it. After a time, like the gloomier forms
of Evangelicalism, a mountain of precepts weighs down heavily on the realities of human nature. As Arnold says of stoicism
in the *Meditations* of Marcus Aurelius, it lacks sweet reasonableness and forgiveness, becoming like the accusations that
drove Cowper mad or the deformed rigidity against which
Dickens was to rebel on behalf of children and ordinary human nature.

As for the literary artist, it is common to say that 17th-cen-

tury theory was distant from its practice to the point of being
ludicrous. Should it be said that any age that is very self-con-
scious about proclaiming a theory or ideal of action does so in
order to let its practice be what it will? Like Mr. Micawber's
pecuniary obligations, might one not draw up a minute catalogue of regulations to govern a poem down to its last word,
and then cheer up, allowing the poem itself to become what
it could? In literature the works most widely covered by neoclassical theory, tragedy and epic, were not much attempted—
at least not in their traditional forms. Instead of formal epics
and tragedies, the Restoration combines them with changes
adapted to special needs, mainly in its "Heroic" plays, which
are often attempted epics, or treatments of epic qualities. Here
the practice does not falter through rebellious refusal; it is
simply not able to carry out what theory calls for, the theory
itself being derived from examples so good as to be out of
reach. High tragedy and epic are not often tried because the
best work of the age could not be done in them. The best
work was done in areas that freshly released its energy, genres,
or combinations of genres not covered in detail by theory and
rule. This in some measure accounts for the brilliant success
of *Absalom and Achitophel,* a poem so conceived as to be
whatever Dryden had the talent to make it.

In this view theory and rule become something that no one
tried to follow, since they governed what no one could attempt. The artist would be like Gulliver tied down by numberless little threads. Thus in order to get anything done the
poet has to embark on forms not covered by explicit rule; the
rules put things beyond reach by being derived from master-
pieces that could not be surpassed. We must wonder whether
the Augustans would have subscribed to the demand to subject imagination to judgment if they had been writing in the
higher, more heroic genres. Dryden would allow a freer scope
to imagination in epic poetry. Does the age not write epic
then because its demand to curb the imagination forbade
trying a form that needed so much imaginative energy? Or
does it avoid epic because epic theory is too strict, and prac-

tice already so great that attempts would be futile or ridiculous? Poets would then try lower forms, because these could be carried out within general theories of artistic control and created less of a tension between the imaginative faculties needed to write in them and the rules set up to govern them. In the higher forms, the chance to know the theory well from preceding practice is just what prevents the Augustans from going ahead in the same forms themselves. They could do nothing new in these areas, so they decided that anything new is not desirable. Their theory thus prevents them from carrying it out.

If we think of neoclassical rules as representing what a poet would do if he could, we will find that their spirit was enough, without strict pursuit of their letter. A poet sitting down to write was not consciously bound by a vast network of rules; he might not be aware of the limitations on him or, as Van Doren says, be conscious that they were limitations. He wrote in an atmosphere of discipline. The rules did not pretend to make an ideal poem in any case, but they were a useful guide to those who needed them, a set of principles if not statutes. They could be variously interpreted, and as Edward Hooker says, probably no two Augustans meant exactly the same thing by the word "rules." Then, too, a hierarchy of rules obtained, just as there was a hierarchy of genres, and Dennis would allow a poet to violate a lesser rule to save a greater one. Most important, the rules themselves expressly provided for their own violation. The immortal Horace at once confined the poet and invited him to let himself go, to adorn his work with a lavish hand. Boileau in fact offers it as a rule, not to observe any rule at all in some poems. He is willing to modify and balance his doctrines by allowing for the special demands of various genres, especially the lower ones. He sees the need of emotional movement to give some pleasure to the reader. A "brave disorder" may obtain, and Boileau like Horace seems to admit the impossibility of his ideal as he expresses it; it is final, yet tentative and uncertain.

Raymond Havens has exposed the danger of seeing Augus-

tan writers as all bound by a rigid and intolerant neoclassicism; this is nothing more than "an abstraction begotten by
Confidence on Inadequate Information." And certainly there
is evidence to justify not believing in the universal control of
energy so far reviewed. Going first to Horace as usual, we see
the *Epistles* warning against a too slavish pursuit of ancient
authority; the rules of composition are not supposed to be
chains. Quintilian warns against following the very rules he
is at such pains to lay down; rules are helpful in showing us
the direct way, but they are not to restrict us to the ruts of
our predecessors. And within neoclassicism in England itself,
opposition to formalism and ancient authority goes back to
the early 16th century, as Spingarn shows, greatly accelerating
with St. Evremond and those "whigs of criticism," Howard,
Butler, Temple, and even Dennis at times. Although Rymer
held sway with an austere formalism based on his ideas of
common sense, there was always a battle for freedom in progress, or at least a desire like Dryden's to avoid extreme slavish-
ness to rule while living within its safety. The scientific movement, of course, lost no chance to denounce a stunted learning
based too much on the ancients. Ridicule is heaped on the
common notion that everything ancient is good and everything good must be ancient. Glanvill despises this "doting on
antiquity," reverence for gray-headed doctrine, and for opinions that have nothing but charity to uphold them. And
Cowley in his poem *To the Royal Society* makes it a chief
praise of Francis Bacon, that he never

> . . . suffered living men to be misled
> By the vain shadows of the dead.

To be sure, every age sets the force of individual energy
against the claims of authority, and neoclassicism itself, the
most explicitly authoritative of systems, found itself always
tested against the pressure of individual talent and impulse.
As for late 17th-century England, it has been argued that the
rules were mostly an importation from France, that they became nothing but exotic growths on the soil of England. Like

Charles II on leaving France and settling in England, the
rules were bound to relax and expand in the free English
air. So much is made of the rules, they are so often repeated
and insisted upon, because they had to be drummed into
English heads that were never really suited to them. A nation
that has produced Shakespeare and goes on loving him will
not cling to regulations that cut down his abundance. Shakespeare was bent on pleasing his audience; when Dryden and
his fellow playwrights saw that they too must please in the
theater, they adjusted themselves to actual theatrical needs
and let the rules govern as best they could. Aside from Shakespeare, the Elizabethans generally seemed attractive, so that
a tension arose between appreciating Elizabethan literature
and the demand to repudiate the Elizabethans as implied in
neoclassical theory. As Paul S. Wood has remarked, modern
English literary criticism had its beginning in trying to recon-
cile these opposite forces.

If native English energy was bound to declare itself, a generous outlet was at hand. If the couplet was a strain, ways of
relieving it were available. Saintsbury says of Roscommon's
love of gambling that he took to cards as relief from the couplet's bondage. While this can hardly be serious, it is true that
games of chance, gambling in card games which contain a
large element of chance, flourished when the dominant zeal
for order left the minimum to chance. While using the couplet itself, one might in fact write in stanzas or verse paragraphs, or vary monotony with Dryden's alexandrines and
triplets. In addition there is enough variety and freedom in
the lyrics to show how the Augustans let themselves go when
they felt the need. Rapin himself allows irregularity and
transport for the ode, it being a "rule" to let the ode go without "rule." While Yvor Winters can say that there is a kind
of tyranny in the use of longer stanzas, the scope offered by
the bigger units of the Pindaric ode was a relief from what
Edward Phillips called "the continued rhapsody of rhyming
couplets." The result might be mediocre verse; something irregular just for the sake of being irregular as an escape from

the couplet was bound to be worse than the monotony it professed to cure. This suggests why the worst romantic poem is supposed to be worse than the worst Augustan poem; consciously free of regulation like the Cowleyan Pindaric, there was nothing to prevent its being as bad as its author's bad taste would permit.

But a vigilant age, looking from literary to general social order, might see other than artistic danger in the license of Pindaric verse. A Tory dialogue of "Jest and Earnest" discusses a proper form in which to set a poem praising the king. Jest says, "I think Pindarique, which is the poet's latitudinarian way or liberty of conscience in verse, is more jaunty; and it . . . may procure our pardon from the dissenting crickets, who cannot in justice condemn us in what they allow themselves." A form that lacks discipline is then appropriate for expressing rebellious sentiments, and suggests how the desire for political and social order led to so much control of literary expression. Behind all the vast structure of rule and law there is a fear lest individual energy, if given any chance at all, will assert itself dangerously. Hence the attack on such displays of energy as eloquence, vigorous figurative language, powerful original thought or speculation, and, worst of all, the force of human imagination, which might lead into a whole complex of dangers suggested by the term "enthusiasm."

The ancients had explored oratorical eloquence, seeing clearly its power and its danger. Aristotle in the *Rhetoric* justified oratory and its devices because most people could not learn from reason and scientific proof; weak judgments respond to oratorical means of persuasion. Quintilian is himself eloquent in his praise of the art he so greatly admires. A favorite theme of his discourse emphasizes the qualities in man that distinguish him from other creatures—mainly reason and the powers of speech. Should we not consider, then, that the special virtue of man lies just as much in eloquence as it does in reason? In establishing the orator's ideal Quintilian appeals to the sense of balanced dualism. Each term in a series of eight is held in check by a negative, with sixteen words ending in *a*, each pair joined by *non*, every virtue to be cultivated balanced by a fault to be avoided: "Sic erunt magna non nimia, sublimia non abrupta, fortia non temeraria, severa non tristia, gravia non tarda, laeta non luxuriosa, iucunda non dissoluta, grandia non tumida." The sound here echoes the sense, and along with this sobriety and measure, we are not astonished to find Quintilian insisting that no one can be a proper orator who is not also a good man; thus the evils that might come of his power are accidents outside his own nature. His last term, "tumida," however, implies a danger to Longinus, who while celebrating sublime eloquence warns against tumidity as one of the most difficult faults of oratory to avoid. And Tacitus in his masterly dialogue on oratory has to say that eloquence flourishes best in times of unrest, being quite hushed in the reign of Augustus. He might be writing on behalf of the conservative myth of late 17th-century England when he says in effect that eloquence must be curbed for the sake of peace:

> . . . really great and famous oratory is a foster-child of licence, which foolish men called liberty, an associate of sedition, a goad for the unbridled populace . . . Devoid of reverence, it is insulting, off-hand, and overbearing. It is a plant that does not grow under a well-regulated constitution . . . at Rome, so long as the constitution was unsettled, so long as the country kept wearing itself out with factions and dissensions and disagreements . . . the growth of eloquence was doubtless sturdier . . . oratory has less prestige and smaller consideration where people are well-behaved and ready to obey their rulers . . . What is the use of one harangue after another on public platforms, when it is not the ignorant multitude that decides a political issue, but a monarch who is the incarnation of wisdom?

For Dennis, the ancient mastery of eloquence is due to the opportunity it then gave to personal ambition; love of glory may be as strong in men as ever, but there are no tumults of applause from popular assemblies now to recompense the flaming orator. Rapin sees that oratory is no longer the road to distinction; it leads to no prize, and Wotton observes that the oratorical style declines in ages of close authority. After Macedon and Rome fall under the sway of emperors, Demosthenes and Cicero are not possible, and nowadays it is expected that men will hold their tongues when they have spoken to the point in few words. Let us beware of the golden tongue in a subtle head, Osborne tells his son; such a union does best under a republic. In a more controlled scheme of things large numbers of people need not be considered or appealed to, and a more concentrated style will suffice to address the sensible few. Even if the scientific movement for a style easily understood by anyone has a democratic effect of wider appeal, it is never intended to go beyond use and understanding, never aimed at arousing emotional response. Those wishing to let their eloquence have free play will find scope in the literature of flattery called for by a courtly society; poems of tribute and panegyric, glowing dedications, were quite uninhibited, so that it might be said of some writers that they wrote books to make an occasion for composing a profitable dedicatory tribute to the great. For the rest, "innovators and seditious orators" had caused trouble enough, and the power of oratory to cause dissension and to inflame the turbulent was so great that Rapin, invoking Quintilian, is sure that none but a good man ought to be an orator. And the biblical Sprat sees so much danger in "superfluity of talking" that "eloquence ought to be banished out of all civil societies, as a thing fatal to peace and good manners."

Similar fears account partly for the attack on pulpit eloquence. The general call for a simpler prose was bound to alter the style of sermons, since clearly a sermon must make its effect when given, not at some uncertain future time. If their hearers call for a change of tone, sermons must therefore respond. Like other branches of literary prose, sermons will change under the many influences then active, from science and the Royal Society, through the taste of the court and the educated classes, back to native English influences based on tradition or popular journalism. The special needs of the pulpit, however, made for a great variety of tone and language. Common distinctions emerge in Abraham Wright's *Five Sermons in Five Several Styles* (1656). A preacher may well require the various qualities of a scholar, poet, philosopher, and apostle, in order to adapt himself to the responses and abilities of any sort of audience. Thus sermons will vary with the religious sect involved, something that gave Sir William Petty a chance for comic mimicry. According to Evelyn, Petty is said to have amused Charles II with successive imitations of the court pulpit, the Presbyterian, Independent, Anabaptist, Quaker, Fanatic, Friar, and Jesuit styles of preaching. This suggests that preaching split up into a variety of manners suited to the special audience of each, thus allowing the use of any devices that seemed necessary. General reform of style would bring about some of these changes and adaptations, leaving other modes of address much the same as they chose to be. It seems clear at least that more elaborate sermons gave way to the more "plain and practical," which could in turn be split into the variations ridiculed by Petty.

If sermons became simpler, they did so in order to be more clearly understood, and to avoid the dangers of excited passion or emotional upheaval. John Spencer's essay "Ministers to Preach Plainly as well as learnedly, to the Capacity of their Hearers" (1658), sounds the common note of appeal to ordinary capacities, the address "to the apprehensions of the meanest." The success of John Tillotson's pulpit style did much for the cause of functional prose in general and showed how effective "plain" preaching could be. Bishop Burnet would have matters adjusted to the lowest common denominator in the parish, with nothing carried beyond the ordinary observation of mankind. In 1670 John Eachard had explored reasons why the clergy and religion were fallen into contempt. His work made him seem to Spingarn like the Jeremy Collier of corrupt pulpit rhetoric, and he makes a strong demand for seeing the preacher's audience for what it is. It serves no purpose to pretend that the audience knows more than it does. One must preach so as to instruct ignorance in terms that will neither confuse nor disturb the people. And true to his scientific bias, Glanvill would have nothing mysterious or speculative uttered from the pulpit. He is unscientific but typically conservative in saying that preaching is not supposed to teach men new things, but rather to bring known things to the mind for consideration. "Mysterious notional preaching" has caused some conceited persons to meddle with what they do not understand. It has "filled them with air and vanity, and made them proud, fantastical, and troublesome, disobedient to their governors and contemptuous to their betters." Swift will soon express a similar view by means of his "Aeolists," suggesting notions of fear and disdain, of the need for control in society for the sake of order, men being what they are.

If the preacher is not to be obscure, he should also avoid stirring the emotions of his hearers. Imagination and passion are centers of disorder, and Meric Casaubon had pointed out that wise men suspect whatever is joined with passion. Rapin instructs the preacher, then, to avoid any obvious attempt to move his audience; a passion too long continued is always false. Burnet himself was charged by his contemporary George Hickes with showing too great a strain. His sermon on the death of Tillotson was forced eloquence; Burnet used the figures of a young declaimer, transported by the heat of rhetoric. This recalls the caution of Hobbes that preaching of their duty to the people should be done by "grave, discreet, and ancient men," and much of the concern over the dangers of pulpit eloquence shades into the strong anticlericalism shared by Dryden and violently asserted by the deists. Long after there was a great danger from this source, the deist Thomas Woolston could charge that teachers of religion have been the pest of mankind, the bane of society, sometimes by their sermons overturning the very governments they should have sustained. It was certainly dangerous, Hobbes thought, to allow a set of men to harangue the people every Sunday and oftener; let the state be sure of their sobriety then.

This fear of eloquence must seem strange when so many preachers of the old florid style gave no sign of rebellious sentiment at all, but on the contrary were devoted royalists. Yet such was the dread of emotional or imaginative appeal that, once more, control of individual energy must obtain. Whether one says that prose changed for scientific or for religious reasons, the result in clearness and order will be the same. If all is so clear that everyone can understand it, there can be no disputes over what it means. Again, if the preacher avoids high-flown language with elaborate figures that tend to stimulate the imagination, no one will be stirred to a dangerous frenzy. Religion must not grow too poetical.

Ancient commentary on figurative language seemed at once to allow its virtues and to warn against misuse of its power. The Abbé Bouhours, in accepting imagery as a source of delight, finds that Aristotle had seen our common pleasure in comparing one thing with another through metaphor. Horace had cautiously rejoiced in his own tendency to be economical in style, and Quintilian in deploring high-flown, extravagant expressions, warns against the "shame of artifice," and against the notion that genius cannot express itself in direct, natural terms. Demetrius' *On Style* permits metaphors under special conditions, for which he gives precise rules. He would have them natural, based on true analogy and usage, and applied from the greater to the less. In general he regards the simile as the less daring device. Longinus, to be sure, sees that "the sublime" has to invoke the aid of "artifice," and that "sublimity" needs metaphorical language for its effect of grandeur. Yet metaphor is like any other beauty of style in that it tempts one to excess, as witness the deplorable linguistic intoxication so often remarked in Plato. In the end, the burden of proof is on the use of metaphors. They atone for themselves only by achieving the sublime effect at which they aim; unless they carry us away so that we do not notice them, they are not legitimate.

But the age of Dryden did not allow itself to be carried away, as it feared the danger of transport and emotion. Its

ideal of pleasure would allow poetical language to make wholesome lessons more agreeable, and it would accept Lansdowne's
cautious *Essay upon Unnatural Flights in Poetry* (1701):

> Mistake me not: No figures I exclude,
> And but forbid intemperance, not food.

At times too, the very attack on figurative language so agitates
its enemies that they become the comic victims of their own
fears. In his censure of Platonic philosophy Samuel Parker denounces metaphors as unable really to express the nature of
things, achieving only some fanciful resemblance. Hence philosophical theories using metaphor are not real truths:

> Thus their wanton and luxuriant fancies climbing up into
> the bed of reason, do not only defile it by unchaste and il-
> legitimate embraces, but instead of real conceptions and
> notices of things, impregnate the mind with nothing but
> airy and subventaneous phantasms.

But whether they could avoid it themselves or not, cautious
men of the Restoration were opposed to such excess—the extravagance, as they saw it, of their predecessors. The lack of
common sense leads to a demand for it; the uninhibited Elizabethan debauch, in this view, called for a rest cure. There
was simply too much of everything in the prose that came
down through Donne and Browne and Jeremy Taylor. It was
not all bad in the same way, but things had to become simpler.
One hears the adjective "swollen" applied, meaning that
prose was unnaturally enlarged in the number of words, and
in the number of meanings carried by heavily charged figurative language. With his translation of More's *Utopia* (1684),
Burnet reviews the fulsome pedantry, the "dark and unintelli-
gible wit," the coarse extravagance of canting, the corruption
of English by strong but false rhetoric. It is now happily more
"natural and proper" than ever before. This suggests that the
condition seeks the remedy, and England first suffers from
excess or license before adopting fully the neoclassical cor-

rective of rule and decorum. An age gets a desired classicism only after it has gone too far with its opposite, and retreats from a too advanced position, going back to something more secure, something preferably that has always been there—in this case, a functional medium of expression.

Here again the scientist blends with the critic, the preacher, and the rhetorician to curb the energy of figurative language. "I study matter, not words," says Alexander Ross, invoking the familiar battle between words and things. Language itself, the mere fact of using words at all, was a defect. All language seemed to obscure reality, instead of describing it clearly. Ordinary, literal words seemed far enough from the things they were supposed to stand for. Even worse are terms that possess many different meanings, that mean the same as others, or that in their willful energy seem to invite comparisons which in turn make language more obscure and unreal than ever. In religious discourse, elaborate language is liable to the same objection offered by the deists against excessive ceremony; it gets in the way and substitutes itself for what it should convey, obscures the reality to be understood. Therefore Eachard would appeal to plain English and common sense, would avoid metaphors that rely on special arts or areas of experience known only to certain groups; he would return to the practice of Christ himself, who took his references from the salt of the earth, from things so plain and familiar that they must be known to any man who has lived in the world as it is. For eloquence Thomas Blount would encourage metaphor but confine it sharply to what is clear and appropriate. One should speak through common notions, and remember, as Rapin says in warning against metaphors, antitheses, and epithets, that "what shines most in a discourse, is commonly the greatest cheat." There is no virtue in striving to make a thing seem great by the use of high-flown terms. Le Bossu scorns those who think they are creeping, "unless they soar above the clouds: and little dream that when they quit the earth, they part with what is solid to embrace an airy phantom."

Language, too, like all other forms in which human energy might get itself expressed, must then be driven down and brought within the scope of easy understanding and control. And the same fear governs this attempt at control, like all others. Hobbes desires to curb metaphors because they are *ignis fatui,* whose end is "contention, sedition, or contempt." Sprat denounces "this vicious abundance of phrase, this trick of metaphors, this volubility of tongue, which makes so great a noise in the world" as a source of general mischief, and Samuel Parker favored an act of Parliament to abolish metaphors and so end the distempers of the age. Style becomes almost a matter of life and death, and even the attempts to defend metaphors impose strict rules on their use, as R. F. Jones says, ransacking "all the principles of rhetoric for precautions in the use of metaphors and similitudes," so that the principle of control is maintained even while recommending what seems to violate it. The villain here emerges ever more clearly as a certain faculty of the mind, a gift which enables men to create the more energetic, hence the less controllable, hence the more dangerous forms of expression. A line passes from creative imagination, to rhetoric, to energetic figures of speech, to stirring up people's emotions, to causing controversies and factions, to larger divisions, and finally to public outbreaks against the established order.

If it is dangerous to be eloquent, for the eloquent man it is then dangerous to possess the abilities of mind and spirit that engender his power. In the conservative myth to this day, nothing is more steadfastly maintained than the paradox of superior gifts as futile and dangerous. Alas, Tacitus remarked in his determined way, one cannot have both great renown and great repose, and Thucydides had long before decided that a man is more happy and fit for governing a commonwealth if his spirit is somewhat below mediocrity. The over-quick and ingenious, the too elevated spirit, torments himself and others; the danger he poses for the world gets a classical statement from Charron:

. . . we cannot but see, that they that have any extraordinary vivacity and rare exellency . . . are, for the most part, lawless both in opinion and manners. There are very few of whose guide and conduct a man may trust, and in the liberty of whose judgments a man may wade without temerity, beyond the ruled and governed; it is a dangerous sword which a man knows not well how to guide; for from whence come all those disorders, revolts, heresies and troubles in the world, but from this?

Great ability means energy resisting control, and the sober Elizabethan Daniel sees no way but to conclude that "the greatest spirits were ordained to endanger the world, as the gross are to dishonor." As we might expect, the plodding Sprat is more afraid of excess "in the subtlety of men's wits, than in their thickness."

Too much ability is inconvenient in turn because it leads to pursuit of learning, to kinds of knowledge that mankind is better off without. Montaigne had conceded that learning has its place, but too much of it is folly. Indeed the thirst for knowledge led to the first downfall of mankind, and nowadays it is clear that knowledge is a prime source of misery. In the history of Rome one sees in the first centuries a steady growth in virtue and valor; as soon as Rome grew learned, it fell into corruption and civil war. It is better not to know much beyond what is useful, and Burnet, as befits his calling, prefers a great measure of piety with a small proportion of learning. And suspicion of learning is bound to extend to the citadels thereof. Hobbes compared the universities to the wooden horse that led to the ruin of Troy. Orators trained at the universities had misled the people into disobedience, instead of teaching them absolute loyalty to the laws of the king. The case against learning and the kind of men who possess it is so explicitly stated by Thomas Pope Blount that his language seems about to turn into its opposite and become ironic. He sees learning as the enemy of virtue and innocence; all the troubles of the world have risen from men of knowledge. As soon as learning has a chance to diffuse itself among the vulgar, they become restless and begin to argue with their superiors. Princes therefore keep their subjects ignorant, and the subtle, crafty James I of England was often heard to say that the thinking man made the worst of all subjects.

So Daniel can say, "I thank God that I am none of these great scholars." He is content to go "plodding on the plain tract I find beaten by custom and the time, contenting me with what I see in use . . . it is ever the misfortune of learning, to be wounded by her own hand." Learning leads on to speculation, and as Halifax says, speculative knowledge is too fine for use; it is unnecessary and possibly dangerous. This was just the most telling of the charges against the old "philosophy of the schools," as Glanvill said. Here Aristotle becomes the villain, Bacon and Descartes the heroes who show the way down from the clouds of speculation and theory to the world of things as they are. It is commonly observed of Descartes that he was intellectually bold but practically timid, unwilling to push to their farthest ends the implications of his method. He disavows large changes in practice, and seems to support the improvement of life in detail without forcing logic to go beyond. Hence his utility as an antidote to the old philosophy, the speculative mode that filled the mind with monstrous chimeras, confusing it with ambiguous and equivocal terms offensive to a discreet and wary spirit, and betraying men into fighting and contending.

If such is the tendency of superior gifts, the world had best exclude the sagacious of wit from its governing councils. The bookish man, the learned scholar, the speculative theorist— all may be gifted, they may come fresh from the university, they may have set up the best schemes, methods, and precepts ever imagined. But let them confront particular matters, see the nature of men as it is and not as it should be, appear at court and face the problems of civil prudence and present emergencies. They discover that doctrine or theory cannot govern practice, they hesitate and wax astonished and see that their knowledge miscarries, for as Osborne tells his son in many different ways, "experience is a better tutor than Buchanan." A comparison suggests itself here between the agony over words and the defeat of general ideas. Words, too, are hard facts, particular realities against which our ideas are always casting themselves and maiming themselves in the attempt. There being no precisely right word for anything, the process of searching for it leads us farther from what we wish to say. The search continues in loss, in multiplication of words with diminishing effect.

But human vanity too often betrays men into folly before the useful lessons of experience have done their work. The attack on the various forms of human pride has a history as long as any aspect of the wise, realistic distrust of our common nature. If vanity here is placed after individual ability, it is because vanity is part of what makes the individual believe in his own rightness, become confident of his own opinions, and depart, as Montaigne says, from the common path to embrace novelties. We have then paid a high price for our capacity of judging and knowing. It leads the individual into illusory notions of himself and of the world, betrays him into insolence, separates him from other men, and inflames the spirit to the point of madness.

The nearness of great wit to madness carries a number of ominous implications. Great wit as containing imagination was, to be sure, allowed by many to function in its proper sphere. Dennis sees the imaginative faculty as proper for poetry and pleasure, if not in business and politics, and Charleton's *Two Discourses* (1669) allows the faculty opposite to judgment free play in its right sphere—in poetry, in eulogy or panegyric. In actual practice the conflict between intellect and imagination bothered the 17th century less than Cartesian philosophy seemed to imply. Men went on imagining vividly while thinking clearly and acutely. Still, those minds concerned to expose possible dangers to order leveled the standard charges against the imaginative faculty. Imagination more than passion is evil; it is various and inconstant, a rebel within the spirit; as Charron has said, using images of noise, the imagination makes all the stir, clatter, and perturbation of the world, and leads to every mischief and disorder. For Henry More its enormous strength seems to be in our power, as respiration is; but it can work without our leave, and "hence men become mad and fanatical whether they will or no." It is deceptive and hence an uncertain guide, bound up with dangerous psychological states, shading into melancholy and madness. All the more reason, then, to distrust the man who seems gifted with the more intense forms of individual energy and genius. There is no way of knowing what excesses such a man is capable of. Let him therefore not be elevated to power, and let the large majority of mankind be content with commoner talents, safer for themselves and others.

The constant fears lest personal energy as seen in the intellectual, emotional, or imaginative faculties get beyond a safe control, converge finally upon the term "enthusiasm." From suggesting a high form of religious contemplation, "enthusiasm" finally draws to itself the meaning of all the accumulated fear-words of the conservative myth: passion, imagination, poetical inspiration, emotion, rhetoric, eloquence, and figurative language, and the various ways in which vanity brings on self-assertion—these and all their accompanying dangers that the late 17th century thought it had reason to fear seem implied by "enthusiasm." Neither in the creation nor in the criticism of poetry was the individual to rely on mere "divine" inspiration, sensitiveness of response, subjective impression, but on the virtues that led to orderly statement: rational power, deliberate use of principle and knowledge, judicious reading, and careful consideration. Neither poet nor critic was to be an "enthusiast," to give way to inspiration or zeal—to go his own way, that is.

If art was to exercise authority against the pressure of individual talent or impulse, in religion it was vastly more important to hold down the everlasting impulse to break away toward one's own feeling and persuasion, since religious control had to sustain the whole structure of law and order in society. Anyone who insists on his own way in religion, who is conceited or proud of his special views or insights simply cannot be a good subject or a good neighbor. All extraordinary callings, secret motions, inspired or extempore prayers outside the standard forms, preachings, windy humors and fumes that rise to the mind and bring on fluency and eloquence—all the myriad forms in which enthusiasm in religion may show itself are to be avoided as the worst possible dangers to the general welfare. For this reason Hobbes objected to making the Bible generally available; it could lead only to diverse opinions, which in turn mean rebellion. He is part of a vast chorus that cries out against differences, contentions, controversies, argumentations, schisms, disputes, and contrarieties, singularities, or innovations in religion. Diversity of religions, says Alexander Ross in a typical passage, begets "envy, malice, seditions, factions, rebellions, contempt of superiors, treacheries, innovations; disobedience" and other mischiefs that invoke the judgment of God upon the state permitting contrary religions, since "whilst every one strives to advance his own religion above the other, all these distempers . . . must needs follow."

The peaceful centrality of Deism supports these endlessly repeated features. Tolerance in Chesterton's view is the virtue of men who do not believe in anything; thus the Deists could reject the idea that truth consists in any one system or persuasion. They desired to compose differences, to avoid theories or speculations in favor of a few simple, generally understood and acceptable truths. Their language abounds in goodness, virtue, peace, the light of common reason, universal consent, the common fatherhood of God. Indeed their God is a mosaic of ingredients from mythical conservatism: He never changes, He cares nothing for particular ceremony, private revelations, miracles or prophecies or other nonessential peculiarities; He is always simple and clear to everyone.

For God too, then, the enemy is anything that makes for division or trouble, with the result that He must share the anticlericalism of the Deists and other peaceful elements—a

suspicion that "priests of all religions" as Dryden says, are the
same in posing a danger to established order. In their reading
of Scripture priests cannot agree; they divide into numberless
sects, and indeed leaders of the same sect cannot agree in their
opinions, and are even capable of fraud in imposing their contradictory views on others. As expected, Hobbes thought that
rebellion had been openly taught from pulpits in the past, but
even if this had not been so, it would be dangerous to allow
the clergy to preach or publish the materials of their own
endless dissensions. Bishop Burnet himself deplores the restless clerical spirit, and a long experience of the malice and
falsehood of mankind has forced him to think the worst of
men and parties—especially of the ill nature, peevishness, and
ambition of the clergy. Burnet quotes the anecdote of Shaftesbury, who was once heard to say that men of sense are really
of but one religion; on being asked which religion it was, the
Earl replied, "men of sense never tell it."

They never tell it precisely because they are men of sense,
unlike the common enemy, the enthusiasts. We are forced
back here to the language of disease as applied to these dangerous social elements, moving from physical into mental disorder to absolute madness at last. We have before us, as Glanvill says, the things that have been done "by the ecstatic priests
of the heathen oracles, and the madmen of all religions; by
sybils, lunatics, poets, dreamers, and transported persons of
all sorts." From their melancholy brains have come visions,
voices, and revelations. They have been the victims of epilep-
tical raptures and ecstasies, fits, hypochondriacal distempers,
spiritual drunkenness. Nothing is more dangerous than the
well-meaning zealot who becomes bold and furious, giddy
and inflamed, while his head grows distempered with religious
lunacies. Giving power to such an individual is like placing
a sword in the hands of a madman under whose influence the
ignorant multitude, so easily excited and misled, may fall into
no one knows what degree of insane violence themselves.

As in Swift's *Tale of a Tub,* our review of danger for the
age of Dryden finally centers on this pervasive language of

madness. The energy displayed in great individual ability, taking as it does so many forms difficult to control, leads to self-assertion, the break-up of corporateness, division of men into contending groups, disturbance of the unruly and changeable mass of mankind into final upheaval, disruption, rebellion—what is all this but madness? In the conservative myth, it is literally insane to do anything which might possibly overturn the established order. And on this, with all of its kindred associations, Dryden was to draw heavily in creating *Absalom and Achitophel.*

CHAPTER 3

The Downfall of the Good Old Cause

Now this effort to deplore separation and to praise unity, authority, and harmony appears justified by historical events as well. The Restoration that was to compose all past disharmony left many problems unsolved, and went on to create or intensify others. It was agreed that division was fatal; nothing could be worse for England than parties, factions, cabals, colliding interests, disputes between high and low. Yet as Glanvill lamented, in spite of hating disputes he is engaged in one amid "a squabbling and contentious age." Like the Deists, the nation in general had hoped for common agreement, a view of things large enough so that everyone might be at peace within it. Let there be agreement after contention, order after disorder, peace after war; let England be rid of all that divides and cling to all that unites men. Yet sources of friction became more sharply defined than ever. Religious divisions became worse when Charles II sided with the Bishops against dissenters; the new tests and conditions would never be agreeable to nonconformist scruples, so differences were sharpened instead of composed. An age whose entire aim and need was to get into agreement developed a spirit of disorder, as Henry Tubbe declared, in families, schools, colleges, and churches. Fairfax sees that "an ill willed and frampled waspishness has broken forth, to the royling and firing of the age wherein we live," and Butler sees a harmonious inclination, "Of all degrees to Reformation." A surface frivolity meant concealed anxiety, and as the reign of Charles II wore on, the reasons for fear became ever more obvious and more clearly justified. As F. J. C. Hearnshaw says in studying the element of fear in the conservative temper, there are some things that men ought to be afraid of, and toward the middle of the age of Dryden the standard English fears of France, Rome, and Hell converged upon the obsessive fear of Civil War.

Such a work as Bishop Samuel Parker's *History: Or the Tory's Chronicle* of the years from 1660 to 1680 pictures a troubled reign for Charles II even in the early "honeymoon" years after the Restoration. Conspiracies, treacheries, plots, and schisms are carried on by hot fanatics, threatening the King's peace and his very life itself. The 1675 version of our modern "loyalty oath" demands that anyone enjoying beneficial office—ecclesiastical, civil, or military—must swear his abhorrence of the thing most to be feared:

> I . . . do declare, that it is not lawful upon any pretence whatsoever to take up arms against the King, and that I do abhor that traiterous position of taking arms by his authority against his person, or against those that are commissioned by him in pursuance of such commission. And I do swear, that I will not at any time indeavour the alteration of the government either in Church or State. So help me God.

In giving *A Compendious View of the late Tumults and Troubles* of the years 1678 to 1685, James Wright creates a vivid sense of the mounting tension of these years of intrigue and desperate struggle. He cannot pretend to give a full account of all the "narratives, discoveries, trials, executions, speeches, votes, accusations, examinations, commitments, tumultuous elections, petitions, riots, libels and seditious attempts" that disfigured the last years of the reign of Charles II.

Hearnshaw observes that conservatism is relative to whatever danger threatens the established order at a given time. Thus conservatism has no consistent doctrine; it moves in response to its needs, its defense taking a form called for by present danger. As events moved to their climax in 1681, the

dangers seemed to center on Rome and on civil war. "We
dread the effects of a new Civil War," writes Samuel Pordage,
and "We dread Rome's yoke" as well, since there can be no
peace for England without a Protestant king. But the threat
of civil war was in the end to contain all other reasons for
fear, and the conservative myth was to concentrate on a theme
which had long been essential to its force. Basil Willey has
shown that nearly every statement found in Hobbes arises
from hatred of schoolmen and clerics, from the fear of civil
war and the longing for an ordered, stable society. His views
are shared by those who find any tyranny better than civil war;
better a century of tyrants than a single year's rebellion. And
the memory of England's own mid-century upheaval was still
vivid. Anything done after 1660 that resembled anything done
in the 1640's was supposed to have the same result. One could
discredit any action merely by saying that it recalled something done in the late civil war. All revolts are the same, they
begin in the same way for the same reasons, and are certain
to have the same results—witness the English civil war. All
elements agreed on this, and kept accusing each other's actions
and motives as tending to this unforgivable offense against
England. The old civil war had given conservatism its perfect
defense: what happened yesterday will happen again. L'Estrange and other Tory propagandists especially warn against
the extremities of another war, denounce presbytery and enthusiasm, start in alarm over a recurrence of the late unnatural rebellion and its miseries, England's "preternatural in-
testine jars," and ring all the changes possible on the "martyrdom" of Charles I and its threatened repetition. In the
volume of *One Hundred Eighty Loyal Songs* (1680) written
since 1678 and the Popish Plot, the reader is asked "Have you
not heard of forty-one, Sir?" and is warned constantly against
reformers, Whigs, zealots, rebels, dissenters, and associators.
"The Downfall of the Good Old Cause" has this refrain:

> Charles the first they murdered,
> And so they would the other.

The civil war that had preceded Charles II had been also a good omen, since it encouraged the resemblance seen between Charles and the Roman Augustus by the indispensable Sprat. Augustus was fortunate in succeeding a long civil war, since "the minds of all men were easily composed into obedience by the remembrance of their past misfortunes"; yet this was no match for the felicity of England once Charles II had returned. But composure into obedience gave way to something that resembled the preceding tumult, and the parallel between the mid-century civil war and any move that seemed to involve radical change was to hold individual energy in check for generations. Dennis likened the conflict in man between reason and passion to a kind of civil war, and for him too the English upheaval was "a universal conspiracy of fools against right reason." As Montaigne had written against the background of violent civil war in France and so arrived at his classical views of order and stability, Dryden and his age could not help recalling what must under no circumstances be allowed to happen again. Therefore, L'Estrange solemnly warns, "let every man look behind him, and lay his finger on his mouth."

Now if civil war was always the same in result, it was always the same in its origins and the means taken by men bent on rebellion, who will rebel regardless of the consequences. Given the intimacy between religion and the state, any man willing to risk civil war cannot avoid clashing with, or making use of, religion in some form. Bishop Parker thinks that there has hardly been a civil war in the Christian world that did not have some religious coloring; no matter what murder, treason, or rebellion a man commits, he will see it as justified by his religious conscience. There will be an attack on religion generally so as to weaken its influence; there will be a pretense of religion in order to deceive others; or some special religious opinion will be urged that has the effect of dividing and stirring up animosity beyond control.

Traditional praise of the usefulness of religion maintained that religion teaches all the virtues essential to the good cit-

izen: sincerity, modesty, meekness, and submission to the
higher powers being among these, it follows that anyone who
teaches irreligion is a public enemy whether he wills it or not;
and certainly anyone bent on public disturbance will best
succeed by undermining religion and its custodian, the
church. He will be impious and profane, will deny God, snarl
at his Maker, and oppose the heavenly power in order to
shake its earthly counterpart. Since the church never promotes
changes in the civil order, rebels try to weaken the church or
simply to get control of it, for their own purposes. They are
skilled in the arts of pretending and will promote their knavish designs under the guise of religious feeling. Men are repeatedly warned against sly and crafty incendiaries, conven-
ticlers, and atheistical persons, plausible hypocrites who pose
as angels of light to the people like the master of all such, Oliver Cromwell—in short, all who hide the aim of violence behind the borrowed titles of religion.

But the masquerade that misleads, we are told, is not far
from the zealous pursuit of some special form of dissent that
breaks up into warring elements or tries to substitute its new
mode of worship for the old. The line from dissent into rebellion becomes entirely clear from England's own experience
with Puritans and Presbyterians. They first insist that religion
as now practiced is defective and must be reformed by the use
of force if need be. From unobtrusive beginnings through a
gradual movement of increasing boldness, self-assertion, and
insolence, with demands for change arousing discontent, and
arbitrary insistence on themselves and their own way leading
to a total subversion of the general order—such for the Tories
was the Puritan progress. Having reformed the practice of
Sunday, they insisted on new priests, new prayers, new faith,
new catechism, new assemblies, new forms of government to
sustain their special brand of fanaticism. From the church
they drove out the most orthodox, canonical, grave, and
learned ministers, all who were constant and loyal; their record is one of treason and rebellion, in short, and it could not
be otherwise given the nature of rebellion itself.

This portrait of rebellious dissenting ministers looks toward the ambitious politician who will practice any form of deception to obtain power. Religion may be employed again in the pretense of sheltering the people against Rome, as when a great clamor arose against Popery, the popular fear of which enabled ambitious schemers to shake the crown and undermine the established church. In speaking of Popery, Marvell observes that "to introduce that which is absurd, there must be something done that is barbarous." In turn, since to make a successful rebellion there has to be fraud, every rebel leader must resemble Dryden's "false Achitophel." Such men are personally ambitious, and since they have lost the right sense of corporateness and care only for their own advantage and power, they will engage in any form of misleading behavior to gain their ends. As good writers and orators are, or should be, good men, so the leaders of plots and conspiracies are likely to be "bad, poor, unliking, and revengeful men. Whereof the worst shall destroy the best." In the end, as the King asserts in *Absalom and Achitophel,* the nature of schism and faction will turn the leaders against themselves, they will be unable to agree among so many units of selfish and wicked impulse, their conspiracy will break into clashing fragments. For all such men are vain, opinionated, unable to see any goal but their own, and willing to sacrifice the public welfare "to get some office" for themselves. As Dennis says, "a patriot designs the good of his country, but one of a party intends his own." Radical changes are always a danger, even when sincerely intended. But experience shows that schemes of innovation proceed from turbulent, ambitious spirits, demagogues uttering specious phrases and slogans, promoting private designs by appeal to public alarm or hope. It is then not too much for L'Estrange to say, "Never did private party band against a public settlement, with an intent to mend it."

Since all rebellious leaders think only of their own preferment, the defenders of order assume that rebellion has to proceed by fraud. An evil so monstrous, so totally devoid of mitigation as civil war, can have begun only as a result of

falsehood. Since truth can never serve the ends of a scoundrel, as the Deist Anthony Collins says, it follows that rebellion employs dissimulation, hypocrisy, artifice, imposture, all
manner of deceit and subtle contrivance. Ambition covers
over rebellion with gaudy attractions, and the crafty leader
with smooth language deceives the people by plausible argument, and like those modern Pharisees the Presbyterian ministers, he makes his ruinous course appear like a defense of
public welfare. The means to power, then, are painfully, necessarily always the same, and ambitious men will seek popular
favor by seeming to care for the people, bemoaning their sufferings, lamenting the vices of the king, asserting a great love
of country, and adopting an air of virtuous gravity until their
wicked ends are achieved.

Such men, to be sure, have ability, and we meet again the
dangers of intellect, imagination, superior energy in public
leaders whose madness here may consist in the ease with which
they can deceive the foolish, unstable mass of mankind. Thus
a clever man can hardly avoid being selfish and dishonest. Intellect may be detrimental in alliance with imagination that
inspires theories or schemes too far from reality; then, too, a
strong mind plus the temptations offered to superiority will
inspire selfish ambition. Ability becomes an excuse for seeking power, since ability can wield power so readily. Worst of
all, the weakness of others less gifted seems to invite the fraud
so easy for a superior man to practice upon them. Again the
record of the late civil war shows how the people were prepared, duped, confused into fear, gulled from day to day by
fresh impostures. Rebellion is, then, the triumph of knavery
over unstable popular feeling.

But rebellion also assumes someone ready to be deceived by someone willing and able to practice fraud: someone
has to be stupid and someone else clever. We return to the
weak majority of mankind; the temptation to be wicked and
selfish is almost irresistible in the face of so many available
fools. Their ignorance, which should make them more docile,
may also lead, as Davenant says, to disobedience which is the

path to civil war. The dangers of misleading the people are expressed in a variety of images. References to plague, disease, poison, and fever are to be expected, and the motives of wicked leaders are often likened, as Simon Patrick has it, to making commotion so that they may fish in troubled waters. Chiefly the fear of releasing energy beyond control is carried by the language of fire and flood, of powerful bodies of water irresistibly bursting forth against ordinary restraints. Bishop Burnet's statement of his purpose carries just the right combination of excess, madness, death, flood, and fire. His *History* has been exact, he says, in exposing error, so as "to warn posterity from falling into the like excesses, and to make it appear how mad and fatal a thing it is to run violently into a torrent, and in a heat to do those things which may give a general disgust, and to set precedents to others."

This reasoning accounts for the fear of sudden and uncontrollable extremes. The slightest concession, any remote beginning of free popular demand, any opening however small to the spirit of change is certain to get beyond control. There seemed to be no moderation between absolute control and violent chaos. As R. F. Jones remarked concerning the fear of science as endangering traditional education, "The fear that if one plank were loosened in the intellectual edifice, the whole would crash to the ground represents the most constant element in conservatism." The architectural image suggests that no one can foresee the consequences of any popular move for change; if the building gives ever so slightly anywhere, the whole structure may collapse. Consider for example, what seems an innocent approach to those in authority: the petition. The very nature of petitions, however, makes them certain to end in tumult. L'Estrange, citing "his late Majesty" as authority, finds that the rude people "are taught first to petition, then to protest, then to dictate, and at last to command." Factions use petitions like the tools of a housebreaker: to get in little by little, without much noise, and then rob the house. A popular petition becomes a link in the inevitable chain of rebellion. It lets the multitude interfere in

matters of state which are none of their affair and of which
they are ignorant. Even if it comes of good faith, a petition
always goes through a progress into leagues, covenants, protes-
tations, oaths, and agreements leading to direct action against
the king; there is bound to be some conspiracy on hand to
make use of the petition, and some wicked and rebellious
intent will profit. The final outcome is certain to be uncontrollable violence, just as it was during the last civil war.

The lessons of English history show that it is best not even
to think changes necessary or desirable, let alone to take part
in formal demands for alteration. Beware of the unruly populace, for like a raging tide they press where the bank is weak-
est and in an instant overrun all. Samuel Parker in his *Pre-
existence of Souls* used with powerful effect the flood image
for the danger of releasing popular energy:

> . . . if they be suffered to run without restraint, they will
> break down all the banks of law and government; and
> therefore 'tis the main wisdom and policy of governors . . .
> to check the violence of the tide, by swaying them back-
> wards by contrary laws, and to keep them fluctuating be-
> tween both extremes, and so by alternate fluxes and re-
> fluxes, to preserve the Commonwealth from popular in-
> undations.

They must be neither too ignorant nor too knowing, lest they
be drawn into plots and designs of reformation "that usually
proceed to rebellion, and end in a deluge of civil wars, as the
experience of all ages sufficiently attests, and our own too
sadly demonstrates."

The danger of flood that cannot be contained is like the
danger of fire that cannot be quenched. Images of warmth and
heat support the requirements of our myth as they lead to
notions of rage, fury, fever, or madness. Indeed Horace had
spoken against the first heat of the mind in favor of care and
time and skill. We hear of ungovernable fire, heated fancies,
the inflamed imagination, and in ordinary poetical counter,
of the fire of love, the coals of affection, the flame of passion.

Rapin distinguishes his various responses to past poetic greatness by saying that "Homer animates me, Virgil heats me, and
all the rest freeze me, so cold and flat they are." This seems
harmless, if typical language, and far from the fiery zeal, the
hot rage that will start whole kingdoms into the combustion
of revolt, setting the world in a blaze and reducing it to ashes.
At one point, it was found necessary to forbid bonfires in
honor of the Restoration of Charles II on May 29, these bonfires seeming by the mere symbolism of their heat and destruc-
tiveness to become occasions of tumult. Indeed, L'Estrange
wishes to know in his *The Growth of Knavery* (1677), do we
not strike fire now as we did in 1641? Are not the people as
much tinder now as they were then? The answer must be yes,
for "zeal was the flint and ambition the steel, out of which the
sparks of rebellion have in our days kindled the most fatal
mischiefs."

If the merest hint of change releases a flood, the merest
spark of zealous fire leads to the insanity of civil war, there is
only one course open to sensible men. With endless variations,
the myth returns to its everlasting admonition: don't give up
what is certain for what is uncertain; do not abandon a present
guide until a better is at hand; consider how much better a
thing you give up than whatever it is you seek; as the proverb
says, don't start into a precipice to avoid a feather; know that
to insist on mending something is to invite its being spoiled;
don't surrender present happiness for future inconvenience,
and beware at all times lest the remedy for distemper be far
worse than the disease. Certainly in public affairs the world
must yield to government of and by men as they are. Experience shows that any tyrant is better than rebellion; for some
of Dryden's contemporaries, the worst prince that ever ruled,
the most depraved Nero or Caligula, should be obeyed rather
than hazard the dissolution of order. Stay within the present
settlement, because an attempt to change it will certainly
make it worse, and after the ensuing confusion passes, life
will settle once more into its everlastingly defective condition.

So the Restoration, alive with fresh energy, making discov-

eries in science and declaring the modern temper, establishing
the lines for so much modern practice, has nonetheless laid
down the classical principles of control. Recent English history and the chance that its power would break into violence
made the Restoration go back and draw upon a long-accumu-
lated set of observations and conclusions from experience,
giving to ancient lessons restated for modern guidance the
force of myth. In Dryden the myth found its ideal voice, and
Absalom and Achitophel draws together with remarkable fidelity the various elements of conservative mythology, pausing
in fact at its turning point, to offer a little essay which relies
on the very images we have met with throughout. One of its
most solemn lines declares that "innovation is the blow of
fate," and behind it lies a varied suspicion of, and attack upon,
things that are "new."

Conservatism being a defensive position, it saw in "novelty"
of any sort a possible threat and tried to place the burden of
proof on anything "new." Hobbes had written that he and
Fear were twins, and Fear in others of like mind showed itself
against the dangers posed by novelty, innovation, and the various schemes of projectors, undertakers, or reformers. Novelty
is specious in appeal, and lovers of novelty, when they come
to chew this wind, find nothing in it. Writers plead innocent
to novelty or singularity; John Wilkins is not "tainted" by
the affectation of novelty, Meric Casaubon seeks truth, not
novelty, and others are happy in avoiding novelty of language
or inspiration. Similarly, the term "innovation" bears all
the wrong associations. One does not wish to appear "guilty"
of innovation in language; innovation always falls short, it
fails to perform what it promises, it becomes an unprofitable
fancy and those who believe in it are finally ridiculous. The
very term "reformer" has become so odious, it is better not
to apply it, but rather to speak of one as an "amender" or "re-
storer" in religious affairs lest some new alteration be suspect-
ed. The age seems fallen into "convulsions of newness," and
the Deists, who were supposed to offer some danger to the prevailing order themselves, show their scorn for the pretenders

to revelation from above who profess new ideas of God, new doctrines, new commands, new ceremonies and modes of worship. A steady rain of blows continues to descend upon the word "new," each use of it a stroke like the impaling of a victim's name in the satiric use of accent and rhyme in the couplet. An ancient statute had said that anyone wishing to bring in a new law should declare it publicly with a halter around his neck; if his law is not fit for the general good, he may presently be hanged for his desire of innovation. John Spencer sees his world afflicted with an unhappy vertigo, a passion for newness that will encounter the judgment of God:

> We are all for invention, and new devices of sin, altogether unknown to the ages of our forefathers; new lords, new laws; new lights, new doctrines; new fashions, new faces; nay almost new kinds of men and women . . . new devices for gain, new ways of cheating, new ways of breaking; so that without all doubt, God is devising some new manner of judgment.

The familiar plea of literary orthodoxy, its defense of the past and honor of its heritage from antiquity, resembles religious and political caution. Ben Jonson would have no pursuit of "fierce undertakers" in the search of truth, and even Boileau's famous principle that nothing new is to be allowed except in the expression, does not govern the ridicule of Dryden in *The Rehearsal*. Here the most ridiculous passages are explained as "the new way of writing," as if to say that the effort to be new and different is in itself absurd, and is bound to result in nonsense. It violates the general sense of normal people like the interlocutors of Bayes, whose names are the commonest possible: "Smith and Johnson" are metaphorical terms to suggest the views of all sensible, reasonable people, men who are like everyone else, that is. Act v, scene 1, shows Bayes being proud of the unheard-of uniqueness of his method in stopping the battle—the very quality which to Smith and Johnson must seem most outlandish. Bayes will stop the battle by an eclipse, "Which, let me tell you, is a kind of fancy that was yet never so much as thought of, but by myself, and one person more, that shall be nameless." Something never heard of before thus seems absurd for no other reason than its newness.

What would seem to lead into liberal views from advanced scientific or skeptical positions actually came to rest in the accepted orthodoxies as well. At one point Glanvill seems to ridicule the common fear of the bugbear novelty, the timid apprehension that frightens men away from sober verities; but men are repeatedly assured that science, too, like so many English appearances of radicalism, will appeal to or make its peace with earlier practice. In defending the usefulness of experimental philosophy, Robert Boyle shows that the new science is not a danger to established religion; he constantly cites authority from the past as he glorifies the opportunities of the present; assuring one and all that religion as it is has nothing to fear from the new science before he has explored what the new science actually implies. When Sprat defends the Royal Society, his first concern is to answer the charge of newness. He is afraid of ridicule as injuring science because it is new, as if a new thing were absurd on the face of it and therefore subject to ridicule. Apart from this, Sprat is not "frighted" he says, over "the hazard of alteration, and novelty." He shows the English that this new thing is not really new at all, or if it is, that it will be "inoffensive to all the various ways of living, already in use; and thereby I shall secure all the ancient proprietors in their rights." His most telling point shows that the Church of England and the Royal Society both were a Reformation; both proceeded to their ends in the same way, both were accused by their enemies of novelty, yet clearly both are loyal to the same sovereign.

Sprat does well to seek protection alongside the church, of all institutions the most resistant to individual energy, to separate opinion that goes its own way. If the Royal Society is like the church, it is safe indeed no matter how "new" it seems; for the church knows that "every opinion must make a sect, and every sect a faction, and every faction, when it is able, a war." The church preaches the great acknowledged truths, and private opinion is never the standard for these truths. In its "preface" *The Book of Common Prayer* states that men given to change show more regard for "their own private fancies and interests" than for public duty. These "men of factious, peevish, and perverse spirits" assert their own will. All such victims of pride, ambition, of the spirit of contradiction and innovation should come under the discipline of the church; its order will regulate luxurious wits and so maintain the general peace. Indeed a chief inconvenience even now is that there is not "common prayer" and preaching enough. Sir William Petty would make London a single great parish, with a thousand copies of "one judiciously and authentically composed sermon" to be read each week in each single chapel, with no later repetition of the same; everyone going to church would then hear the same sermon and take part in a uniform exercise that would put a stop to the near million of different discourses now to be heard throughout the year. As for the dissenters, they clearly dislike the common liturgy, because in their obstinate individualism they cannot pray as follows: "From all error, heresy and schism, from all sedition, privy conspiracy and rebellion, Good Lord deliver us."

CHAPTER 4

Dryden's Own Temper

Dryden quite rightly complained that he had been the object of unusually bitter attack throughout his career. We can learn much concerning him from these attacks and the possible reasons for them. Dryden was almost continuously involved in defending himself at a time when, as Rymer and others have said, critical abuse had achieved extreme violence and brutality. Some of Dryden's best work has emerged from the need to reply, especially to a persistent enemy like Thomas Shadwell. If we omit the abuse that Dryden suffered on becoming a Roman Catholic, and the replies that his religious poems inspired, there is ample abuse at hand in the fierce, insulting diatribes written in 1681 and 1682. Most of these performances try to apply to Dryden himself the charges he has leveled against others in his own satires—especially charges of instability, selfishness, and vanity. Both Whigs and Tories adopt the same virtues, and each accuses the other of being the faction that divides, the party that disturbs the general peace. Ironically Dryden is supposed to be, then, the false, ambitious, vain, inconsistent opportunist for whom his own satire had shown no mercy. To be sure, after the Restoration a stock object of satire was the man who had gone all out for Cromwell and then had changed to praising the king; Dryden here has some embarrassing company, including his victim,

Flecknoe. After *Absalom and Achitophel,* Dryden's enemies lose no time in reminding him of his seeming ease in changing from one loyalty to another, and some might say that he had this coming to him. At one point, Dryden is made to seem, "Like a mad dog" as

> . . . he runs about the streets,
> Snarling and biting every one he meets.

Certainly he could use his own weapons so well that our sympathy may turn to his enemies. They now denounce him bitterly. His poetic soul is vast, takes in right and wrong, truth and falsehood easily; he is like Judas Iscariot, or like the wind, able to range anywhere. He is vain, boastful, treacherous, a cowardly mean-spirited hireling, false as water, the creature of those able to pay his fee. In *The Medal of John Bayes* (1682), Shadwell runs through the worst in the standard catalogue of epithets: Dryden is a hired libeler, an executioner of men's reputations. He steals from the writings of other men; he is the impudent, bawdy, wretched mercenary, Bayes, a fawning coward and slave.

After making every allowance for the heat of political or literary battle in an age that took a great deal of abuse for granted, there still seems a gratuitously bitter note in the violence of Dryden's enemies. There must have been something personally and professionally offensive about him to inspire the kind of persistent rancor under review here. Let us explore what was likely to be the response to a man of conspicuous ability who was an obvious success, who at the same time knew that he was superior to his rivals and could afford a certain diffidence and reserve.

Dryden had the marks of a true professional, the mind, the fluency and energy, the versatility of the gifted man of letters who could do everything his profession demanded and do it better than anyone else in his age. Such a man is certain to arouse envy at any time, especially in a period of fierce competition for what little preferment one could obtain from

literary work. It was a new thing for anyone to be truly professional as a writer, and the first man to make a success of it
was bound to be a target. What was easy for Dryden was impossible for his enemies. The demands of professional compe-
tence were clear; he met them and others could not; so except
for the young, they envied and disliked him.

Some men, like Shakespeare apparently, can surpass their
contemporaries and inspire love nonetheless. Despite early
satiric thrusts, Shakespeare may have been so high above all
others as to afford sweetness of temper. His rivals may not have
realized how much better he was, or their envy has not been
written down and preserved as in Dryden's case. Then, too,
the towering genius can be written off as an accident of nature
for which there is no accounting, and comparison with which
is not expected of anyone else. But a man like Dryden who is
simply superior at doing what should come within the reach
of others making similar attempts—such a man must be reduced in size. His enemies pounce on any sign of weakness
and insist on its worst possible implications. Thus Dryden has
to be shown as an odious turncoat, failing to meet his own
professions. Yet compared with someone like Waller, he seems
a model of sensible action. Waller degraded himself to escape
from a wrong political choice. A time-server with no aim but
worldly success, he finds himself on the wrong side in 1643
but manages to save his life while more innocent men are
hanged. Ten years later he petitions Cromwell for leave to
return, and so seeks advantage between two positions with
far worse implications than Dryden was to be guilty of. But
his rivals could not compare Dryden fairly to other men. Had
they done so, he would emerge better than if tested by an
abstract, theoretical standard of consistency and uprightness.
Few if any in his day would stand comparison with the practice of other men more readily than Dryden. Yet mediocrity
seldom likes to admit that a superior man achieves success
simply because he is superior. Hence the enemy must charge
Dryden with a variety of contemptible actions which he had
been guilty of in order to ensure his success. It must be made

to seem as if he got to high place by shifts and dodges: by plagiarism in literature, and by flattery or inconsistent change at other levels. It is true that these are among the standard charges made by satire and to be expected in this age. Yet they are urged with such consistency, and are so often repeated with such violence against Dryden that another explanation seems justified.

It must have been irritating that Dryden should stand so clearly above others; even worse was his knowing it and perhaps showing that he knew it. A certain disdain emerges, as of one who is above others and beyond their power to do him harm. Only when it suited him did he show resentment or take notice, as of one so confident of his power to retaliate that he could wait for the right moment to display it; what is small and inferior sinks then more deeply into a sense of being just what it is. Merely being what he was enabled Dryden to accuse others silently for their failures. Hence the malice with which they fell on any sign of inconsistency at the political or religious level, since weakness in other ways did not offer itself to attack. His enemies took a gleeful spite in finding him vulnerable at last, vulnerable as they were always made to feel by Dryden's supremacy as a man of letters.

Dryden was simply one of those men who could not be good at what he was doing without being offensive to others. Though he did nothing or said nothing overt to bring this about, he seemed to make others feel that they were being exposed and obliged to defend themselves. Some factor in his personality, added to his superior attainments, seemed to inspire uneasiness or dislike. Perhaps merely by never saying anything he could give the impression of silent disdain. He was quiet, modest, and reserved in manner, not inclined to take others into his confidence; hence he was likely to suffer misunderstanding or dislike from not being well known as a person. It is easy to misunderstand and so dislike a man who does not explain himself, who except as a professional writer kept to himself, minded his own affairs and seemed self-sufficient. Such a man is irritating, since others wish to get at him and make him act like themselves, find out what goes on in him and make sure that it is nothing disturbing to their own self-esteem.

Dryden's character, his solid human worth and substance, thus kept to a certain reserve and modesty that disdained to come out of itself just to satisfy others. He showed the strength of his character in overcoming his various troubles, being at his best when overworked, weary, and impoverished. After losing everything in 1688, he struggled back to his own feet, and so belied his enemies then, as he had done before, by his dignity and silence. His strength and independence irritated his rivals, but attracted young men. Like Socrates, he was beloved of the young who desired only to gain from his superiority, to profit from him without wishing to unseat him or reduce him to their size. In company Dryden was a reserved listener, not a gifted talker, not entertaining or lively, and so liable to the suspicion of lesser men. When he did say anything it was brief and to the point, perhaps sharp or aggressive to cover up his bashfulness. What he said might irritate by its quality of sense and intelligence, its suddenness or surprise, its tendency to make lesser things seem even more foolish than ever. Dryden strove to make words count, and seen as a whole even apart from his function as a satirist, he did little to make others think better of themselves or their own merits. Such a man will be disliked, especially if he is usually right.

These qualities of versatile talent, professional superiority, personal reserve yet ready confidence are allied with others often remarked by Dryden himself and students of his career. He is candid and dispassionate about his own faults and virtues, genial and flexible. He is very much an Englishman in respecting tradition and authority, past inheritance rather than new systems, sets of grand principles or inspired missions. He is described as having a vigorous intellect, which nonetheless produced unsystematic, unoriginal thought. Dryden was too realistic for a coherent system that would take him away from things as they are, here and now, the dry hard things of classicism. Systematic intellectual constructions would hinder a mind which desires to remain as flexible as the reality to which it must always adjust itself. A mind bent on taking the world as it is will not insist on rounded symmetry.

More than any other quality, this coming to terms with what is immediately so has impressed students of Dryden. Some deplore and others praise this facile and accommodating mind; Dryden adapts, absorbs, assimilates, we are told—"adjusts" most frequently. While he constantly tried new literary forms and devices and was too restless to go on doing what he had already done well, this mood of alteration did not extend beyond his literary practice. The desire to be inoffensive and reconciliatory emerges in his letters, and was an easy object of ridicule in *The Rehearsal*. Here Mr. Bayes loves agreement, compromise, and avoidance of all strife. In Act II, scene 3, Smith says, "That's very complaisant, I swear, Mr. Bayes, to be of another man's opinion, before he knows what it is." This does not describe Dryden's criticism, which was combative when need be, or his satire in defense of order, tradition, or authority. Yet all Dryden's effort was like that of an advocate, as Lowell says. He was always convinced of his present way of thinking; he argued well, argued in fact better than he reasoned. He did not have a good analytical mind, but he could concentrate powerfully on what was immediately before him, could take on the color of what he was doing and adjust himself to theme and purpose as immediately needed.

This pliable quality was important for a man having to make his own way in the world. Dryden has to be seen standing among the men who wrote in his time to show his superiority as an artist and as a man having to live as best he could, saving himself amid the violent upheavals of the 17th century. Besides having the ambivalent attitude of any sober intellectual to public acclaim he was in a difficult position; he often says that he despises popular applause, yet he must succeed by appealing to it. Dryden's young friend John Oldham writes "A Satire Dissuading from Poetry," which, while obliged to Juvenal, shows that a poet must now either starve or beg:

> Preach, plead, cure, fight, game, pimp, beg, cheat,
>   or thieve;
> Be all but poet, and there's way to live.

A man who must rely on himself in an aristocratic age under court control soon adopts a mood of realistic pliability. He cannot afford lofty ideals strictly adhered to in such a world. Even in the democratic era of opportunity open to all talent, anyone wishing to succeed must get along with many different kinds of people, must seem to believe or accept things that he considers dubious. In an age of contraction and narrow choice, such a man as Dryden must adapt himself to things as they are. His ambition would then force his conformity, even if his temperament were less inert or realistic than it was.

Seen from different angles, Dryden's poetic practice is adaptable and various. As a poet, he sees himself as falling between the Elizabethans and the Restoration. On one hand he discloses an immense variety of verse forms and meters, yet he settles on the couplet, absorbs the advances in its use made up to his time, and compels it to be his own instrument. Depending on the argument of the moment or the use for which he needs the couplet, Dryden will defend rhyme as being no constraint and then object to its bondage, its fetters, or its "slavery." The couplet suited him in fact as being disciplined yet easy to manage. It restrained a lawless imagination and curbed a luxuriant fancy; "Yet rashness is a better fault than fear," he says, and in the end Dryden has all the room he needs for what "rashness" he is inclined to within his own version of the couplet.

Literary study has learned to be careful in interpreting a given poet's use of imagery. We must beware of concluding something from Dryden's images that we might prefer to think is so; the images must be related to the use made of them in the places where they are found. The early metaphysical figures are of little significance for a poet who matured very late. Then, too, various plays and poems demand special figures which reveal little or nothing of Dryden's total practice. A great deal of current poetical counter emerges as well, figures used by everyone taken from a common stock. Related to these are images derived from ancient classics and other poets referred to by all learned writers addressing a select, civilized audience which expects and recognizes allusions to common knowledge. Extensive use of Ovid, Lucretius, Horace, and other Latin writers so important to neoclassicism generally, and in particular a heavy and conscious reliance on Virgil, are common features of Dryden's imagery. Echoes of Waller and Denham, Cowley, Herrick, Milton, and of course Shakespeare and the Bible reinforce our caution in fixing upon Dryden's characteristic mode. He absorbs and continues the poetic tradition to a marked degree; he has a strong sense of genres and the requirements of each, of poetic conventions and rituals, especially in the elegiac poems whose adornments are deliberately traditional.

The use of inherited materials, and of current poetical figures ready to hand, increases our sense of Dryden's conservatism. He falls into common, average usage, and chooses to do what everyone else does. The images for love in *Aureng-Zebe* show how figures apply to nothing outside the moment of their use, common as they are in other Restoration plays. Flame or fire equals love; wounds, darts, swords, and other military symbols stand for love and what it does to people; love images may come from navigation where the lover is a mariner and his condition resembles a crisis in a sailor's life. While it is true that many images in the plays are ambivalent and suggest deeper attitudes on Dryden's part, we must be sure of their importance before isolating them from what is only standard machinery.

Keeping in mind these cautions and adding that Dryden's images will vary with the subject and occasion, we may still find something characteristic of what we know to be the general tendency of his mind and temperament. As we should expect of a realistic man, writing to please other men who are distinctly of this world, Dryden's imagery seems concrete, material, factual—of his own time and place of existence. It is said that Dryden seldom looked up from the real world in which he lived to get material for his images. He derives little from Heaven or other out of the way places, save when he has to elevate his subject for a special purpose as in some of his dedications. The 17th-century influence demanding the control of energy in figurative language joins with Dryden's themes and his own imaginative temper to keep his images to the world as it is. The doctrine prescribed by Sprat, Hobbes, Eachard, Wilkins, Parker, and others does not eliminate figurative language from Dryden's text, but gives another reason for its being what it was, drawn from the material world of daily experience, the simple, homely, and useful areas of life. As Van Doren says, "he proceeds painfully to scour the surface of life for allusions," observing an adult world and the affairs of normal, sensible men within it. In spite of absorbing so much of the literary and classical tradition, Dryden's images show Johnson's observation, that he learned more from experience and life than from books. His figures refer to daily life and the occupations of men, their professions and trades, their government and labor, or to the recreation and entertainment of any upper-class person in his day. Dryden's sources are common property, and his comparisons obvious and available to anyone; little that is remote or startling emerges either in the materials used or in the manner of their use. His figures are down where he can see and control them as called for by the revolt of his age away from a more complex literary practice, and as agreeable to his own mind and character. So also Dryden's subject matter for occasional writing about the world around him kept his figures turned toward men and events in his own day. His audience desired to read clear poems about itself, its own actions and affairs; its poet laureate was exactly the man to satisfy the need.

In the theater Dryden was successful in providing a desired commodity; yet as with so many other dilemmas in his career, the need to be popular bothered him. On some occasions he made no pretense of writing for anything but hire, as befitted a professional author who wrote on order whatever was called for by the taste he had at the moment to satisfy. At other times, he would seem to repent of having written to satisfy popular taste. He never apologized for catering to the taste or desire of the court, to be sure, but he is quite vehement in, for example, the dedication of *The Spanish Friar* (1681). Having written passages bad enough to please, he now repents of his sins, and is resolved to "settle myself no reputation by the applause of fools." His ambition is undiminished, but he scorns "to take it from half-witted judges." No matter to whom this refers, or whether it lumps together all men of bad taste including those of the ruling classes, the plays remain within Dryden's over-all loyalty to the establishment in his time. Even those written not expressly to support the establishment have little to show that endangers it. The degree of Dryden's commitment to write directly in support of things as they were varies only enough to clarify his general line. As Joseph Krutch has said, early Restoration comedy aimed to take men as they are, not to reform or improve them; it has no ideal to uphold nor any standard by which to change a world which it assumes will go on as it is. Dryden's comedies certainly do not suggest that the world ought to improve its existing arrangements, and his more serious plays would satisfy the standard requirement of John Dennis, "that the instructions which we receive from the stage ought to be for the benefit of the lawful established government." The magnificent *All for Love* departs from Dryden's usual mode, yet it remains on the side of authority and moral instruction as demanded by neoclassical theory. The play seems to portray the danger of uncontrolled passion. The subtitle, "The World Well Lost," is more Antony's than Dryden's acceptance. The play can be read as teaching wholesome lessons of restraint by showing the unhappy end of persons who gave way to the desires of unlawful love. If these are its "lessons," the play could afford to go its own way in other respects, and leave the fetters of the couplet for blank verse.

Dryden's heroic plays have been read as heavily ambivalent, seeming to praise heroic idealism while at the same time ridi-

culing it, and having as their real aim to make the actions and
characters absurdly comic. They have also been read as conscious attempts to defend the political and social ideas of
Hobbes and to show belief in Hobbes' gloomy view of human
nature. In turn, the plays are read as having no important reliance on Hobbes and his political absolutism, their orthodoxy
being only the commonplace sentiment of all royalists and
easily found in a dozen writers besides Hobbes. The plays,
like others of their kind, respond to three principal conflicts
of the age, all closely related: Catholics and Protestants, Whigs
and Tories, King and Parliament. In writing the sort of thing
called for, Dryden keeps to his general loyalty. What little is
to be assumed of a playwright's own ideas from the speeches of
certain characters will show that Dryden's plays generally
follow his characteristic thoughts and feelings concerning the
established order. Certainly heoric plays that celebrate the
aristocratic ideal will glorify royalty and the court, enhancing
the supposed elevation of thought and conduct on the part of
Charles II and his courtiers. Davenant in *The Siege of Rhodes*
had monarchic sentiment and scorned the crowd, glorifying
the high and denigrating the low; so also Dryden will stay
with these and similar conventions expected of the genre.

In addition, Dryden, being sensitive to passing demand,
would write political plays when these seemed the only thing
to get people back into the theater during and after the Popish
Plot frenzy. The theaters had lost their public to the great
interest in politics, and the playwrights like everyone else
divided themselves between the two camps and wrote Whig
or Tory plays according to their persuasion. The government
intensified its already great control by censorship and licens-
ing, severely challenging anything offensive to the court, and
even suspecting a loyal work like *The Duke of Guise* before
permitting its production. Dryden had in fact already sketched
a play on this subject some twenty years before; in 1682 he
got out his old scenes and joined forces with Nathaniel Lee to
produce *The Duke of Guise* as we know it today. It had therefore both preceded and followed *Absalom and Achitophel* and

bears a strong relationship to the poem's celebration of the conservative myth. It had been Dryden's first play after the Restoration in 1660, aiming to expose the late rebellion and to warn posterity against similar errors in the future. Dryden's pen was here at the service of the king just as it was in 1681 when the dangers that seemed too remote in 1660 to need the play's warning now had grown to be a fearful threat of new civil war. Like *Absalom and Achitophel, The Duke of Guise* supports the establishment by showing many of the same forces in action: the set of rebel conspirators; the curate of St. Eustache ready to swear to anything like Oates; the rebellious rabble courted by Guise himself, who bows amiably this side and that to the crowd; the rightful king who is just and clement of course, and dangerously merciful; the necessary pretense of religious zeal by the rebels; the alliance of the devil and sedition, and the vast strength of the popular cause as against the loyal few supporting the king. *The Duke of Guise* may then be said to begin and end the first half of Dryden's career, from 1660 to 1682, and to show him at work in his most characteristic manner—the professional writer producing on demand at any given moment, supporting the royal cause and at the same time responding to general interest in politics along with other playwrights. He stays with his convictions and yet does the thing that will pay—as he must.

Of three main divisions of Dryden's work—poems, plays, and prose criticism—the last has inspired many of the standard remarks about Dryden's mind and character. In the chaos of the essays, the man himself shows forth most clearly suspended. A variegated mass of commentary is found to display Dryden in terms of his own character, the needs of his career, and his many-sided relationship to the age and its influence. The essays, as he says, lay down his present thoughts; they display a mind that has been described as plastic, clever, patient, acute, versatile, facile, and accommodating as befits a man in the process of defining his own position. The *Essay of Dramatic Poesy* is a dialogue "sustained by persons of several opinions, all of them left doubtful," in the effort to see what truth there is in different positions, some of which are not left as "doubtful" as Dryden, wishing to be unhampered, implies. The essays are considered a desert relieved by some graces of style; they are largely hack work, we are told, derived from the neoclassical scriptures as interpreted by their mainly French prophets. Others find Dryden stable in his principles but various and flexible in application. He seems a man of the world suited to his own time, all things to all men, a conformist able to see things from many sides. The critical inconsistency so much remarked supports his conservative temperament that looks to the fact, the real thing at any given moment which may call for a response unlike what the facts demanded yesterday. If the English conservative takes his cue from reality and not from rigid principle or theory, he must change as reality changes; he will seem to contradict himself in shifting his position according to the way things are. Unlike the steadfast line of his political royalism, Dryden's literary view alters with the problem before him. His opinion is free to be what its immediate object seems to demand; it applies here and now, as befits a realistic mind. And the same mind is politically steadfast while it is critically variable, and probably nothing would astonish Dryden more than that this should seem remarkable to us. Dryden is both committed and free—because he had to be and could be so.

Although he seems to search for the kind of order under which he could be at ease, the general movement of his criticism pursues freedom, after absorbing nearly every attitude available in a critically disorderly age, after holding well-nigh every position possible to neoclassicism. From essays freely appreciative and enthusiastic, through much *ad hoc* defense of his actual practice in the heroic drama under court influence, into a phase of exploring rules drawn from literature but not imposed on it, becoming at last an open, uncommitted, and assured reader offering some of his most valued judgments—such a general pattern will allow most of the numerous observations about Dryden's criticism, each with its fraction of the truth. Dryden is elusive, at once the champion

of neoclassicism, its chief voice, yet sharing its contradictions
and ambivalence so much that he becomes one of the forces
that undermined it. Dryden's temper simply let him fall into
paradoxes that he could not fully resolve. He finds himself
at various times trying to be just to both past and present, to
England and France, rule and freedom, anarchic taste and
objective principles or standards, learning and genius, theory
and practice or the need of immediate success and appeal. At
any one time he may seem entirely dogmatic or entirely dis-
engaged; only when taken as a whole will his criticism show
a general balance, a coming to rest in the undogmatic middle
ground.

A perceptive student of Dryden, George Williamson, remarks that Dryden's taste was a coarse sieve that let the finest
delicacies escape, and kept back only the larger, cruder experiences. Dryden is in this view an honest amateur as a critic,
unlike his position as a professional playwright, satirist, or
translator. Nevertheless we seem interested now mainly in
his verdicts, not in his method or doctrine, principle or learning. For Dryden, the rules are essential, but as a means to
successful poetic creation; authority supports individual taste,
the rules assist genius; so Dryden has it both ways, as his temper demanded. The best things he has left us in the coarse
sieve of his reading remain the freely expressed opinions and
feelings about literature that came to him in the moment of
reading.

Our review of Dryden's temper may well end on this note
of freedom. It emerges especially in the critical essays where
Dryden speaks in his own person most directly in a genre not
yet developed enough to have clear requirements, and where
he needs to serve no other purpose than to explain what he is
doing and why, and what he thinks about it. He seems at
times like an inquiring scientist, looking for the truth rather
than asserting that he already has it—unlike his political, and
later on his religious, view, both of which, after much waver-
ing, move toward authority. Dryden's use of the term "essay"
itself seems to show how open or undogmatic he or anyone else

is, who uses it—a thing of wide appeal, allowing many different opinions, a sort of Broad Church for sensible men
everywhere. There is bound to be a certain amount of truth
in anything that a sensible man chooses to declare, and Dryden was the sort of man who could see the element of truth
in a great variety of ideas that seemed to oppose each other.
He says of himself, "As I am a man, I must be changeable,"
recalling Terence no doubt; but this holds only in matters of
judgment or critical opinion. The fluent ease with which he
writes his criticism; the sense of keeping a large part of the
old central vocabulary of prose; his maintaining the corporate,
professional attitude while striking into new ways; the naturalness that developed a common body of English available
to all sorts and conditions of men; his carrying prose forward
into modern usage without depriving it of anything essential
to its versatility and energy—all of these achievements have
made his prose criticism precious to us even though his own
contemporaries did not take it seriously. The numerous tributes paid to him after his death in 1700 say little of his distinction as a prose critic, of his immense achievement in
bringing prose style closer to its object and greatly enlarging
the areas of life available to literary comment.

It is said that Dryden's prose is not greatly different in
1700 from what it was in 1665; it is that of a free man at any
time. He seldom writes like an artist under duress, with vivid
powers straining at the leash—a genius contained within
limits only at desperate expense to itself. He seems to be
making no sacrifice of any kind, even though he speaks of the
restraint of the couplet, the fetters of rhyme or rule. He could
write under neoclassicism with complete self-fulfillment, even
though not all of our common humanity is satisfied now by
the neoclassical result. Yet no one is a complete man, a full
summary of all human needs and possibilities. If one is by
nature as Dryden was, at ease under the demand for order,
one may go forward with no sense of loss or human cost. Rule,
dogma, restraint, formula; established opinion, orthodoxy,
and all manner of conventional obligation—Dryden absorbs

all that the conservative myth demands. He respects all this so much that he can never be eccentric or outlandish, nor even wish to be so. He can end as a free man, and never so clearly choosing what suits him best as in committing himself to an authoritative political and social order.

After all, literature is even less inclined than politics to remain within its own prescriptions. Dryden makes us feel that he has done as he pleased in literature by testing the rules and trying out various positions. In politics he gives us the same sense of having done as he pleased, but here by staying within rule and principle. For the sake of the general order, he is willing to be confined, sees that he must be and should be so confined by rule, common sense, and experience. Even when he suffers after 1688 for his convictions, he does not repent of his constancy, "since I am thoroughly persuaded of the justice of the laws, for which I suffer." Experience only intensifies the beliefs that have cost him so much. Having lost all for honesty, and merit and belief, he seems almost belligerent in claiming these virtues for himself. He convinces himself, by praising his honor, that he took the best course after all, and virtue becomes more precious after he has lost all in its service.

Yet like Luther he could not have done any other; he ends as a free man at ease within the authoritative order he constantly sought. *Absalom and Achitophel* will show Dryden's view of life as inevitable, will show him as ideally suited to express it, and make us wonder how he could have believed anything else. It will show, too, how lucky Dryden was. He could be all that was required by the conservative myth, could be the ideal voice to express it, and yet come to the end of his career a free agent. His conservatism is freely chosen, the natural unforced result of what he was.

PART TWO

The Poem Itself

ABSALOM
AND
ACHITOPHEL.

A

POEM.

--------*Si Propius ftes*
Te Capiet Magis----------

The Second Edition ; Augmented and Revifed.

LONDON,

Printed for *J. T.* and are to be Sold by
W. Davis in *Amen-Corner*, 1 6 8 1.

Absalom and Achitophel

A POEM

Si propius stes
Te capiet magis.

To the Reader

'T is not my intention to make an apology for my poem: some will think it needs no excuse, and others will receive none. The design, I am sure, is honest; but he who draws his pen for one party must expect to make enemies of the other. For wit and fool are consequents of Whig and Tory; and every man is a knave or an ass to the contrary side. There's a treasury of merits in the Fanatic Church, as well as in the Papist; and a pennyworth to be had of saintship, honesty, and poetry, for the lewd, the factious, and the blockheads; but the longest chapter in Deuteronomy has not curses enough for an anti-Bromingham. My comfort is, their manifest prejudice to my cause will render their judgment of less authority against me. Yet if a poem have a genius, it will force its own reception in the world; for there's a sweetness in good verse, which tickles even while it hurts, and no man can be heartily angry with him who pleases him against his will. The commendation of adversaries is the greatest triumph of a writer, because it never comes unless extorted. But I can be satisfied on more easy terms: if I happen to please the more moderate sort, I shall be sure of an honest party, and, in all probability, of the best judges; for the least concern'd are commonly the least corrupt.

And, I confess, I have laid in for those, by rebating the satire (where justice would allow it) from carrying too sharp an edge. They who can criticise so weakly, as to imagine I have done my worst, may be convinc'd, at their own cost, that I can write severely with more ease than I can gently. I have but laugh'd at some men's follies, when I could have declaim'd against their vices; and other men's virtues I have commended, as freely as I have tax'd their crimes. And now, if you are a malicious reader, I expect you should return upon me that I affect to be thought more impartial than I am. But if men are not to be judg'd by their professions, God forgive you Commonwealth's-men for professing so plausibly for the government. You cannot be so unconscionable as to charge me for not subscribing of my name; for that would reflect too grossly upon your own party, who never dare, tho' they have the advantage of a jury to secure them. If you like not my poem, the fault may, possibly, be in my writing (tho' 't is hard for an author to judge against himself); but, more probably, 't is in your morals, which cannot bear the truth of it. The violent, on both sides, will condemn the character of Absalom, as either too favorably or too hardly drawn. But they are not the violent whom I desire to please. The fault on the right hand is to extenuate, palliate, and indulge; and, to confess freely, I have endeavor'd to commit it. Besides the respect which I owe his birth, I have a greater for his heroic virtues; and David himself could not be more tender of the young man's life than I would be of his reputation. But since the most excellent natures are always the most easy, and, as being such, are the soonest perverted by ill counsels, especially when baited with fame and glory; 't is no more a wonder that he withstood not the temptations of Achitophel, than it was for Adam not to have resisted the two devils, the serpent and the woman. The conclusion of the story I purposely forbore to prosecute, because I could not obtain from myself to shew Absalom unfortunate. The frame of it was cut out but for a picture to the waist, and if the draught be so far true, 't is as much as I design'd.

Were I the inventor, who am only the historian, I should certainly conclude the piece with the reconcilement of Absalom to David. And who knows but this may come to pass? Things were not brought to an extremity where I left the story; there seems yet to be room left for a composure; hereafter there may only be for pity. I have not so much as an uncharitable wish against Achitophel, but am content to be accus'd of a good-natur'd error, and to hope with Origen, that the Devil himself may at last be sav'd. For which reason, in this poem, he is neither brought to set his house in order, nor to dispose of his person afterwards as he in wisdom shall think fit. God is infinitely merciful; and his vicegerent is only not so, because he is not infinite.

The true end of satire is the amendment of vices by correction. And he who writes honestly is no more an enemy to the offender, than the physician to the patient, when he prescribes harsh remedies to an inveterate disease; for those are only in order to prevent the chirurgeon's work of an *ense rescindendum,* which I wish not to my very enemies. To conclude all; if the body politic have any analogy to the natural, in my weak judgment, an act of oblivion were as necessary in a hot, distemper'd state, as an opiate would be in a raging fever.

ABSALOM AND ACHITOPHEL

IN pious times, ere priestcraft did begin,
Before polygamy was made a sin;
When man on many multiplied his kind,
Ere one to one was cursedly confin'd;
When nature prompted, and no law denied
Promiscuous use of concubine and bride;
Then Israel's monarch after Heaven's own heart,
His vigorous warmth did variously impart
To wives and slaves; and, wide as his command,
Scatter'd his Maker's image thro' the land.   10
Michal, of royal blood, the crown did wear;
A soil ungrateful to the tiller's care:

Not so the rest; for several mothers bore
To godlike David several sons before.
But since like slaves his bed they did ascend,
No true succession could their seed attend.
Of all this numerous progeny was none
So beautiful, so brave, as Absalon:
Whether, inspir'd by some diviner lust,
His father got him with a greater gust;   20
Or that his conscious destiny made way,
By manly beauty, to imperial sway.
Early in foreign fields he won renown,
With kings and states allied to Israel's crown:
In peace the thoughts of war he could remove,
And seem'd as he were only born for love.
Whate'er he did, was done with so much ease,
In him alone 't was natural to please:
His motions all accompanied with grace;
And paradise was open'd in his face.   30
With secret joy indulgent David view'd
His youthful image in his son renew'd:
To all his wishes nothing he denied;
And made the charming Annabel his bride.
What faults he had, (for who from faults is free?)
His father could not, or he would not see.
Some warm excesses which the law forbore,
Were construed youth that purg'd by boiling o'er,
And Amnon's murther, by a specious name,
Was call'd a just revenge for injur'd fame.   40
Thus prais'd and lov'd the noble youth remain'd,
While David, undisturb'd, in Sion reign'd.
But life can never be sincerely blest;
Heav'n punishes the bad, and proves the best.
The Jews, a headstrong, moody, murm'ring race,
As ever tried th' extent and stretch of grace;
God's pamper'd people, whom, debauch'd with ease,
No king could govern, nor no God could please;
(Gods they had tried of every shape and size,

That god-smiths could produce, or priests devise:)   50
These Adam-wits, too fortunately free,
Began to dream they wanted liberty;
And when no rule, no precedent was found,
Of men by laws less circumscrib'd and bound;
They led their wild desires to woods and caves,
And thought that all but savages were slaves.
They who, when Saul was dead, without a blow,
Made foolish Ishbosheth the crown forego;
Who banish'd David did from Hebron bring,
And with a general shout proclaim'd him king: 60
Those very Jews, who, at their very best,
Their humor more than loyalty express'd,
Now wonder'd why so long they had obey'd
An idol monarch, which their hands had made;
Thought they might ruin him they could create,
Or melt him to that golden calf, a State.
But these were random bolts; no form'd design,
Nor interest made the factious crowd to join:
The sober part of Israel, free from stain,
Well knew the value of a peaceful reign;   70
And, looking backward with a wise affright,
Saw seams of wounds, dishonest to the sight:
In contemplation of whose ugly scars
They curs'd the memory of civil wars.
The moderate sort of men, thus qualified,
Inclin'd the balance to the better side;
And David's mildness manag'd it so well,
The bad found no occasion to rebel.
But when to sin our bias'd nature leans,
The careful Devil is still at hand with means;   80
And providently pimps for ill desires.
The Good Old Cause reviv'd, a plot requires:
Plots, true or false, are necessary things,
To raise up commonwealths, and ruin kings.
    Th' inhabitants of old Jerusalem
Were Jebusites; the town so call'd from them;

And theirs the native right——
But when the chosen people grew more strong,
The rightful cause at length became the wrong;
And every loss the men of Jebus bore,   90
They still were thought God's enemies the more.
Thus worn and weaken'd, well or ill content,
Submit they must to David's government:
Impoverish'd and depriv'd of all command,
Their taxes doubled as they lost their land;
And, what was harder yet to flesh and blood,
Their gods disgrac'd, and burnt like common wood.
This set the heathen priesthood in a flame;
For priests of all religions are the same:
Of whatsoe'er descent their godhead be,   100
Stock, stone, or other homely pedigree,
In his defense his servants are as bold,
As if he had been born of beaten gold.
The Jewish rabbins, tho' their enemies,
In this conclude them honest men and wise:
For 't was their duty, all the learned think,
T' espouse his cause, by whom they eat and drink.
From hence began that Plot, the nation's curse,
Bad in itself, but represented worse;
Rais'd in extremes, and in extremes decried;   110
With oaths affirm'd, with dying vows denied;
Not weigh'd or winnow'd by the multitude;
But swallow'd in the mass, unchew'd and crude.
Some truth there was, but dash'd and brew'd with lies,
To please the fools, and puzzle all the wise.
Succeeding times did equal folly call,
Believing nothing, or believing all.
Th' Egyptian rites the Jebusites embrac'd;
Where gods were recommended by their taste.
Such sav'ry deities must needs be good,   120
As serv'd at once for worship and for food.
By force they could not introduce these gods,
For ten to one in former days was odds;

So fraud was us'd (the sacrificer's trade):
Fools are more hard to conquer than persuade.
Their busy teachers mingled with the Jews,
And rak'd for converts even the court and stews:
Which Hebrew priests the more unkindly took,
Because the fleece accompanies the flock.
Some thought they God's anointed meant to slay   130
By guns, invented since full many a day:
Our author swears it not; but who can know
How far the Devil and Jebusites may go?
This Plot, which fail'd for want of common sense,
Had yet a deep and dangerous consequence:
For, as when raging fevers boil the blood,
The standing lake soon floats into a flood,
And ev'ry hostile humor, which before
Slept quiet in its channels, bubbles o'er;
So several factions from this first ferment   140
Work up to foam, and threat the government.
Some by their friends, more by themselves thought wise,
Oppos'd the pow'r to which they could not rise.
Some had in courts been great, and thrown from thence,
Like fiends were harden'd in impenitence.
Some, by their monarch's fatal mercy, grown
From pardon'd rebels kinsmen to the throne,
Were rais'd in pow'r and public office high;
Strong bands, if bands ungrateful men could tie.
    Of these the false Achitophel was first;   150
A name to all succeeding ages curst:
For close designs and crooked counsels fit;
Sagacious, bold, and turbulent of wit;
Restless, unfix'd in principles and place;
In pow'r unpleas'd, impatient of disgrace:
A fiery soul, which, working out its way,   ⎫
Fretted the pigmy body to decay,   ⎬
And o'er-inform'd the tenement of clay.   ⎭
A daring pilot in extremity;
Pleas'd with the danger, when the waves went high,   160

He sought the storms; but, for a calm unfit,
Would steer too nigh the sands, to boast his wit.
Great wits are sure to madness near allied,
And thin partitions do their bounds divide;
Else why should he, with wealth and honor blest,
Refuse his age the needful hours of rest?
Punish a body which he could not please;
Bankrupt of life, yet prodigal of ease?
And all to leave what with his toil he won,
To that unfeather'd two-legg'd thing, a son;   170
Got, while his soul did huddled notions try;
And born a shapeless lump, like anarchy.
In friendship false, implacable in hate;
Resolv'd to ruin or to rule the State.
To compass this the triple bond he broke;   ⎫
The pillars of the public safety shook;   ⎬
And fitted Israel for a foreign yoke: ⎭
Then seiz'd with fear, yet still affecting fame,
Usurp'd a patriot's all-atoning name.
So easy still it proves in factious times,   180
With public zeal to cancel private crimes.
How safe is treason, and how sacred ill,
Where none can sin against the people's will!
Where crowds can wink, and no offense be known,
Since in another's guilt they find their own!
Yet fame deserv'd no enemy can grudge;
The statesman we abhor, but praise the judge.
In Israel's courts ne'er sat an Abbethdin
With more discerning eyes, or hands more clean;
Unbrib'd, unsought, the wretched to redress;   190
Swift of dispatch, and easy of access.
O, had he been content to serve the crown,
With virtues only proper to the gown;
Or had the rankness of the soil been freed
From cockle, that oppress'd the noble seed;
David for him his tuneful harp had strung,
And Heav'n had wanted one immortal song.

But wild Ambition loves to slide, not stand,
And Fortune's ice prefers to Virtue's land.
Achitophel, grown weary to possess   200
A lawful fame, and lazy happiness,
Disdain'd the golden fruit to gather free,
And lent the crowd his arm to shake the tree.
Now, manifest of crimes contriv'd long since,
He stood at bold defiance with his prince;
Held up the buckler of the people's cause
Against the crown, and skulk'd behind the laws.
The wish'd occasion of the Plot he takes;
Some circumstances finds, but more he makes.
By buzzing emissaries fills the ears   210
Of list'ning crowds with jealousies and fears
Of arbitrary counsels brought to light,
And proves the king himself a Jebusite.
Weak arguments! which yet he knew full well
Were strong with people easy to rebel.
For, govern'd by the moon, the giddy Jews
Tread the same track when she the prime renews;
And once in twenty years, their scribes record,
By natural instinct they change their lord.
Achitophel still wants a chief, and none   220
Was found so fit as warlike Absalon:
Not that he wish'd his greatness to create,
(For politicians neither love nor hate,)
But, for he knew his title not allow'd,
Would keep him still depending on the crowd:
That kingly pow'r, thus ebbing out, might be
Drawn to the dregs of a democracy.
Him he attempts with studied arts to please,
And sheds his venom in such words as these:
   "Auspicious prince, at whose nativity   230
Some royal planet rul'd the southern sky;
Thy longing country's darling and desire;
Their cloudy pillar and their guardian fire:
Their second Moses, whose extended wand

Divides the seas, and shews the promis'd land;
Whose dawning day in every distant age
Has exercis'd the sacred prophets' rage:
The people's pray'r, the glad diviners' theme,
The young men's vision, and the old men's dream!
Thee, Savior, thee, the nation's vows confess,   240
And, never satisfied with seeing, bless:
Swift unbespoken pomps thy steps proclaim,
And stammering babes are taught to lisp thy name.
How long wilt thou the general joy detain,
Starve and defraud the people of thy reign?
Content ingloriously to pass thy days
Like one of Virtue's fools that feeds on praise;
Till thy fresh glories, which now shine so bright,
Grow stale and tarnish with our daily sight.
Believe me, royal youth, thy fruit must be   250
Or gather'd ripe, or rot upon the tree.
Heav'n has to all allotted, soon or late,
Some lucky revolution of their fate;
Whose motions if we watch and guide with skill,
(For human good depends on human will,)
Our Fortune rolls as from a smooth descent,
And from the first impression takes the bent:
But, if unseiz'd, she glides away like wind,
And leaves repenting Folly far behind.
Now, now she meets you with a glorious prize,   260
And spreads her locks before her as she flies.
Had thus old David, from whose loins you spring,
Not dar'd, when Fortune call'd him, to be king,
At Gath an exile he might still remain,
And Heaven's anointing oil had been in vain.
Let his successful youth your hopes engage;
But shun th' example of declining age:
Behold him setting in his western skies,
The shadows lengthening as the vapors rise.
He is not now, as when on Jordan's sand   270
The joyful people throng'd to see him land,
Cov'ring the beach, and black'ning all the strand;

But, like the Prince of Angels, from his height
Comes tumbling downward with diminish'd light;
Betray'd by one poor plot to public scorn,
(Our only blessing since his curst return;)
Those heaps of people which one sheaf did bind,
Blown off and scatter'd by a puff of wind.
What strength can he to your designs oppose,
Naked of friends, and round beset with foes?   280
If Pharaoh's doubtful succor he should use,
A foreign aid would more incense the Jews:
Proud Egypt would dissembled friendship bring;
Foment the war, but not support the king:
Nor would the royal party e'er unite
With Pharaoh's arms t' assist the Jebusite;
Or if they should, their interest soon would break,
And with such odious aid make David weak.
All sorts of men by my successful arts,
Abhorring kings, estrange their alter'd hearts   290
From David's rule: and 't is the general cry,
'Religion, commonwealth, and liberty.'
If you, as champion of the public good,
Add to their arms a chief of royal blood,
What may not Israel hope, and what applause
Might such a general gain by such a cause?
Not barren praise alone, that gaudy flow'r
Fair only to the sight, but solid pow'r;
And nobler is a limited command,
Giv'n by the love of all your native land,   300
Than a successive title, long and dark,
Drawn from the moldy rolls of Noah's ark."
    What cannot praise effect in mighty minds,
When flattery soothes, and when ambition blinds!
Desire of pow'r, on earth a vicious weed,
Yet, sprung from high, is of celestial seed:
In God 't is glory; and when men aspire,
'T is but a spark too much of heavenly fire.
Th' ambitious youth, too covetous of fame,
Too full of angels' metal in his frame,   310

Unwarily was led from virtue's ways,
Made drunk with honor, and debauch'd with praise.
Half loth, and half consenting to the ill,
(For loyal blood within him struggled still,)
He thus replied: "And what pretense have I
To take up arms for public liberty?
My father governs with unquestion'd right;
The faith's defender, and mankind's delight;
Good, gracious, just, observant of the laws:
And Heav'n by wonders has espous'd his cause.   320
Whom has he wrong'd in all his peaceful reign?
Who sues for justice to his throne in vain?
What millions has he pardon'd of his foes,
Whom just revenge did to his wrath expose?
Mild, easy, humble, studious of our good;
Enclin'd to mercy, and averse from blood;
If mildness ill with stubborn Israel suit,
His crime is God's beloved attribute.
What could he gain, his people to betray,
Or change his right for arbitrary sway?   330
Let haughty Pharaoh curse with such a reign
His fruitful Nile, and yoke a servile train.
If David's rule Jerusalem displease,
The Dog-star heats their brains to this disease.
Why then should I, encouraging the bad,
Turn rebel and run popularly mad?
Were he a tyrant, who, by lawless might
Oppress'd the Jews, and rais'd the Jebusite,
Well might I mourn; but nature's holy bands
Would curb my spirits and restrain my hands: 340
The people might assert their liberty;
But what was right in them were crime in me.
His favor leaves me nothing to require,
Prevents my wishes, and outruns desire.
What more can I expect while David lives?
All but his kingly diadem he gives:
And that"—But there he paus'd; then sighing, said—

"Is justly destin'd for a worthier head.
For when my father from his toils shall rest,
And late augment the number of the blest,   350
His lawful issue shall the throne ascend,
Or the *collat'ral* line, where that shall end.
His brother, tho' oppress'd with vulgar spite,
Yet dauntless, and secure of native right,
Of every royal virtue stands possess'd;
Still dear to all the bravest and the best.
His courage foes, his friends his truth proclaim;
His loyalty the king, the world his fame.
His mercy ev'n th' offending crowd will find;
For sure he comes of a forgiving kind.   360
Why should I then repine at Heaven's decree,
Which gives me no pretense to royalty?
Yet O that fate, propitiously inclin'd,
Had rais'd my birth, or had debas'd my mind;
To my large soul not all her treasure lent,
And then betray'd it to a mean descent!
I find, I find my mounting spirits bold,
And David's part disdains my mother's mold.
Why am I scanted by a niggard birth?
My soul disclaims the kindred of her earth;   370
And, made for empire, whispers me within,
'Desire of greatness is a godlike sin.' "
    Him staggering so when hell's dire agent found,
While fainting Virtue scarce maintain'd her ground,
He pours fresh forces in, and thus replies:
    "Th' eternal God, supremely good and wise,
Imparts not these prodigious gifts in vain:
What wonders are reserv'd to bless your reign!
Against your will, your arguments have shown,
Such virtue 's only giv'n to guide a throne.   380
Not that your father's mildness I contemn;
But manly force becomes the diadem.
'T is true he grants the people all they crave;
And more, perhaps, than subjects ought to have:

For lavish grants suppose a monarch tame,
And more his goodness than his wit proclaim.
But when should people strive their bonds to break,
If not when kings are negligent or weak?
Let him give on till he can give no more,
The thrifty Sanhedrin shall keep him poor;   390
And every shekel which he can receive,
Shall cost a limb of his prerogative.
To ply him with new plots shall be my care;
Or plunge him deep in some expensive war;
Which when his treasure can no more supply,
He must, with the remains of kingship, buy.
His faithful friends, our jealousies and fears
Call Jebusites, and Pharaoh's pensioners;
Whom when our fury from his aid has torn,
He shall be naked left to public scorn.   400
The next successor, whom I fear and hate,
My arts have made obnoxious to the State;
Turn'd all his virtues to his overthrow,
And gain'd our elders to pronounce a foe.
His right, for sums of necessary gold,
Shall first be pawn'd, and afterwards be sold;
Till time shall ever-wanting David draw,
To pass your doubtful title into law:
If not, the people have a right supreme
To make their kings; for kings are made for them.   410
All empire is no more than pow'r in trust,
Which, when resum'd, can be no longer just.
Succession, for the general good design'd,
In its own wrong a nation cannot bind;
If altering that the people can relieve,
Better one suffer than a nation grieve.
The Jews well know their pow'r: ere Saul they chose,
God was their king, and God they durst depose.
Urge now your piety, your filial name,
A father's right, and fear of future fame;   420
The public good, that universal call,

To which even Heav'n submitted, answers all.
Nor let his love enchant your generous mind;
'T is Nature's trick to propagate her kind.
Our fond begetters, who would never die,
Love but themselves in their posterity.
Or let his kindness by th' effects be tried,
Or let him lay his vain pretense aside.
God said he lov'd your father; could he bring
A better proof, than to anoint him king?   430
It surely shew'd he lov'd the shepherd well,
Who gave so fair a flock as Israel.
Would David have you thought his darling son?
What means he then, to alienate the crown?
The name of godly he may blush to bear:
'T is after God's own heart to cheat his heir.
He to his brother gives supreme command,
To you a legacy of barren land:
Perhaps th' old harp, on which he thrums his lays,
Or some dull Hebrew ballad in your praise.   440
Then the next heir, a prince severe and wise,
Already looks on you with jealous eyes;
Sees thro' the thin disguises of your arts,
And marks your progress in the people's hearts.
Tho' now his mighty soul its grief contains,
He meditates revenge who least complains;
And, like a lion, slumb'ring in the way,
Or sleep dissembling, while he waits his prey,
His fearless foes within his distance draws,
Constrains his roaring, and contracts his paws;   450
Till at the last, his time for fury found,
He shoots with sudden vengeance from the ground;
The prostrate vulgar passes o'er and spares,
But with a lordly rage his hunters tears.
Your case no tame expedients will afford:
Resolve on death, or conquest by the sword,
Which for no less a stake than life you draw;
And self-defense is nature's eldest law.

Leave the warm people no considering time;
For then rebellion may be thought a crime.   460
Prevail yourself of what occasion gives,
But try your title while your father lives;
And that your arms may have a fair pretense,
Proclaim you take them in the king's defense;
Whose sacred life each minute would expose
To plots, from seeming friends, and secret foes.
And who can sound the depth of David's soul?
Perhaps his fear his kindness may control.
He fears his brother, tho' he loves his son,
For plighted vows too late to be undone.   470
If so, by force he wishes to be gain'd;
Like women's lechery, to seem constrain'd.
Doubt not: but, when he most affects the frown,
Commit a pleasing rape upon the crown.
Secure his person to secure your cause:
They who possess the prince, possess the laws."
      He said, and this advice above the rest,
With Absalom's mild nature suited best:
Unblam'd of life, (ambition set aside,)
Not stain'd with cruelty, nor puff'd with pride;   480
How happy had he been, if destiny
Had higher plac'd his birth, or not so high!
His kingly virtues might have claim'd a throne,
And blest all other countries but his own.
But charming greatness since so few refuse,
'T is juster to lament him than accuse.
Strong were his hopes a rival to remove,
With blandishments to gain the public love;
To head the faction while their zeal was hot,
And popularly prosecute the Plot.   490
To farther this, Achitophel unites
The malcontents of all the Israelites;
Whose differing parties he could wisely join,
For several ends, to serve the same design:
The best, (and of the princes some were such,)

Who thought the pow'r of monarchy too much;
Mistaken men, and patriots in their hearts;
Not wicked, but seduc'd by impious arts.
By these the springs of property were bent,
And wound so high, they crack'd the government.   500
The next for interest sought t' embroil the State,
To sell their duty at a dearer rate;
And make their Jewish markets of the throne,
Pretending public good, to serve their own.
Others thought kings an useless heavy load,
Who cost too much, and did too little good.
These were for laying honest David by,
On principles of pure good husbandry.
With them join'd all th' haranguers of the throng,
That thought to get preferment by the tongue.   510
Who follow next, a double danger bring,
Not only hating David, but the king:
The Solymæan rout, well-vers'd of old
In godly faction, and in treason bold;
Cow'ring and quaking at a conqu'ror's sword;
But lofty to a lawful prince restor'd;
Saw with disdain an Ethnic plot begun,
And scorn'd by Jebusites to be outdone.
Hot Levites headed these; who, pull'd before
From th' ark, which in the Judges' days they bore,   520
Resum'd their cant, and with a zealous cry
Pursued their old belov'd Theocracy:
Where Sanhedrin and priest enslav'd the nation,
And justified their spoils by inspiration:
For who so fit for reign as Aaron's race,
If once dominion they could found in grace.
These led the pack; tho' not of surest scent,
Yet deepest mouth'd against the government.
A numerous host of dreaming saints succeed,
Of the true old enthusiastic breed: 530
'Gainst form and order they their pow'r imploy,
Nothing to build, and all things to destroy.

But far more numerous was the herd of such,
Who think too little, and who talk too much.
These, out of mere instinct, they knew not why,
Ador'd their fathers' God and property;
And, by the same blind benefit of fate,
The Devil and the Jebusite did hate:
Born to be sav'd, even in their own despite,
Because they could not help believing right.   540
Such were the tools; but a whole Hydra more
Remains, of sprouting heads too long to score.
Some of their chiefs were princes of the land:
In the first rank of these did Zimri stand;
A man so various, that he seem'd to be
Not one, but all mankind's epitome:
Stiff in opinions, always in the wrong;
Was everything by starts, and nothing long;
But, in the course of one revolving moon,
Was chymist, fiddler, statesman, and buffoon: 550
Then all for women, painting, rhyming, drinking,
Besides ten thousand freaks that died in thinking.
Blest madman, who could every hour employ,
With something new to wish, or to enjoy!
Railing and praising were his usual themes;
And both (to shew his judgment) in extremes:
So over-violent, or over-civil,
That every man, with him, was God or Devil.
In squand'ring wealth was his peculiar art:
Nothing went unrewarded but desert.   560
Beggar'd by fools, whom still he found too late,
He had his jest, and they had his estate.
He laugh'd himself from court; then sought relief
By forming parties, but could ne'er be chief;
For, spite of him, the weight of business fell
On Absalom and wise Achitophel:
Thus, wicked but in will, of means bereft,
He left not faction, but of that was left.
    Titles and names 't were tedious to rehearse

Of lords, below the dignity of verse.   570
Wits, warriors, Commonwealth's-men, were the best;
Kind husbands, and mere nobles, all the rest.
And therefore, in the name of dulness, be
The well-hung Balaam and cold Caleb, free;
And canting Nadab let oblivion damn,
Who made new porridge for the paschal lamb.
Let friendship's holy band some names assure;
Some their own worth, and some let scorn secure.
Nor shall the rascal rabble here have place,
Whom kings no titles gave, and God no grace: 580
Not bull-fac'd Jonas, who could statutes draw
To mean rebellion, and make treason law.
But he, tho' bad, is follow'd by a worse,
The wretch who Heav'n's anointed dar'd to curse:
Shimei, whose youth did early promise bring
Of zeal to God and hatred to his king,
Did wisely from expensive sins refrain,
And never broke the Sabbath, but for gain;
Nor ever was he known an oath to vent,
Or curse, unless against the government.   590
Thus heaping wealth, by the most ready way
Among the Jews, which was to cheat and pray,
The city, to reward his pious hate
Against his master, chose him magistrate.
His hand a vare of justice did uphold;
His neck was loaded with a chain of gold.
During his office, treason was no crime;
The sons of Belial had a glorious time;
For Shimei, tho' not prodigal of pelf,
Yet lov'd his wicked neighbor as himself.   600
When two or three were gather'd to declaim
Against the monarch of Jerusalem,
Shimei was always in the midst of them;
And if they curs'd the king when he was by,
Would rather curse than break good company.
If any durst his factious friends accuse,

He pack'd a jury of dissenting Jews;
Whose fellow-feeling in the godly cause
Would free the suff'ring saint from human laws.
For laws are only made to punish those   610
Who serve the king, and to protect his foes.
If any leisure time he had from pow'r,
(Because 't is sin to misimploy an hour,)
His bus'ness was, by writing, to persuade
That kings were useless, and a clog to trade;
And, that his noble style he might refine,
No Rechabite more shunn'd the fumes of wine.
Chaste were his cellars, and his shrieval board
The grossness of a city feast abhorr'd:
His cooks, with long disuse, their trade forgot;   620
Cool was his kitchen, tho' his brains were hot.
Such frugal virtue malice may accuse,
But sure 't was necessary to the Jews;
For towns once burnt such magistrates require
As dare not tempt God's providence by fire.
With spiritual food he fed his servants well,
But free from flesh that made the Jews rebel;
And Moses' laws he held in more account,
For forty days of fasting in the mount.

　　To speak the rest, who better are forgot,   630
Would tire a well-breath'd witness of the Plot.
Yet, Corah, thou shalt from oblivion pass:
Erect thyself, thou monumental brass,
High as the serpent of thy metal made,
While nations stand secure beneath thy shade.
What tho' his birth were base, yet comets rise
From earthy vapors, ere they shine in skies.
Prodigious actions may as well be done
By weaver's issue, as by prince's son.
This arch-attestor for the public good   640
By that one deed ennobles all his blood.
Who ever ask'd the witnesses' high race,
Whose oath with martyrdom did Stephen grace?

Ours was a Levite, and as times went then,
His tribe were God Almighty's gentlemen.
Sunk were his eyes, his voice was harsh and loud,
Sure signs he neither choleric was nor proud:
His long chin prov'd his wit; his saintlike grace
A church vermilion, and a Moses' face.
His memory, miraculously great,   650
Could plots, exceeding man's belief, repeat;
Which therefore cannot be accounted lies,
For human wit could never such devise.
Some future truths are mingled in his book;
But where the witness fail'd, the prophet spoke:
Some things like visionary flights appear;
The spirit caught him up, the Lord knows where;
And gave him his rabbinical degree,
Unknown to foreign university.
His judgment yet his mem'ry did excel;   660
Which piec'd his wondrous evidence so well,
And suited to the temper of the times,
Then groaning under Jebusitic crimes.
Let Israel's foes suspect his heav'nly call,
And rashly judge his writ apocryphal;
Our laws for such affronts have forfeits made:
He takes his life, who takes away his trade.
Were I myself in witness Corah's place,
The wretch who did me such a dire disgrace,
Should whet my memory, tho' once forgot,   670
To make him an appendix of my plot.
His zeal to Heav'n made him his prince despise,
And load his person with indignities;
But zeal peculiar privilege affords,
Indulging latitude to deeds and words;
And Corah might for Agag's murther call,
In terms as coarse as Samuel us'd to Saul.
What others in his evidence did join,
(The best that could be had for love or coin,)
In Corah's own predicament will fall;   680

For *witness* is a common name to all.
   Surrounded thus with friends of every sort,
Deluded Absalom forsakes the court;
Impatient of high hopes, urg'd with renown,
And fir'd with near possession of a crown.
Th' admiring crowd are dazzled with surprise,
And on his goodly person feed their eyes.
His joy conceal'd, he sets himself to show,
On each side bowing popularly low;
His looks, his gestures, and his words he frames,   690
And with familiar ease repeats their names.
Thus form'd by nature, furnish'd out with arts,
He glides unfelt into their secret hearts.
Then, with a kind compassionating look,
And sighs, bespeaking pity ere he spoke,
Few words he said; but easy those and fit,
More slow than Hybla-drops, and far more sweet.
   "I mourn, my countrymen, your lost estate;
Tho' far unable to prevent your fate:
Behold a banish'd man, for your dear cause   700
Expos'd a prey to arbitrary laws!
Yet O! that I alone could be undone,
Cut off from empire, and no more a son!
Now all your liberties a spoil are made;
Egypt and Tyrus intercept your trade,
And Jebusites your sacred rites invade.
My father, whom with reverence yet I name,
Charm'd into ease, is careless of his fame;
And, brib'd with petty sums of foreign gold,
Is grown in Bathsheba's embraces old;   710
Exalts his enemies, his friends destroys;
And all his pow'r against himself imploys.
He gives, and let him give, my right away;
But why should he his own and yours betray?
He, only he, can make the nation bleed,
And he alone from my revenge is freed.
Take then my tears, (with that he wip'd his eyes,)

'T is all the aid my present pow'r supplies:
No court-informer can these arms accuse;
These arms may sons against their fathers use: 720
And 't is my wish, the next successor's reign
May make no other Israelite complain."
    Youth, beauty, graceful action seldom fail;
But common interest always will prevail;
And pity never ceases to be shown
To him who makes the people's wrongs his own.
The crowd, that still believe their kings oppress,
With lifted hands their young Messiah bless:
Who now begins his progress to ordain
With chariots, horsemen, and a num'rous train;   730
From east to west his glories he displays,
And, like the sun, the promis'd land surveys.
Fame runs before him as the morning star,
And shouts of joy salute him from afar:
Each house receives him as a guardian god,
And consecrates the place of his abode.
But hospitable treats did most commend
Wise Issachar, his wealthy western friend.
This moving court, that caught the people's eyes,
And seem'd but pomp, did other ends disguise: 740
Achitophel had form'd it, with intent
To sound the depths, and fathom, where it went,
The people's hearts; distinguish friends from foes,
And try their strength, before they came to blows.
Yet all was color'd with a smooth pretense
Of specious love, and duty to their prince.
Religion, and redress of grievances,
Two names that always cheat and always please,
Are often urg'd; and good King David's life
Endanger'd by a brother and a wife.   750
Thus in a pageant shew a plot is made,
And peace itself is war in masquerade.
O foolish Israel! never warn'd by ill!
Still the same bait, and circumvented still!

Did ever men forsake their present ease,
In midst of health imagine a disease;
Take pains contingent mischiefs to foresee,
Make heirs for monarchs, and for God decree?
What shall we think! Can people give away,
Both for themselves and sons, their native sway?   760
Then they are left defenseless to the sword
Of each unbounded, arbitrary lord:
And laws are vain, by which we right enjoy,
If kings unquestion'd can those laws destroy.
Yet if the crowd be judge of fit and just,
And kings are only officers in trust,
Then this resuming cov'nant was declar'd
When kings were made, or is for ever barr'd.
If those who gave the scepter could not tie
By their own deed their own posterity,   770
How then could Adam bind his future race?
How could his forfeit on mankind take place?
Or how could heavenly justice damn us all,
Who ne'er consented to our father's fall?
Then kings are slaves to those whom they command,
And tenants to their people's pleasure stand.
Add, that the pow'r for property allow'd
Is mischievously seated in the crowd;
For who can be secure of private right,
If sovereign sway may be dissolv'd by might?   780
Nor is the people's judgment always true:
The most may err as grossly as the few;
And faultless kings run down, by common cry,
For vice, oppression, and for tyranny.
What standard is there in a fickle rout,
Which, flowing to the mark, runs faster out?
Nor only crowds, but Sanhedrins may be
Infected with this public lunacy,
And share the madness of rebellious times,
To murther monarchs for imagin'd crimes.   790
If they may give and take whene'er they please,

Not kings alone, (the Godhead's images,)
But government itself at length must fall
To nature's state, where all have right to all.
Yet, grant our lords the people kings can make,
What prudent men a settled throne would shake?
For whatsoe'er their sufferings were before,
That change they covet makes them suffer more.
All other errors but disturb a state,
But innovation is the blow of fate.   800
If ancient fabrics nod, and threat to fall,
To patch the flaws, and buttress up the wall,
Thus far 't is duty: but here fix the mark;
For all beyond it is to touch our ark.
To change foundations, cast the frame anew,
Is work for rebels, who base ends pursue,
At once divine and human laws control,
And mend the parts by ruin of the whole.
The tamp'ring world is subject to this curse,
To physic their disease into a worse.   810
    Now what relief can righteous David bring?
How fatal 't is to be too good a king!
Friends he has few, so high the madness grows:
Who dare be such, must be the people's foes.
Yet some there were, ev'n in the worst of days;
Some let me name, and naming is to praise.
    In this short file Barzillai first appears;
Barzillai, crown'd with honor and with years.
Long since, the rising rebels he withstood
In regions waste, beyond the Jordan's flood: 820
Unfortunately brave to buoy the State;
But sinking underneath his master's fate:
In exile with his godlike prince he mourn'd;
For him he suffer'd, and with him return'd.
The court he practic'd, not the courtier's art:
Large was his wealth, but larger was his heart,
Which well the noblest objects knew to choose,
The fighting warrior, and recording Muse.

His bed could once a fruitful issue boast;
Now more than half a father's name is lost.   830
His eldest hope, with every grace adorn'd,
By me (so Heav'n will have it) always mourn'd,
And always honor'd, snatch'd in manhood's prime
B' unequal fates, and Providence's crime;
Yet not before the goal of honor won,
All parts fulfill'd of subject and of son:
Swift was the race, but short the time to run.
O narrow circle, but of pow'r divine,
Scanted in space, but perfect in thy line!
By sea, by land, thy matchless worth was known,   840
Arms thy delight, and war was all thy own:
Thy force, infus'd, the fainting Tyrians propp'd;
And haughty Pharaoh found his fortune stopp'd.
O ancient honor! O unconquer'd hand,
Whom foes unpunish'd never could withstand!
But Israel was unworthy of thy name;
Short is the date of all immoderate fame.
It looks as Heav'n our ruin had design'd,
And durst not trust thy fortune and thy mind.
Now, free from earth, thy disencumber'd soul   850
Mounts up, and leaves behind the clouds and starry pole:
From thence thy kindred legions mayst thou bring,
To aid the guardian angel of thy king.
Here stop, my Muse, here cease thy painful flight;
No pinions can pursue immortal height:
Tell good Barzillai thou canst sing no more,
And tell thy soul she should have fled before.
Or fled she with his life, and left this verse
To hang on her departed patron's hearse?
Now take thy steepy flight from heav'n, and see   860
If thou canst find on earth another *he:*
Another *he* would be too hard to find;
See then whom thou canst see not far behind.
Zadoc the priest, whom, shunning pow'r and place,
His lowly mind advanc'd to David's grace.

With him the Sagan of Jerusalem,
Of hospitable soul, and noble stem;
Him of the western dome, whose weighty sense
Flows in fit words and heavenly eloquence.
The prophets' sons, by such example led,   870
To learning and to loyalty were bred:
For colleges on bounteous kings depend,
And never rebel was to arts a friend.
To these succeed the pillars of the laws;
Who best could plead, and best can judge a cause.
Next them a train of loyal peers ascend;
Sharp-judging Adriel, the Muses' friend;
Himself a Muse—in Sanhedrin's debate
True to his prince, but not a slave of state:
Whom David's love with honors did adorn,   880
That from his disobedient son were torn.
Jotham of piercing wit, and pregnant thought;
Endued by nature, and by learning taught
To move assemblies, who but only tried
The worse a while, then chose the better side:
Nor chose alone, but turn'd the balance too;
So much the weight of one brave man can do.
Hushai, the friend of David in distress;
In public storms, of manly steadfastness:
By foreign treaties he inform'd his youth,   890
And join'd experience to his native truth.
His frugal care supplied the wanting throne;
Frugal for that, but bounteous of his own:
'T is easy conduct when exchequers flow,
But hard the task to manage well the low;
For sovereign power is too depress'd or high,
When kings are forc'd to sell, or crowds to buy.
Indulge one labor more, my weary Muse,
For Amiel: who can Amiel's praise refuse?
Of ancient race by birth, but nobler yet   900
In his own worth, and without title great:
The Sanhedrin long time as chief he rul'd,

Their reason guided, and their passion cool'd:
So dext'rous was he in the crown's defense,
So form'd to speak a loyal nation's sense,
That, as their band was Israel's tribes in small,
So fit was he to represent them all.
Now rasher charioteers the seat ascend,
Whose loose careers his steady skill commend:
They, like th' unequal ruler of the day,   910
Misguide the seasons, and mistake the way;
While he withdrawn at their mad labor smiles,
And safe enjoys the sabbath of his toils.
    These were the chief, a small but faithful band
Of worthies, in the breach who dar'd to stand,
And tempt th' united fury of the land.
With grief they view'd such powerful engines bent,
To batter down the lawful government:
A numerous faction, with pretended frights,
In Sanhedrins to plume the regal rights;   920
The true successor from the court remov'd;
The Plot, by hireling witnesses, improv'd.
These ills they saw, and, as their duty bound,
They shew'd the king the danger of the wound;
That no concessions from the throne would please,
But lenitives fomented the disease;
That Absalom, ambitious of the crown,
Was made the lure to draw the people down;
That false Achitophel's pernicious hate
Had turn'd the Plot to ruin Church and State;   930
The council violent, the rabble worse;
That Shimei taught Jerusalem to curse.
    With all these loads of injuries oppress'd,
And long revolving in his careful breast
Th' event of things, at last, his patience tir'd,
Thus from his royal throne, by Heav'n inspir'd,
The godlike David spoke: with awful fear
His train their Maker in their master hear.
    "Thus long have I, by native mercy sway'd,

My wrongs dissembled, my revenge delay'd: 940
So willing to forgive th' offending age;
So much the father did the king assuage.
But now so far my clemency they slight,
Th' offenders question my forgiving right.
That one was made for many, they contend;
But 't is to rule; for that 's a monarch's end.
They call my tenderness of blood, my fear;
Tho' manly tempers can the longest bear.
Yet, since they will divert my native course,
'T is time to shew I am not good by force.   950
Those heap'd affronts that haughty subjects bring,
Are burthens for a camel, not a king.
Kings are the public pillars of the State,
Born to sustain and prop the nation's weight;
If my young Samson will pretend a call
To shake the column, let him share the fall:
But O that yet he would repent and live!
How easy 't is for parents to forgive!
With how few tears a pardon might be won
From nature, pleading for a darling son!   960
Poor pitied youth, by my paternal care
Rais'd up to all the height his frame could bear!
Had God ordain'd his fate for empire born,
He would have giv'n his soul another turn:
Gull'd with a patriot's name, whose modern sense
Is one that would by law supplant his prince;
The people's brave, the politician's tool;
Never was patriot yet, but was a fool.
Whence comes it that religion and the laws
Should more be Absalom's than David's cause?   970
His old instructor, ere he lost his place,
Was never thought indued with so much grace.
Good heav'ns, how faction can a patriot paint!
My rebel ever proves my people's saint.
Would *they* impose an heir upon the throne?
Let Sanhedrins be taught to give their own.

A king 's at least a part of government,
And mine as requisite as their consent;
Without my leave a future king to choose,
Infers a right the present to depose.   980
True, they petition me t' approve their choice;
But Esau's hands suit ill with Jacob's voice.
My pious subjects for my safety pray;
Which to secure, they take my pow'r away.
From plots and treasons Heav'n preserve my years,
But save me most from my petitioners!
Unsatiate as the barren womb or grave;
God cannot grant so much as they can crave.
What then is left, but with a jealous eye
To guard the small remains of royalty?   990
The law shall still direct my peaceful sway,
And the same law teach rebels to obey:
Votes shall no more establish'd pow'r control—
Such votes as make a part exceed the whole:
No groundless clamors shall my friends remove,
Nor crowds have pow'r to punish ere they prove;
For gods and godlike kings their care express,
Still to defend their servants in distress.
O that my pow'r to saving were confin'd!
Why am I forc'd, like Heav'n, against my mind,   1000
To make examples of another kind?
Must I at length the sword of justice draw?
O curst effects of necessary law!
How ill my fear they by my mercy scan!
Beware the fury of a patient man.
Law they require, let Law then shew her face;
They could not be content to look on Grace,
Her hinder parts, but with a daring eye
To tempt the terror of her front and die.
By their own arts, 't is righteously decreed,   1010
Those dire artificers of death shall bleed.
Against themselves their witnesses will swear,
Till viper-like their mother Plot they tear;

And suck for nutriment that bloody gore,
Which was their principle of life before.
Their Belial with their Belzebub will fight;
Thus on my foes, my foes shall do me right.
Nor doubt th' event; for factious crowds engage,
In their first onset, all their brutal rage.
Then let 'em take an unresisted course;   1020
Retire, and traverse, and delude their force;
But, when they stand all breathless, urge the fight,
And rise upon 'em with redoubled might;
For lawful pow'r is still superior found;
When long driv'n back, at length it stands the ground."
    He said. Th' Almighty, nodding, gave consent;
And peals of thunder shook the firmament.
Henceforth a series of new time began,
The mighty years in long procession ran:
Once more the godlike David was restor'd,   1030
And willing nations knew their lawful lord.

CHAPTER 5

Absalom and Achitophel: A Poem

When the political-religious crisis of 1681 gave Dryden his supreme opportunity as a man of letters, he was ready for it. He is supposed to write in the main, "sound specimens of the uninspired," to have an unoriginal, receptive, too assimilative mind. But his skill in adapting what was at hand to immediate uses becomes a virtue in a poem that must express the conservative myth in a strikingly fresh and persuasive form. Dryden now displays the full intellectual and literary resources of his time. The less he has to invent the better, for the poem must seem a reassuring summary of belief and feeling given in such a way as to confirm beyond any further question the truth of what it says. It has to raise the great issues of all societies and answer them finally. It must refer to an incident or situation of the moment like a newsletter in verse; yet it must be resonant with echoes of other worlds, in Mr. Brower's phrase, suggesting larger manners and events. A wide range of instruments comes into play from the English and European literary traditions. A blending of styles, a variety of literary, philosophical, religious, and political allusions, will appeal to all shades of taste and knowledge.

Absalom and Achitophel then becomes a great synthetic effort of creation. We are struck by an air of assurance; if the poem is not the culmination of Dryden's own work, it is the final act in the events that it describes. For it gains enormously by its tone of coming after a victory already won. It supports

a cause already successful, gives added reasons for believing
in what has already prevailed. The king has in fact dealt with
his enemies in disbanding Parliament in April 1681. The
event has justified the assurance with which Dryden asserts
his view of a scheme of things that has prevailed because it
must. The rhetoric by which he seems to beg the question,
blandly assuming that the position adopted is the only one
possible for men of sense—this seems proper in the light of
what has actually taken place. The king's enemies are dis-
persed, and only their leader has now to be tried and sentenced
to what the poem has shown to be his just deserts.

Dryden comes to his task, then, with all the necessary material ready, his cause safely won; he has also had enough literary practice to make the most of these given advantages. His
literary instruments are ready after the writing of a dozen
poems, a score of prologues and epilogues with as many plays,
the translation of three Epistles from Ovid, and the fluent
composition of some thirteen critical essays. Saintsbury has
said that Dryden was trained at this point like a professional
athlete in a championship test. Certainly by now he had mas-
tered the couplet and could move freely within it, even anticipating the time when the couplet would give way before
freer verse forms. He could observe the strict march of couplet
verse with each two-line unit making its statement, containing
its member of the periodic grouping that made up the standard, perfect sentence of his day. He could avoid monotony by
occasional triplets, alexandrines, irregular or imperfect lines,
parentheses, quatrains, and verse paragraphs. He could observe the "separation of styles" as demanded by the constant
movement of his poem—shifting from one aspect of the conspiracy to another, moving amid a variety of people and portraits, expressing ideas clearly, and enlarging the poem's experiences by highly concentrated language, by manifold allusion, and by absorbing so many elements of the conservative
myth. Miltonic things like the temptation of Achitophel and
David's speech contrast with more colloquial tones in the Corah portrait with its direct personal address and scornful tone.

These emphasize Mr. Dobrée's remark that *Absalom and Achitophel* must be read aloud for full effect. Such verse will not do on the stage where it is merely heard; its intensity requires concentration while Dryden is free of all stage requirements and may employ his medium for the lessons and the influence he wishes to establish in the existing political situation. His couplet, then, is so ready and under his control that it carries a functional narrative, a series of sententiae, flowing blank-verse effects, statements of idea and attitude, oratorical eloquence, antithesis and balance as in the praise of James II, anticlimax and surprise as in the Shimei portrait, concentrated analysis of character as in the great lines on Zimri and Achitophel.

We encounter Dryden's freedom once more. And the extraordinary sense that *Absalom and Achitophel* gives of an artist triumphantly succeeding results from the freedom that Dryden has in fact declared for himself on the very title page. *Absalom and Achitophel: A Poem,* we read, not "a satire" as with *Mac Flecknoe* and *The Medal.* The word "poem" in Dryden's age meant a long story in verse, an epic or heroic poem, or a play like an epic. If this is the poetic norm in the late 17th century, Dryden naturally would see the heroic poem as the greatest work of human nature, and the heroic play would try to be more like epic than like ancient tragedy. The distinction between "poem" and "satire" was clear. Satire had the specific aims and limitations proper to itself as a lower genre, and was not expected to have so large a moral responsibility, to show the scope and freedom or to attempt what was proper only to the higher forms. Boileau explicitly admitted that his verse was bred in satire, not daring to attempt greater things. Dryden's own view of satire as fine raillery, inoffensive decapitation, is a long way from his concept of a heroic poem, and in *Absalom and Achitophel* the contemptuous ridicule of satire is not the principal element, being directed mainly at figures below the chief protagonists. Aristotle's distinction between poetry and history applies here, if *Absalom and Achitophel* is more than a special attack on particular individuals

at a certain moment in history. A satire has to be below a poem
because its reference is more particular, being contaminated
by history. We are allowed a more flexible "imitation" also if
Absalom and Achitophel is seen as a "poem." It then imitates
something beyond what simply is, and Dryden may imitate an
order he simply hopes for, may recommend an order more
stable than what in fact has been possible in a turbulent age.
Thus the poem will see its good men as better, its bad men as
worse than they are, while its order recommends things as
they ought to be, not as they are. Therefore when he says
that this will be a poem, Dryden becomes free to make a general criticism of life. He is free of any occasion that called the
poem forth or of any one historical situation. He is not bound
to any special opinions of his own as a person, so that the
views uttered in the poem may apply generally to human affairs in the light of experience. He does not have to follow
any special literary genre, while at the same time he is free to
draw on the entire literary tradition, to use any or all of the
genres that will suit the poem's requirements. The word
"poem" sets him above the very circumstances that cause him
to write at all, yet his work is a tract for the times governed by
civic uses, a tract for a certain month, week, even day in trying
to influence a decision that must be made after a specific action: the trial of Shaftesbury. Yet it symbolizes more than it
states, embodying as it does a myth assembled from throughout the neoclassical universe. True, if Shaftesbury and Monmouth had not threatened civil war, Dryden would have had
no reason to write the poem; we know that conservatism does
not declare itself unless in fear of some danger. Yet once called
for by events, *Absalom and Achitophel* invites reading as an
imagined scheme of things. If rebellion occurs, it must take
some such form as this, the poem persuades us. As Dryden uses
names like Absalom, Achitophel, and David, we see them as
old enough in use and memory to have the force of literary
terms with associations far beyond what could be suggested
by giving these individuals their actual names of Monmouth,
Shaftesbury, and Charles II. The actual names might gain

satiric force, as the use of Shadwell in *Mac Flecknoe* does, or as Pope obtains it in *The Dunciad* and elsewhere. Yet for Dryden now, real names would limit the poem to its own place and time, make it in fact less a poem. The names used are poetic terms adopted because their meanings and suggestions are not controlled by contemporary events. So also with other materials. The familiar biblical story, plus the historical effect of the civil wars, the false politician and his usual followers, his young instrument of royal blood, the king himself with his ideal qualities, the multitude, the discontented conspirators of all sorts and the loyal few—all these become poetic terms, heavily charged with application to Dryden's world, but now ready at his hand after generations of development. At no time, then, is Dryden the poet in greater ascendancy than while repeating accepted commonplaces of the myth touching the divine sanction of kings, celebrating the virtues of the man who happened to be king of England at the time, or exposing the vices of those rebelling against him. The poem goes beyond its occasion and penetrates to the elements inseparable from the human condition and the way in which its affairs must be governed. Its poetic fusion of so many elements in the service of established order is a brilliant adaptation of means to ends.

We keep saying "Dryden" as if he were assumed to be responsible for whatever the poem says, as if the narrator in the poem were necessarily the poet himself. We have learned to read Augustan poems, however, with a constant ear for the implied dramatic speaker, a device used by Pope with such masterly effect. The poet is always speaking in Dryden's masterpiece, to be sure, in that he controls the entire effect and marshals the poem's materials toward a view of things we know to be his own. *Absalom and Achitophel* may be seen as an oratorical structure with a number of main speakers, including the poet, but with no single dramatic speaker. If we agree that the poem needs to be read aloud, Van Doren is right in saying that someone seems all the while to be reciting. A public issue is presented on both sides; the poem as a whole takes the Tory side hoping to influence the outcome of Shaftesbury's trial. The five main speeches formally given, that make up a third of the poem, are subtly changed in tone, depending on who is speaking. For the rest, the poet himself may be heard as the speaker, presenting the issues clearly, commenting on the speeches and actions of the others, and tempering his own passionate convictions with the moderation that his intended lesson calls for. We could distinguish here between the passion of one side of the narrator-poet and the moderation of the speaker who lays down the careful lessons of the poem. Outbursts of anger, abrupt exclamation, a tone of outrage suggest oratorical rhetoric by a speaker invented by Dryden for conscious effect. As we "listen" to the poem rendered through a number of voices or speakers, we should then be cautious about assuming that the central narrator is always Dryden. When we have heard the poem to the end, we cannot mistake where Dryden himself is to be found; but he is not the equivalent of any one voice in a complex harmony, or interchange.

So also, returning to the subtitle "A Poem," we must be glad that *Absalom and Achitophel* does not hold to the demands of any particular genre. It has some qualities drawn from epic and satire, panegyric and elegy, character writing, biblical allegory, and oratory with its argumentative rhetoric. In quantity it divides itself into thirds: the portraits, the five speeches, the narrative-descriptive passages. Now free of the stage, Dryden nonetheless keeps some dramatic elements where these suit his aims: dramatic situations, clashes and contrasts, presentation of character in speech and action. This deliberate choosing among genres and modes, while avoiding any form that would hold him to fixed requirements, raises the old question of the Augustan hiatus between theory and practice. If it is true that the Augustans do their best work when free of their own principles, we see again that they get round the need of reconciling theory and practice by attempting things for which a governing theory is not yet well developed, by avoiding forms which would hold them to severely defined rules. This does not prevent them from believing in the rules as laid down; perhaps they believe in them so much that they avoid trying things which they could not perform under existing rules, rather than seem to be violating them.

For Dryden, even if we say that he chose the genre of narrative or Varronian satire for *Absalom and Achitophel,* there is still a large degree of freedom in a kind of satire with so little existing theory to govern its practice. If he had written a declared epic, he certainly would have tried to follow its theory; when he writes poems that have a standard set of requirements, he keeps within them, as in the Killigrew *Ode* conspicuously. Since the rules are derived from past practice in established genres, Dryden for *Absalom and Achitophel* has to develop a mode not explored enough before to have an exhaustive theory derived from it. His epic attempts show him hampered by rules and theory, and his best tragedy is all by itself among his plays. He will now do his best free of the rules for a given kind, yet keeping the virtues of many different kinds, adapting them freely.

Still Dryden is shrewd enough to exploit tradition when it strengthens his poem. The established lines from many directions carry associations of great value. The character portraits benefit especially; the imagery drawing on the familiar areas of disease, navigation, and architecture does a great deal of the poet's work for him, offering to the reader a whole freight of suggestion and implication as befits poetic language well employed. Tradition comes in again most effectively through the biblical story, used as an allegory. Cowley had urged the virtues of the Bible to replace ancient classical tales of Gods and heroes; as story material the Bible would yield more variety, and for Dryden now its familiarity would help the poem's lesson, making it clearer and giving it a holier sanction. The biblical materials greatly enlarged Dryden's possibilities; he could be less direct than in conventional political satire, simpler, more objective, more elevated, wider by far in application. The censure against persons like Shaftesbury and Buckingham is enlarged poetically so as to discredit a whole way of looking at things, while the praise of King David in turn celebrates the opposite view. Dryden can thus praise and blame, destroy and build at once.

The biblical allegory enforces the satire which is by nature allied to allegory and which in this poem may resemble a morality play. A struggle between vice and virtue for the soul of man, a sharply defined conflict between good and evil, certainly passes before us. The struggle is resolved in the end by the speech of Godlike David, and Absalom, like the protagonist of a morality play, is offered forgiveness for repentance. We see clearly the skill with which Dryden hit upon just the formula that would offer him the greatest freedom as well as the greatest benefit from tradition. He wishes to write a satire, but the genre had some severe limitations and distinctions. He wishes to write, then, a poem, which does not suffer from these limitations by having to stay entirely within them, while at the same time it profits from them where needed. Since Dryden cannot allow satire to be seen as a subpoetic mode, he can get the best of all possibilities by calling his work "A Poem" and then making it highly satiric. The satirist, poet, artist, and moralist combine in a poem that profits from the nature and function of satire without being limited to it.

We see now why *Absalom and Achitophel* so often gives the effect of heroic or epic poetry. Dryden sees a close kinship between satiric and heroic materials, and here satire becomes a species of heroic poetry. *Absalom and Achitophel* is, then, written instead of the heroic or epic poem that Dryden had been hoping for years to write. It is often remarked how fortunate for Dryden and for English literature it was that he wrote the best poem of its kind in English instead of a pedestrian, second-class imitation of what had already been better done by others. Instead of settling for ancient heroic materials or for something on the Black Prince or Prince Arthur, Dryden chooses to elevate contemporary men and events to an heroic level. We can be glad as well that he did not go on with the heroic poem mentioned in the dedication of *Aureng-Zebe* to Mulgrave in 1675. Charles II and James were to be the heroes, along with most of the ancient English nobility; the whole was to be neither too far nor too near its own age in time.

It was better to bring the English public debate on to a larger stage, reaffirming the public role of the ancient classic poets. This is done by skillful use of the Bible and by drawing on the epic manner of Virgil and Homer and Milton. The explanatory opening before the declamations of Achitophel; the epic catalogue of the conspirators and of the loyal few; the last word of warning from the king, like a sentence pronounced by Zeus and ratified by a sign from above in the thunder—these devices join with numerous Virgilian echoes to preserve the high, heroic tone. The elegy in honor of Barzillai's son keeps the note of Virgil amid the satire and sustains the grandeur of *Absalom and Achitophel* as a poem. The tone of heroic poetry is in keeping with Dryden's tribute to the loyal few so necessary to his argument. They all seem worthy of the ideal as Dryden uses the inherited associations of epic greatness and dignity in contrast to the rebellious individuals in his own day whom he wishes to discredit. Thus the poem does its work in contemporary politics, while remaining above its subject.

The sense of high, manly satire, of a poem trying to get above what it is in fact doing, is hard to maintain. But Dryden can lower the key when he wishes to ridicule Corah, for example, although he tends to avoid the double rhymes common in low satire like *Hudibras;* he uses only three double rhymes throughout. If we insisted on the austerity of French epic criticism, we might say that Dryden's use of sententiae goes beyond the limits of decorum in heroic poetry. But he uses them moderately enough to stay within English tolerance —functional, transitional, connective tissue as they are. They tend to support Dryden's rhetoric as well, in giving a sense of dispassionate wisdom in action, leading the reader to accept the general lesson.

A closer look at the sententiae makes us wonder at poetic standards that could find them dangerous to epic decorum.

They blend skillfully with narrative transitions to maintain
a continuous movement. Before its intermission at line 752
the poem simply pauses several times for reflection and summary. These divisions and reflections succeed each other, and
lead into the verse essay, 752–810; taken together these materials carry the didactic meaning of the poem. The narrator
steps aside from the poem's action to say what should be
learned from it. After the first picture of Absalom and the
relationship to his father, we hear,

> But life can never be sincerely blest:
> Heav'n punishes the bad, and proves the best. (42–43)

After exposure of "the Jews," another reflection follows, beginning with the word "but" to give an added sense of warning or contrast:

> But when to sin our byast nature leans,
> The Careful Devil is still at hand with means;
> And providently pimps for ill desires.   (79–81)

Such reflections work transitionally, since what follows illustrates the truth of what has just been said or looks forward
to what will come. The next three lines (82–84) look back
to the Civil War just mentioned (71–74) and look ahead to
the "plot" which according to the myth is necessary before
rebellion:

> The Good Old Cause, reviv'd, a plot requires:
> Plots, true or false, are necessary things,
> To raise up commonwealths, and ruin kings.

After the portrait of Achitophel, another contrast follows:

> But wild ambition loves to slide, not stand,
> And fortune's ice prefers to virtue's land.   (198–99)

The transition again suggests what is to come, as in 303–8,
after the temptation speech of Achitophel. The parts of the
poem as divided by these connecting passages, illustrate the
truth of what is said in them:

What cannot praise effect in mighty minds,
When flattery soothes and when ambition blinds!
Desire of pow'r, on earth a vicious weed,
Yet, sprung from high, is of celestial seed:
In God 'tis glory; and when men aspire,
'Tis but a spark too much of heavenly fire.   (303–8)

The transition from the temptation scene to analysis of the rebellious elements stays within the poem's own story without offering a general lesson or reflection. Absalom determines to strike while zeal is hot, and "popularly prosecute the plot." Then:

To farther this, Achitophel unites
The malcontents of all the Israelites;
Whose differing parties he could wisely join
For several ends, to serve the same design.   (491–94)

Lines 494–752 picture these very malcontents, including Zimri, Shimei, and Corah. At line 683 "deluded" Absalom makes his progress among the people and speaks to them, 698–722. The crowd's response and Achitophel's exploitation of it lead to the didactic passage reviewing the entire position which the poem exists to maintain, 752–810. Here the general meaning is laid down in a series of sententiae, no longer transitional but sufficient to convey the moral lesson of an epic poem.

These preliminary suggestions of the depth and variety in *Absalom and Achitophel* make us ready to hear the poem read with the respectful ears its quality demands. There used to be a standard set of objections to Dryden, so long held and often repeated that they grew into a kind of myth themselves. Modern literary study has shown how much is lost by leaving such positions unexamined, yet the old image of a faulty, unequal, inconsistent poet will not fade. Dryden is not supposed to have any constructive, architectural faculty; he cannot plan anything, he writes good poetry but bad poems, of course. C. S. Lewis says that Dryden, "being rather a boor, a gross vulgar, provincial, misunderstanding mind," simply lacks the cultivated gentility to write the higher forms of poetry to which he aspires, to move at ease in his chosen world. He does well enough at satire, but even here he loses force by a fatal lack of architectonic power. As we turn now to hear the fine opening of *Absalom and Achitophel,* let us see whether some of these complaints against Dryden so often and so powerfully urged are not forced to give way.

CHAPTER 6

What Is the Law?

Dryden likes to begin well, and he has never done so more brilliantly than in the opening lines of *Absalom and Achitophel,* charged with irony, echoing the sharp tone of a Donne elegy, catching our attention in the smoothest of verses. Yet nothing in the poem is more integral to its meaning than these urbane, cynical lines. The work begins by stating that Monmouth is a bastard, and so carries its necessary end in its beginning. The law says that a prince cannot legitimate his bastard son to the prejudice of a lawful heir. Even if Charles II therefore wished to let Monmouth follow him, he could not do so. This is recalled simply by mentioning that Monmouth is not legitimate. As in the end the king needs only to speak in order to prevail, at the outset the poem needs only to say one thing about Monmouth to carry its point. The narrator can afford to seem flippant about it, when its force is so irrevocably fixed in law and custom.

In 1603 Thomas Craig had written in *The Right of Succession:* "Neither can any man legitimate his bastards either begotten in adultery, or simple fornication only, so as thereby to prejudice the right of others." Alas, the fornications of Charles were more complex and compound than simple, but no matter how construed, their result could never inherit his throne. Gaily and delightfully the poem opens, hiding its irrevocable point behind the Old Testament allowance. What Gibbon was to call "the gallantries of David" now carry an important symbol: illegitimacy, no matter how explained or excused, is the first incontrovertible fact. Everything possible will be done to make the person of Monmouth himself excusable and agreeable. The fact remains that Monmouth is not the legitimate heir and nothing under the sun can make him so. Against this position nothing will prevail; in the face of it there can be only one conclusion. The first ten lines govern the poem as if they were the wintry setting in *Ethan Frome* or Egdon Heath in *The Return of the Native,* where nothing can take place out of keeping with their gloom and terror. The rebellion that follows is doomed, because it rests on what can never be allowed to prevail, something that violates law and order, custom and divine sanction.

But the opening lines show, too, why a rebellion could center upon Monmouth. The "injustice" of his exclusion inspires his revolt, as he says in answer to Achitophel's first temptation. Thus for Absalom as well as for the poet-narrator the illegitimacy is central; it must be immediately clear, and yet the king must not be condemned for the promiscuity of which Absalom himself, and the established order, are the victims. The problem is solved by witty use of the Old Testament, saying indirectly what would be too ridiculous and offensive if stated in a high, heroic idiom. The illegitimacy is passed off not as another sign of the king's scandalous immorality but as following from polygamy. A question was never more neatly begged, nor was it ever more clearly suggested that the question is in fact pointless and should never be raised in the first place. Polygamy was quite allowable in the Old Testament, and the best way to make it allowable now is to pretend that we are discussing something which took place in those days. Francis Osborne had remarked in *Advice to a Son* that the holy Patriarchs "among their so frequent dialogues held with their Maker, were never reproved for multiplying wives and concubines, reckoned to David as blessing, and to Solomon for a mark of magnificence." So let us assume that the king is David, and a most awkward problem is solved. The usefulness of Old Testament machinery to the poet declares itself at the outset, and it continues to serve him well throughout. Here it has in passing allowed him a slap at the clergy too, these having been placed in the conservative myth as dangerous to the general order.

God has composed the order in the world with care, and it reflects His mind. The need for order creates the obligation to obey. God wills order for the good of man; order comes of obedience to law; therefore, God commands obedience to law and to the authority that endorses it. Thus the various terms of government such as God, king, prince, magistrate, parliament mean in fact any duly constituted authority—that is, the law. Hence the Restoration period asks the Roman question, What is the law? In this sense Coleridge is right to say that Dryden could not have been a Platonist, could not have asked the Platonic question, What is justice? Englishmen are told, to be sure, that they are to obey God and the king and are not to meddle in change, but they are really bound by the law. In a monarchy, the term "king" is used, and monarchy seeming most like the natural government of a family, the ruler becomes king, father, as God is both king and father. The poem then offers us Charles-David as father, king, and God. Absalom violates the law in three forms—moral, social, and religious—in rising against the king. We see again why Absalom's illegitimacy is laid down in the first lines. David is divine in that he represents the order in the universe against which any human force must contend in vain. When David invokes God, he no longer speaks in his own person, but as the law. He can afford to be patient and clement, having on his side the nature of things. Charles can be what he likes as a person, for in the end, he prevails not as man but as king and God—that is, as order. He resembles a wicked pope from whose anointed person not all the water in the rough rude sea can wash the balm.

What is the law? The age of Dryden had to decide its answer for literature, religion, and politics. On November 4, 1680, the second Exclusion Bill against the Catholic James, Duke of York, demanded a political answer. What was the

law? It was that James should succeed his brother to the
throne. The age finally settled on the side of law, but only
after a vast upheaval showing how great was the energy press-
ing against control. *Absalom and Achitophel* seems to reflect
this by its lack of balance between the contending forces in
quantity. The wave of popular disaffection against the law
influenced the actual Commons vote for Exclusion, after a
debate of incredible violence. The law—God, the king, and
order—had the support only of a small group of noblemen as
suggested by the defeat of Exclusion in the House of Lords,
63 to 30. Hence Dryden's poem has all of the loyal few as
noblemen, among them Halifax the mighty Trimmer, to
whose genius in a debate of six hours, the law owed its salvation. In the end, Dryden is typically English in blending the
Greek and Roman questions and showing that the legal, the
orderly and controlled thing is the just thing as well. The
poem finds that what has to be is really what should be; what
is necessary is also what is right, fusing the requirements of
both reason and experience.

Order, then, follows obedience to the law, submission. Individuals like Absalom and Achitophel should remain in their
places, doing what they are called upon to do, never thinking
ambitiously or selfishly of themselves. Charles II himself, before his return to England in 1660, follows the demand of the
royalist party from the civil war and insists on the rule of law.
In his letters to Monck and the House of Commons and in his
Declaration of April 1660 Charles repeatedly urges the law
and the right to be derived from it. He desires to recover his
right "by the laws of God and man"; the army has fought to
preserve "the fundamental laws of the land"; justice demands
for the people a restoring of "the laws of their land to their
due veneration"; and he wishes to see returned to the House
of Lords the authority and jurisdiction belonging to them
"by your birth and the fundamental laws of the land."

In turn Charles-David is inseparable from the refrain that
runs throughout the poem in support of law and order. If the
poem is a plea for law and order, it is therefore a plea for

whoever happens to be the rightful king. *Absalom and Achitophel* begins by seeming to excuse illegitimacy while in fact declaring its doom; and its last three words are "their lawful lord." From beginning to end there occur twenty-six uses of the word "law" or "laws," or the derived adjectives "lawful," "lawless." Seven occur in the king's speech alone, one in the last line as quoted, and four others refer to the king or his relationship to law. The word first comes in line 5, "When nature prompted, and no law denied," and soon we hear that "the law forbore" some warm excesses of Absalom, 37. In turn one of the first remarks made by Absalom concerning the king admits that he is "observant of the laws" (319); David is not a tyrant who "by lawless might" (337) oppressed the Jews, but a good king who is himself subject to the law. Effective use is made of the same rhyme, beginning in 319–20, joining the various associations of goodness or rightness with legitimacy. The relevant passages are as follows:

First,

> Good, gracious, just, observant of the laws;
> And Heav'n by wonders has espous'd his cause. (319–20)

Then, rebellion should,

> Secure his person to secure your cause;
> They who possess the prince possess the laws. (475–76)

Achitophel shows that to be right one must be or seem to be legitimate.

> Whose fellow-feeling in the godly cause
> Would free the suff'ring saint from human laws. (608–9)

The next couplet reinforces with sarcastic irony the connection between law and right:

> For laws are only made to punish those
> Who serve the king, and to protect his foes. (610–11)

"Laws" and "Cause" are joined for the fourth time when Absalom addresses the people:

> Behold a banish'd man, for your dear cause
> Expos'd a prey, to arbitrary laws!   (700–1)

Of the loyal few we hear,

> To these succeed the pillars of the laws;
> Who best could plead, and best could judge a cause.
>
> (874–75)

The sixth and final use of this rhyme poses a key question, in making the idea of laws and the right cause inseparable from the king:

> Whence comes it that religion and the laws
> Should more be Absalom's than David's cause? (969–70)

David goes on insisting, showing that everyone, including a king, his subjects, and a poet of genius, must remain under the law:

> The law shall still direct my peaceful sway,
> And the same law teach rebels to obey.   (991–92)

The king's last words rest his case upon unassailable strength:

> For lawful pow'r is still superior found;
> When long driv'n back, at length it stands the ground.
>
> (1023–24)

In *Amboyna*, the first of Dryden's political plays, Fiscal demands to know, "Pray, what makes anything a sin but law?" (IV,1). Never allowing us to forget what the law is and what it demands, *Absalom and Achitophel* makes a wide-ranging inquiry into the sins that the law has made. The poem devotes in quantity a far greater number of lines to a search into those arrayed against the law and seems to amass a formidable array of forces that threaten the established order. Their numbers, their various motives, the character and intentions of their leaders are all explored in terms familiar to the conservative myth. Rebellion is now seen to take the form it must take; its anatomy cannot be other than what it is now

in 1681 and what it has always been in the light of past experience, especially the recent, still-remembered experience
of England itself. Rebellion has always proceeded from deception, has always been led by selfish, ambitious men, sometimes even gifted and always too daring and impetuous men
who are willing to risk the general good for the sake of their
own rise to power. The bold and turbulent, the unstable, the
Godless and unscrupulous who think to profit from public
upheaval find it necessary to get the support of the multitude,
so easily swayed and deceived, so powerful an ally in its fearful, explosive energy. More important still, they find it impossible to rally their forces except behind some particular
instrument, some man with a color of justice to his cause,
preferably a young man of charm and attractive gifts of nature, of royal blood yet barred through some handicap—sinister or otherwise—from what might be made to seem rightfully his own.

CHAPTER 7

The Anatomy of Rebellion

Absalom

Dryden used most effectively materials growing in the minds of men and ready to work for him through many associations and sanctions. Similarly he chose to express himself through the David-Absalom story, in part for its many-sided usefulness and because it, too, had long served as a vehicle for exposing the nature of rebellion. Of the many anticipations that Dryden found ready, perhaps the clearest and most explicit was by Nathaniel Carpenter, *Achitophel or the Wicked Politician*. A glance at Carpenter's work will show that as early as 1627 some of Dryden's chief lines were already laid down, especially for his aggressors, Absalom and Achitophel themselves.

Carpenter's subtitle strikes the note of falsity in a rebel leader as required by the myth. Indeed both the words "wicked" and "politician" suggest fraud. For our case, he might have omitted "wicked" as unnecessary. No politician nowadays needs to refer to other politicians as "wicked," save for rhetorical—that is, "wicked"—purposes of his own. As a politician he knows all about "wickedness" beforehand, or is simply absurd. Going from Carpenter's title page to the first sentence, we learn that treason works chiefly on ambition and discontent. These three terms of treason, ambition, and discontent invite us to look beyond them fifty-two years later, straight into Dryden's portrait of Achitophel: false, turbulent, restless, daring. Achitophel now plots the ruin of David: "subtlety and secrecy, the two hand-maids of human policy, stood always betwixt his hypocrisy and the king's suspicion." Meanwhile Absalom is shown in the heat and pride of youth, ambitious for the crown, discontented with his disgrace and banishment. There is, of course, no hint of illegitimacy, but we get a reason for Absalom's estrangement from the king, a hint that he had a genuine grievance: "Justice herself seems to claim a part in his traitorous ambition." But he is selfish and therefore deceived: "Such is the prerogative of self-bred actions, to shut out prejudice, and promise to themselves as much success as they find excuse." At this point a conventional image as used by Dryden occurs: policy has taught Achitophel to "strike whilst the iron was hot," a usage that also keeps to the fire or heat image for dangerous energy leading to disruptive revolt. The hope which flatters the ambitious to contemplate success while often betraying them to the worst result also suggests the need of fraud before rebellion. New schemes have always to deceive their projectors as well as their followers—Swift would see this bitterly in *A Tale of a Tub*.

Now the special qualities of Absalom give Achitophel an ideal instrument. His birth, feature, plausibility, and high spirit make him royal material. Yet he is the second son of the king, and so not entitled to the crown by religion or law. But selfish ambition, the desire of private, personal advantage so much abhorred in the myth, ignores the highest good: "their design is not grounded upon God's law, or nature's privilege, but their own seeming advantage." Thus Carpenter isolates "The first and chiefest character of a worldly wise politician" who thinks only of his own advantage, "choosing rather to lose his soul than his wicked purpose." As to Absalom's fair and comely feature, it is a means of attracting the fancy and misleading the discreet judgment, thus appealing strongly to the multitude: "What greater motive could have happened to a seditious multitude, whose affections, led rather by sense than reason, are better taught to fawn on shews than substance, and swallow the most poisonous drugs in golden pills?"

A further analogy exposes the danger of eloquence. A beautiful personage enchants the wisest judgment so that "persuasion is oftener found in the orator than the argument." Thus Absalom flatters and beguiles the people with promises while denouncing the king's government for injustice and oppression. David grows old and diseased, while Absalom sees his chance to make headway with "the giddy multitude . . . as desirous of novelties, as subject to discontent." It is easy to persuade people to think themselves badly governed, as Dryden would say that fools are harder to conquer than persuade. Absalom, of course, hides behind a pretense of religion, as having made a vow to return to Hebron to praise God for his safe return to Jerusalem. This offers him a chance to meet his conspirators and to work on the people more safely than in Jerusalem. As always, deceit and vice go together, stealing the roles of virtue: "Satan transforms himself into an angel of light, when he intends the greatest mischief, and instructs his disciples in the like policy." So the false politician invites comparison with the devil, their designs being much the same. As to the pulpit orators who disturb the passions by their own violence, they are like the crew whom Dryden ignores as beneath the dignity of verse: "such fiery spirits I carelessly pass over scarce worth a scholar's pen."

Carpenter includes some of the more odious aspects of Absalom's behavior from the biblical story, such as the being urged to go in to his father's concubines. Such details would not suit Dryden's more conciliatory line, the tone of half-affectionate regret over a fine young man's being misled, the implied hope that forgiveness is yet ready for repentance. But he shares Carpenter's contrast between the enormous force assembled against the king and the tiny band available to the "weary and weak-handed" David. But it is the wisdom of Providence to let the conspiracy go on, and not to destroy it by a separate act, letting it seem to succeed and then become its own executioner, entangled in its own net. David must prevail, for God is on his side; no matter how great the worldly strength of the conspiracy, it has to lose: "though Absalom's hopes are grounded on his worldly strength, yet David's strength is erected on God's protection."

Many other anticipations of Dryden's poem have made ready for him all that he needs for his brilliant support of Charles II. His portrait of Absalom seems almost automatic, obliged to be what it was, given the Bible story and the qualities demanded in the conservative myth for rebellion. In his own tributes to Monmouth before the crisis of Exclusion, Dryden had in fact drawn together all that he was to say in favor of Absalom in the poem. In 1667 Dryden had dedicated his *Indian Emperor* to the Duchess of Monmouth, and had joined the refrain first sounded in the Bible, celebrating the physical beauty of the young prince: "no part of Europe can afford a parallel to your noble Lord, in masculine beauty, and in goodliness of shape." But when in 1669 Dryden dedicates *Tyrannick Love* to Monmouth himself, the phraseology strains toward the final limit allowed by the conventions of panegyric. No hint of bastardy lies in such terms as "To the most illustrious and high-born Prince, James, Duke of Monmouth and Buccleugh, one of His Majesties most honorable Privy-Council, and Knight of the Most Noble Order of the Garter." The dedication itself makes an interesting use of the architectural image in praise of Monmouth's physical charm. Dryden feels that he should have offered Monmouth an heroic poem instead of this play:

> Heaven has already taken care to form you for an heroe. You have all the advantages of mind and body, and an illustrious birth, conspiring to render you an extraordinary person . . . Youth, beauty and courage (all of which you possess in the height of their perfection) are the most desirable gifts of Heaven: and Heaven is never prodigal of such treasures, but to some uncommon purpose. So goodly a fabrick was never framed by an Almighty Architect for a vulgar guest. He shewed the value which he set upon your mind, when he took care to have it so nobly and so beautifully lodged. To a graceful fashion and de-

portment of body, you have joined a winning conversation, and an easy greatness, derived to you from the best,
and best beloved of Princes. And with a great power of
obliging, the world has observed in you, a desire to oblige,
even beyond your power.

Except for any hint of illegitimacy or selfish ambition, these
lines contain much of the portrait of Absalom: charm, grace,
beauty, desire to please, similarity in all good qualities to his
father, ability, and courage—all but the bad things are here.
The some 175 lines later devoted to Absalom are composed
with great care, celebrating his graces and virtues, and at every
turn reflecting credit on his father, the king. If Absalom is
good, he is so because of his father; if bad, he is so in spite of
his father's generous forbearance and example. Only when
Absalom develops a sense of injustice, a tendency to excuse
himself for ambition, does the portrait show traits that must
be condemned—apparently with great reluctance. Lines 17–
42 offer us an example of beauty, courage, love, grace, ease,
such as inspire the father's indulgence of certain youthful errors and faults; after all, everyone has some faults, and in
spite of young excesses the prince seems quite rightly praised
and loved. Like Juvenal, Dryden urges indulgence for youth:
"indulge veniam pueris." Lines 220–27 show the warlike Absalom becoming the tool of false Achitophel, whose very falsity becomes part of the excuse constantly being made for the
young prince. Lines 303–14 prepare us for Absalom's weakening, but here, too, all is essential virtue, heavenly gift that
ironically invites evil. He will fall through goodness, in his
unwary youth. His first speech that follows (315–72) seems
in the last degree proper for one playing Absalom's double
role of subject and son to King David. The dual relationship
had emerged in the plays such as *The Assignation* (1672),
where the Duke of Mantua and his son Frederick are rivals
in love for Lucretia, and *Aureng-Zebe* (1675), where the emperor considers his son as subject and hence "doubly born my
slave." *Aureng-Zebe* in fact anticipates a line from Absalom's

pious and filial speech (350); the Emperor's son had acted only when he thought his father dead, gone "T'augment the number of the bless'd above." Up to 363, Absalom's speech suggests that he has no ground whatever for complaint against his father-king. David's power is legal, he is a mild ruler, a most generous father; at his death, the law demands succession by his brother, a man with every royal virtue. The enmity between Monmouth and the Duke of York is suppressed here, since Dryden does not wish to offer this old quarrel as a motive on Absalom's part. Absalom then asks, why should he repine at the decree of Heaven? To this point, he has given Achitophel no reason to think that his temptation will succeed.

Now, however, he begins to wish that things were other than they are. He has to delude himself in some way; in the myth rebellion follows only when someone is deceived. He now cries out against the facts that ought to govern him, that have seemed to govern him in his speech so far. A fourfold desire expresses his hopeless quest of the throne. Fate should have raised his birth or have lowered his mind and spirit so that he would aspire to nothing. Fate was wrong to endow him richly within while depriving him by illegitimacy of a chance to fulfill himself. His two objections thus become four, by positive and negative clauses, and give a sense of hopeless drive against the unchangeable or unattainable by use of a subjunctive, conditional form—a hortatory regret in the past perfect verb. Achitophel sees the opening and rushes in with his second temptation that proves effective. Yet even then (477–90) we hear more of Absalom's mild nature, regret over his misfortunes, and lament rather than accusation. Like Almanzor in *The Conquest of Granada* (1670), another's vanity seems noble confidence in him, his soul only too fiery, too great for guidance. Absalom must cry out against Heaven's decree like Torrismond in *The Spanish Friar* (1680), to whom Heaven had given a monarch's soul while clothing it in base plebeian clay.

Poor Absalom is thus a man easily misled by the temptation of Achitophel. In the prose remarks "To the Reader" before

the poem, Dryden excuses Absalom on the ground of his excellent nature, which makes him the soonest perverted by ill
counsels, especially when these are baited with fame and glory
—the sense of a deceptive trap arising from the term "baited."
He thus underlines the poem's reasons why Absalom falls: his
virtue and his illegitimacy, for neither of which he is responsible. As in the nature of the multitude, there has to be something in Absalom which makes him the dupe of the necessarily
false rebel leader. Yet in Absalom it must be something for
which he cannot be blamed, as being the king's son, and as a
symbol in the myth. He cannot be blamed for his fine quality,
for aspiring to what Nature has really equipped him to attain,
in personal ability and grace. Neither can he be blamed for
what is outside himself, his illegitimacy. He says nothing
of the Black Box, supposed to contain proof that the king
had gone through a witnessed marriage ceremony with his
mother. Thus his suffering for the fact of illegitimacy gives
Absalom the shade of a debatable, understandable grievance.
The multitude are misled through something in their own
nature which they cannot help; their foolish instability and
illusion. Absalom is duped by something he cannot help
either: his unlucky birth and misguided talent, for his ambition in itself is not evil if subordinated to higher duty. Even
after he has succumbed and has gone out to rouse the people
to his cause, his character commands elevated, heightened
language. Lines 733–38 tell how fame runs before him, like
a morning star, while as he comes the salutations of joy reach
him from afar: he is received like a young divinity, as befits
his greatness and exciting appeal.

In contrast to these tender considerations of Absalom, the
poem makes no excuse for other leaders of the rebellion. The
best that can be said for them is that they have ability that is
misapplied. Absalom seems deceived, used—an almost passive
instrument of a more cunning force. An interesting contemporary satire against Shaftesbury exposes his plot to change
the royal succession. *Grimalkin, or the Rebel-Cat* (1681) re-
counts a beast fable, suggesting the later *Hind and the Pan-*

ther. Charles II is the Lion, but the king of beasts may be threatened by a seemingly feeble little creature, the cat, who carries just the right suggestions of deception, stealth, and surprise. Monmouth here is a spotted leopard, since his mother was a panther and his spots are the stains of his mother's pollution. Much is made of the leopard's illegitimacy; the father may have been a lion but the mother was nevertheless of baser breed. While the leopard may resemble the lion, they are not to be mistaken or substituted one for the other. Still the role of Monmouth is mollified and excused as it is by Dryden: he becomes like the paw of Grimalkin, the cat. He does not lead the faction against the lion, but in another analogy he is like the forehorse in a team, seeming to lead but in fact pushed on from behind by others.

But if Absalom is deceived and used, he is also a deceiver. Indeed the very attractions that inspire his father's love become the means of the son's betrayal; the qualities that lead to his temptation enable him to deceive others. The first thing said of him (17–18) is present in every tribute to Absalom from the Bible onward:

> Of all this numerous progeny was none
> So beautiful, so brave, as Absalon:

This hyperbole has the sanction of long use in literary portraits, as witness the skill of Chaucer in *The Prologue*. And the 17th-century concern with King David repeats the uniqueness of his son's personal charm. In *David's Troubles Remembered*, Book I (1638), we read,

> In all the kingdoms of the east not one
> Was found, for beauty, like to Absalon.

In the civil war period Samuel Gibson writes of *The Ruin of the Authors and Fomenters of Civil Wars* (1645): "in all Israel there was none to be so much praised as Absalom for beauty ... for fair carriage and winning behaviour, he exceeded other princes." Like a good Augustan, Dryden absorbs this long tradition. His second use of "none" (220) is joined to "warlike

Absalon," letting us recall line 18, while filling in ourselves
the beauty and bravery. We get three adjectives for the price
of one conclusion, namely his fitness as a royal candidate. The
couplet at 17–18 seems inevitable, the name governing the
rhyme and the meaning that leads to it. There was none so
beautiful and brave as Absalon, because his name rhymes with
"none" in the spelling used. The poet gets this sense of an inevitable rhyme and a necessary meaning, by his reader's knowing from the Bible and continued usage that it was so.

In turn, none was so beautiful as Absalon because of his
role in the myth. The more attractive he was, the easier the
deception of those who must be deceived. His beauty suggests
the surface charm of the illusions leading to rebellion. What
is wrong seems at first glance attractive, yet it is fatal to human
welfare. The mass of mankind cannot be expected to see this;
the few must penetrate the specious, dangerously pleasant surface that misleads into illusory change. The beauty of Absalom carries one of the chief moral lessons of the poem; so also
will the language of fraud and agreeable pretense surrounding
the conspirators intensify our sense that men are being misled
into ruinous folly. This Miltonic note of the agreeable surface
of wickedness went on to serve Pope as well in the exposure
of Sporus.

Now all men bent on achieving great power must proceed
in similar ways. For one thing they must ingratiate themselves
into popular favor, and this too has a long history to sustain
Absalom's practice. Tacitus presents Rhadamistus, son of
Pharasmanes, King of Iberia, as a handsome, graceful young
man of intense ambition. Like Absalom he grows impatient,
and with enterprising spirit conciliates the affections of the
people. Unlike Absalom, he is capable of treachery and murder. In Roman history, a candidate for favor was reduced to de-
grading shifts and devices. In his discourse "Of Liberty" Cowley had reviewed the behavior of Catiline from Cicero's ora-
tions. Catiline offers a "general description of all ambitious
men"; he makes himself all things to all men, while his many
vices hide behind the appearance of excellent qualities. Near-

er Absalom's behavior is that of Julius Caesar, as reported by Plutarch. Caesar grows in the affections of the people as he conceals an ambition for absolute power behind a façade of good humor and affability. Absalom himself had been detected by Bishop Hall, who sees the young man as ruined by his beauty and pride. He quickly appeals to vulgar minds; he is easy of access, flatters right and left, praises the multitude and denounces the government:

> Goodliness of person, magnificence of state, gracious affability, unwearied diligence, humility in greatness, feeling pity, love of justice, care of the Commonwealth; the world hath not so complete a prince as Absalom. Thus the hearts of the people are not won, but stolen by a close traitor from their lawfully appointed sovereign.

In *David's Troubles Remembered* (1638) Absalom is also open to all suitors; he hears complaints, denounces the government, appeals to anyone discontented and blames the king for not hearing grievances while he "doth solace with the queen at home." Absalom promises full redress and finally, by a hypocritical pretense of fulfilling a vow, leaves Jerusalem. Nearer the Restoration, the picture of Absalom grows more repulsive, as in William Guild's *Throne of David* (1659), where he is seen a mass of vices, "like a legion of devils, as pride, cruelty, dissimulation, fraud, hypocrisy, unnatural rebellion, atheism, and in a word a mass of monstrous impiety." This diatribe admits that many fine qualities seem to meet in Absalom, but only to serve a last perversion: "goodliness of person, magnificence of state, gracious affability, humility in greatness, fellow feeling sympathy," and so on through all the same qualities listed by Bishop Hall while omitting diligence and adding "exemplary piety"; yet all ends in hypocrisy, "playing with God, that he may deceive men." Achitophel's advice to use the concubines so as to make reconciliation with David impossible is a recurring element in the Absalom story; Dryden includes the concubines to make his point about illegitimacy but never hints that Absalom used them. Absalom has enough

to live down in the poem merely from the associations that
by then must have accompanied his name. In the year of the
Restoration itself Absalom can be shown in Satanic colors. In
one of the many sermons marking the return of Charles II,
William Creed adapts the David-Charles analogy. *Judah's Return to Their Allegiance and David's Return to His Crown
and Kingdom* present Absalom behind a "religious veil and
dress" like the devil pretending to be an angel of light. Here,
too, the plots and designs of the conspirators are the means
of destroying them, while David-Charles remains sweet and
gracious, the soul of love and forgiveness.

If, then, there was an image of a young and beautiful Absalom who is excusable, there is also one of a deliberately scheming hypocrite, bent on achieving power like any other political
scoundrel by whatever means are available—that is, by foul
means. If our reading is valid, that Dryden lets various accumulated associations do his work in the poem, he may not
need to condemn Absalom explicitly; he needs only to let him
be seen doing what he does, needs in fact only to call him Absalom to imply that he is indefensible. In *Advice to a Daughter* (1658), John Heydon cries "how noble a thing is virtue,
when no man dares profess anything else?" He, too, must tell
his daughter that all men bent on ambitious usurpation proceed in the same way: "to dissemble a strong affection to the
country, lamenting the vices of the prince, and miseries of
the people" but only in order to achieve power that they may
abuse it. Dryden himself had told Mulgrave in the dedication
to *Aureng-Zebe* that men who seek popularity do so from base
ambition. The popular man "lies down to everyone he meets
for the hire of praise; and his humility is only a disguised ambition." We think of this when line 490 of *Absalom and Achitophel* explodes in our faces: to "popularly prosecute the plot"
joins two necessary traits of the rebel—plotting and seeking
popular support.

If Dryden could show that Absalom was a knave without
saying it, still he does say it or lets Absalom say it for him in
the second of his speeches, 698–722. This seems addressed to

an uncertain audience, an apparent summary of the kind of thing Absalom said wherever he went on his progress. Absalom's first speech was a careful reply to temptation; the second speech shows that the temptation has succeeded. We should distinguish between what the narrator says about Absalom and what the young man himself says, especially in the "progress" speech. What is said about Absalom shows him as being deceived; what he says in the end shows him as a deceiver, someone going after power as he must. Absalom says things that are more subtly revealing and damaging than what the narrator generously records about him. With his usual skill, Dryden has it both ways. He can seem to forgive Absalom, an attractive but faulty young man, while at the same time leaving a clearly adverse impression. Certainly the "progress" speech shows that after the temptation, wickedness and falsity have grown; opportunity, applause, and flattery have made Absalom a readier tool for clever knaves. His character has grown worse, has changed toward greater boldness and cunning.

Mr. Ian Jack calls this speech a magnificent hypocrisy. Does the narrator know that the tears, the wiping of the eyes are hypocritical? Is he only to carry the surface meaning, while Dryden lets us see the underlying exposure, unknown to the narrator? The narrator then sees his account of Absalom as entirely favorable, as we might accept it up to now, at worst something to be excused or palliated. But now, whether seen by the narrator or not, the real hypocrisy of Absalom shines forth. He bids for popular support on the ground that he is unselfishly devoted to the people's rights and liberties. In the myth we know that a rebel leader is inspired by selfish ambition and must proceed by fraud. Absalom shows himself for what he is: he pretends unselfishness and does what all rebels have to do. He cheats the people into believing that his motives are the opposite of what they are in fact, making them think that he is patriotic and filial. He utters a noble lament, a kind of elegy for the loss of popular liberty and his inability to help it. He begs the question throughout in terms like

"your lost estate," "arbitrary laws," and "my right"; he has no
legitimate right whatever, as he has himself admitted to Achitophel, but now for effect he assumes as proved that he has
such a right. He laments his weak, powerless state, suggesting
that he should have power to do for the people what he is
now unable to do. He tells them how badly off they are, although they would not know this if he did not tell them; like
others of his kind, he partly creates the problems which he
then asks the power to solve. He refers to his own banished
condition, brought on by his patriotic zeal. He deplores what
is happening to liberty, trade, and religion, thus invoking
political, commercial, and religious sanctions. He mourns
over the decline of David, who has, alas, become his own
worst enemy. Though the father gives away his son's right, the
son thinks only of his father and of the people. Yet helpless
as he is, he can offer only his tears.

References to Absalom near the time when the poem was
written show that he is established in the pattern of a selfish
knave bent on power by deceiving the people. In 1680 *Absalom's Conspiracy: or, The Tragedy of Treason* is a warning
to all young men, showing how "ambition, treason and conspiracy" against the lawful government must end. As the poem
would show, Absalom had cultivated popularity, depraved his
father's government, encouraged petitioners against it, and
promised justice to the people should he come to authority.
In *Character of a Rebellion* (1681) Absalom steals the hearts
of the people, "with fair speeches, and flattering pretences."
His behavior toward his father was evil in the eyes of Francis
Gifford in *The Wicked Petition* (1681). He steals away the
hearts of the people from King David by charges of ill government "and other insinuating pretences and courtships." Dryden gives these already clear implications greater power, by
letting Absalom show what he is in the "progress" speech,
which contradicts much of what he has said in private to Achitophel. Although 722–52 imply again that it is all Achitophel's
doing, with the young man a deluded victim of shrewd knavery, nevertheless Absalom stands severely condemned. The

implications being what they are, Absalom is at best a dangerous fool, more likely one who, if he is deceived, is deceived willingly not to say eagerly. Absalom, however, is necessarily wicked. The bid for popular favor, the outcry against present evils, the lament for the king's weakness or vice, the eager listening to grievances with promises of justice and redress—when all becomes clear, Dryden can let this syllogism work for him: It is established in the myth that anyone who does these things is a false and ambitious politician; Absalom does these things; therefore Absalom is a false and ambitious politician. The portrait of Absalom ends on the note of fraud and hypocrisy. Lines 745–52 speak of "smooth pretense," "specious love," "cheat and please," "pageant show," and "masquerade." These words are left in association with Absalom just before the essay on innovation that summarizes the moral of the poem. Absalom is not mentioned again until the king's speech, lines 955–70. Here he is given a way out with a parental offer of forgiveness. But it is more David the father who speaks than David the king, repeating Absalom's own twofold defense of unlucky birth and wrong endowment, excusing him finally as at worst a deluded fool. This indulgence seems, however, to idealize further the Godlike nature of the king; he seems more nobly merciful in the face of so much to forgive in a son who mingles misfortune, deluded folly, and the classical forms of political knavery.

The Multitude

By Dryden's time something referred to by many different names, but in general designating the majority or lower mass of mankind, was so common in the literary tradition as to develop a set of conventions of its own. The "myth" as it concerns the multitude calls for certain qualities, reviewed above (pp. 39–40), which Dryden finds useful in *Absalom and Achitophel*. Particular genres like the heroic play, to be sure, demanded that those on high be idealized and the rest denigrated as something to be kept down through political necessity or fear or both. The Renaissance contempt for those at the bottom of society, fear of mob violence, aristocratic individualism, the example of England's and other civil wars, the influence of Hobbes and related ideas of sovereign control— these would help to explain, apart from literary uses, a kind of ill-natured reviling of the majority in Dryden's age.

Except for the term "masses," a modern coinage, we hear of the many, the multitude, the rout, the crowd, the vulgar, the herd, depending on which of the standard qualities of the majority below requires emphasis. The word "mobile" establishes itself as a noun, abbreviated to mob, since notions of fickleness and instability had become inseparable from the multitude. There is a part of mankind that never rests happily in one steady position, and so is mobile. The term "mob," however, may refer to a particular set of persons, like the Roman mob, or the London mob. Or it may mean crowds excited by some special event, in which sense it has a literary tradition from the mob in Shakespeare's *Julius Caesar* through the mass outbreak in Dickens' *Barnaby Rudge,* or the election riots in George Eliot's *Felix Holt* down to the fearful crush in Nathanael West's *Day of the Locust.* But the standard qualities that apply to the majority have to do with folly, the ease of imposture that Samuel Butler remarks in his character of "A Rabble," the love of novelty, a giddy, headlong temper, a kind of mindless discontent that makes them an easy prey to the inevitably false designs of ambitious rebels. We recall that the possible danger posed by these inherent weaknesses comes through the persistent language of anger and fire; popular anger, rage, fury shades into madness, suggested by images of heat, fever, or fire, with related ideas of something easily kindled, burning, flaming, or inflamed. The sense of something about to burst forth, of sudden combustion, or of an energy that is now or about to be out of control and beyond recovery is inseparable from the endless references to the mass of mankind in Dryden's age.

As we expect, Dryden himself treats the multitude in keeping with its mythical qualities. In his criticism he has looked down upon the crowd which can have only a gross instinct of what pleases or displeases them; he can give little value to the common cry—"nothing but madness can please madmen." The earlier poems offer a choice of approval or contempt depending on how popular energy shows itself. In *Astraea Redux* (1660) the "vulgar" are gulled into rebellion, their blood "warmed"; the "rabble" are compared to winds at sea, or to a monster Cyclops, blind and wild. But in *To His Sacred Majesty* (1661) the people are allowed to show unrestrained joy. They act as a chorus of praise, their great energy taking the form of jubilation. The "people's joyful sound" proclaims the nation's happiness with no hint of the dangers implied in their uncontrolled energy. Again, *Annus Mirabilis* (1667) is ambiguous toward the people. Since one of its aims was to strengthen bonds between nation and king, at first the poem celebrates the people for English qualities of skill and heroism. But later on, as the fire gives a chance for pillage, Londoners have become "the ignoble crowd," the "ignobile vulgus" of Virgil's *Aeneid*. In the heroic plays Dryden treats the multitude according to the conventions of the genre. *The Conquest of Granada* (1670) has the "unthinking crowd," the "mad people's rage," the "many-headed beast," the deaf madness of the people's fear. In *Aureng-Zebe* (1675) we meet "the rabble," the subjects who are "stiff-necked animals," and in the Emperor's words, "The vulgar, a scarce animated clod." In *Oedipus* (1678) the Theban situation is not political, but we meet the usual terms—the mad and fickle multitude, the howling rabble, a wild and bellowing crowd; Creon whispers to Alcander to "head the forces while the heat was in 'em." Dryden's adaptation of *Troilus and Cressida* (1679) shows Hector condemning "the publick" as a herd of vulgar slaves; "the publique sum" is composed of millions of such ciphers.

Much nearer the actual view of the populace taken by *Absalom and Achitophel* are the several references in *The Spanish Friar* (1680). Here Torrismond, Raymond, and the Queen especially draw upon the standard phraseology to describe the fickle, headstrong, and finally dangerous multitude. There are "giddy crowds, changeable as winds"; a "hot mouth'd beast"

that is hard even for a lawful king to break; the gaping crowds,
the rabble listening with their mouths; the bellowing herd
that comes running to the cry of some noisy popular chief;
and the Queen's alarm at the consequences of a cry for liberty
and its release of fiery energy:

> Who knows when fires are kindled for my foes,
> But some new blast of wind may turn those flames
> Against my palace walls: (IV, 2)

Mr. Bredvold has said that "Dryden's whole statement of
Tory belief is a series of variations on the theme that government must save human nature from itself." *Absalom and
Achitophel* says little of human nature as such, but its view
of ordinary human nature in the mass is no different from the
opposing side's. In the 1680's, in fact, both parties specifically
disavow the irrational multitude, as posing a threat to peaceful order; each party tries to show that it commands the loyalty of the sober and prosperous elements of society. Thus the
portrait of the multitude in *Absalom and Achitophel* is
"Tory" only in the sense that the Whigs seemed willing to
use the London mob as an active influence, so much so that
Charles II met Parliament in Oxford to avoid the "Frenzy of
the people," that "unruly and mutinous spirit of the city of
London" so much deplored by Clarendon. A more Tory view
might have continued the line of *Annus Mirabilis* in trying
to strengthen the bonds between people and king. *Absalom
and Achitophel* shows a direct clash between king and people,
especially when it seems that David must go down before the
vast forces arrayed against him:

> Friends he has few, so high the madness grows;
> Who dare be such, must be the people's foes. (813–14)

Opposition to the king is in the end useless; the people are
shown their inferior power and place, nothing is done to lure
or soothe them. The poem sets the king once and for all above
them, after showing that he has done all he could for their
welfare.

Yet the "people" in one term or another figure prominently throughout. We might see them, their claims, their possible power as the king's real antagonists, with the false Achitophel only as the ambitious opportunist using them for his purposes. Certainly the myth demands that all such men as Achitophel get a wide base of support before proceeding with their "designs." The arguments for the popular side are expressed in the poem, as if they were discussable or at least worthy to demand an answer of some kind. There is a popular side, a case for the people, then, even though it should not finally prevail; it deserves to be considered and analyzed, since however unsound, the people are important in an orderly world. Their importance at least emerges in more than fifty various references to the populace. The word "multitude," in fact, occurs only once; aside from possible allusion to Catholic practice, it suggests a mindless, ruminating herd of animals. Concerning the plot, by which general unrest had been fomented, the narrator says,

> Not weigh'd or winnow'd by the multitude;
> But swallowed in the mass, unchew'd and crude. (112–13)

The words "people" or "the people," including the biblical God's chosen people, occur twenty-four times. These words seldom condemn, especially not "the people," even when the narrator is speaking. Achitophel's remarks on "the people," popular rights or liberties, are the standard arguments to justify popular demands. Lines 409–22 especially declare the so-called public good. But anything he says at this point has been discredited by the portrait already given of him in the poem, and by the associations that cling to his very name. The words "crowd" or "crowds" occur thirteen times, twice in the king's speech and never in a complimentary sense—twice in fact with the epithet "factious." "The Jews," "Israel," or "Israelites" come in nine times, referring more directly to the English at the moment, not to a political abstraction or vague general idea. Besides words like "the country" or "nation," we hear of "the vulgar," "rabble," or "rout" each twice—the "throng" or "pack" once each, in the most contemptuous sense.

The weight of these many references leaves no doubt that the king's cause is right and the popular cause wrong, if the word "popular" means what is clearly the doing of Achitophel and other public enemies. The "multitude" in the one reference is not clearly distinguished and might mean any or all who believed in the Popish Plot or who grew discontented and used the Plot as an excuse, just as in neoclassical criticism the multitude is all who have poor taste. The essay on innovation seems at first willing to concede that there is a popular case, but before long the consequences appear disastrous, as seen in the images of disease and madness. Those opposed to the king must seem mad, in that all of them have the uncontrollable energy that marks the violent. Absalom, Achitophel, the multitude, Zimri, Shimei, Corah, and the throng of allied conspirators—all have in common a degree of restless energy, all are after something for themselves and are therefore public enemies.

The multitude itself gets its clearest portrait under the title of "The Jews," showing once again the usefulness of biblical terminology. Lines 44–46, as also 216–19, show these "Jews" as spoiled by freedom, ease, and paternal indulgence. They are satisfied with nothing, given to moody complaints and to shifting toward new political-religious influences. Already free beyond precedent, they "dream," as if asleep, that they are not free and will never be so, short of some wild return to nature. After welcoming King David with apparent enthusiasm, they change mood again, and since rebellion and idolatry are the same, they are bent on destroying what they consider only one more idol, one more false creation of their own to be melted down at their headstrong whim. They are "governed by the moon" indeed, changing their lord every twenty years. Here the poem doubles in ancient Jewish lore and 17th-century history. We have a reference to the moon's prime, also about twenty years in the Jewish calculation of time, and to the English changes of government every twenty years since 1640; the Long Parliament of 1640, the Restoration of 1660, and the Exclusion Bill of 1680. The Old Testament had shown the ancient Jews full of complaints, murmuring against God as the English murmur against the king, setting up idols and false Gods to adore. An interesting passage in *Absalom and Achitophel* (Part II, 374–75) mentions that it is

> A wondrous work, to prove the Jewish nation
> In every age a murmuring generation.

These lines ridicule the justifying of rebellion on the ground that it had been practiced long and often by the Jews. Part I certainly uses the Jews to equal the English, in order to make its point as to the dangers of allowing the multitude to influence political action. The history of the Jews, then, does not justify rebellion; it shows only why the Jews could be such an object lesson to the English, fitting as clearly as they do into the conservative myth. The insanity of rebellion will come only from such as these. If great wits are allied to madness, so also are those with little or no wit. An entire nation may become diseased, and eventually mad, as we learn when the essay on innovation draws together the case against the multitude's instability by concentrating the associations of the "giddy" Jews with the moon and the madness that comes of its influence. A highly effective pun combines these various charges:

> Nor only crowds, but Sanhedrins may be
> Infected with this public lunacy,
> And share the madness of rebellious times,
> To murther monarchs for imagin'd crimes. (787–90)

The multitude seem more weak than evil by nature. The poem does not drive them down below a human level by suggesting something monstrous, many-headed; they are only mindless like cattle, or subject to fits of madness in which they lose what little mind they have. If they are allowed to seem not entirely to blame in order to heap greater discredit on their leaders, they are not like children. Such a comparison might set up overtones too sympathetic; if they are excusable or not accountable for their deeds, they might seem less formidable, more easily dealt with than the rhetoric of the poem demands. But in their instability they are easy prey to the schemes of wicked leaders. It is easier to be evil when one is clever, and the many associations of falsity, wickedness, or actual Satanism cling to the leading conspirators, especially Achitophel. The multitude, then, plays its role in the poem (44–133) when it is misled by religious and political forces to believe in the Popish Plot. This has the added effect of all such events in releasing forms of energy otherwise dormant, providing a chance for various factions and elements to show resentment against the king's rule. The multitude, though unstable, does not break out. Sober men recall the civil wars, and the king's mildness gives no occasion to rebel. Things are held in balance until the Plot arises, the classical, essential plot or fraudulent design without which no rebellion can succeed.

But there can be no plot without men to exploit it. If rebellion has to rest on a large popular base in the multitude, which in turn must by its nature be easily led and deceived into untried ways, there must be men whose character responds to the nature of rebellion. The poem heaps further discredit on the conspirators in showing their necessary popular following as what it is. The qualities given to the multitude are then part of the portraits of their leaders and vice versa. The multitude shares the nature of the men who influence and mislead it. A headstrong, moody, restless race suggests a union of Achitophel and Zimri, of the shifty, unprincipled turncoat Corah, the selfish impiety of Shimei. The discontented opportunism of the unnamed leaders corresponds to the popular willingness to rebel against established order when the chance arises. The rebel leaders are discredited by the nature of their cause, by the quality of their following, and by their own wickedness as called for in the myth.

Achitophel

When Dryden's admirers make much of the brilliance of *Absalom and Achitophel* as an "occasional" poem, they see it in terms of contemporary events which the poem at once describes and hopes to influence. Our pursuit of the conservative myth need not exclude the light derived from actual history. Achitophel is not only a summary of old ideas about politicians; he is Shaftesbury and the poem is something written on assignment by Dryden in a particular set of circumstances, aimed at having a certain effect.

After dissolution of Parliament at Oxford and the triumph of the royal cause, Charles II in June 1681 decided to prosecute the Whig leaders. No fresh popular demand called for this, so the king needed propaganda of his own. He desired to try Shaftesbury for treason, and in order to convict him more easily, the king had to cover him with fresh obloquy. Up to now, Shaftesbury had not been isolated as the main conspirator by an organized campaign. This became Dryden's assignment: so to discredit Shaftesbury that it would be easier to convict him of treason. This fact alone would account for the large space devoted to Shaftesbury in the poem; nearly one fourth of the 1031 lines tell what Shaftesbury is or show him at work. The great portrait (150–215), the two speeches (230–302 and 376–476), and the transitions in 220–29 and 373–75, with other allusions in 566 and 741–46, make well over 250 lines, a third of the section that precedes the essay on innovation wherein the conspiracy is given its full development, and more than the portraits of Zimri, Shimei, and Corah with all the other elements of discontent put together. The summary preceding the king's speech again charges Shaftesbury-Achitophel with one of the worst offenses now to be dealt with by the king; he had "turn'd the Plot to ruin Church and State," 929. He has then played a role impossible to exaggerate, and the time has come in the poem, as in the reign of Charles II, for the king to move against this most cunning and ruthless of his enemies. Except for certain rhetorical purposes Dryden must condemn Shaftesbury without mitigation. The opinion of E. E. Kellett seems mistaken in comparing Dryden with this creation: "like his own Achitophel, he chose the winning cause and abandoned the losing with skill that seemed almost uncanny." But in the poem Achitophel has no such luck in search of the winning cause. His side is absolutely certain to lose, as we learn in the first 16 lines of the poem. One of its chief points is that in spite of a great show of power, Achitophel's cause was at no time likely to win. If he resembled Dryden in making shrewd guesses about successful moves, the resemblance breaks down clearly at this point; he could not have guessed more wildly.

Now if Dryden's assignment was, as Tory spokesman, to discredit Shaftesbury, his own problem as a poet was more difficult. He must use the conservative myth so as to enlarge his reference. He must let the long associations surrounding the name of Achitophel denounce the man as a national leader. Yet Achitophel must also seem gifted, dangerous, and impressive to justify the structure built on him in the poem. Achitophel must appear unreliable, even foolish, yet potentially good, in fact good up to a certain point; then it can be a matter of regret that he is not on the king's side. M. Legouis even sees implied in the poem's "Preface" some charity for Achitophel, inviting a reconciliation between the king and Shaftesbury. In the light of what follows about the final salvation of the devil this seems remote, apart from the king's aim to ruin Shaftesbury by a charge of treason. Still, Achitophel must seem one whom the king would be glad to have with him but who is never to be trusted with power.

Apart from elaborate admissions as to the villain's ability and even his probity at times, the poem must accept a view of Shaftesbury as one who did indeed resolve "to ruin or to rule the state," 174. All of the evidence that in fact Shaftesbury was more "false" in his means than in his real intentions, that he would have sacrificed himself to the common good once he had solved the problem of a protestant succession—this is not allowed in his favor. The concessions are largely rhetorical regrets over something irrevocably lost, and his actual behavior in the poem is past any conceivable forgiveness or royal clemency. The poem suggests that he would in fact have made civil war to get what he was after, that he would defy the law and go on with a session of Parliament after dissolution, that he would enlist the support of the London mob, that as shown in the paper of "Association" seized on Shaftesbury's arrest in July 1681 he was willing to seize the king's person and get control of the armed forces, that he desired to be a kingmaker and chose Monmouth because with such a king Shaftesbury himself would be the real governor—that when he was about to fail he was willing to make use of such unspeakable creatures as Dangerfield with his fraudulent papers against Col. Mansell, and finally of such an obscene perjurer as Titus Oates, whom he protected and championed with monstrous cynicism. When the poem says that Achitophel would rule or ruin the state, it offers in evidence that "the triple bond he broke." This refers to the 1667 alliance of England, Holland, and Sweden against France, undermined by Shaftesbury, or in larger terms to the threefold union of King, nobles, and commons essential to the stable order of England. In either case Shaftesbury stands convicted of disturbing what had been settled, to further his own ends. The speeches of Achitophel, besides drawing on the discourse of Milton's Satan, simply condense current Whig arguments touching the rights of the subject, the will of the people, the contract between rulers and ruled, and especially the idea of 299–302 that one with a poor title makes the best king. Shaftesbury would not scruple to invoke any or all of these ideas to serve his own ambition. He would risk the most radical changes in the existing order. Monmouth's ascent would mean a republic with Parliament and the Whigs in actual control. Civil war would have to precede a change of such magnitude, and while the poem does not refer directly to this, Monmouth's kingship would mean an invasion from the continent on behalf of Mary and William of Orange, always waiting to claim the rightful succession.

If these charges are proper against the historical figure of
Shaftesbury, it does not of course concern Dryden to balance
them by showing that neither side in the dispute was very
scrupulous, that both Whigs and Tories went to highly dubious means to ruin the enemy. If the object is to ruin Shaftesbury, the choice of vehicle could hardly have been more telling. To pass from the contemporary to the mythical frame of
reference shows us again how much Dryden gained by drawing on the sense of knavery and deception that had grown up
around the name of Achitophel. Even without the many 17th-
century commentaries on the biblical story that had fixed the
lines of Achitophel's character, Dryden might have found support in Tacitus, for example, in exposing the special union
of fraud and ambition. In *History* 48 Tacitus presents Titus
Vinius as combining the elements of deceit with boldness and
enterprise. Throughout the work of Tacitus, in fact, Dryden
seems anticipated in the charges of falsity against anyone
whom Tacitus does not approve of. We meet repeatedly the
masks that cover the real intentions or "designs" of men bent
on power for themselves. Tacitus keeps a tone of the sad ob-
server of a scheme of things which he can only deplore, now
that the manly Roman virtues of old Republican days are
gone beyond hope. Augustus and Tiberius are the inevitable
deceivers, operating behind the mask of public virtue to conceal their personal ambition. In *Annals* 1 Sejanus under Tiberius is the "profound dissembler," proud, bold, and enterprising, nourishing unbounded ambition in his heart, inde-
fatigably industrious but in the service of a lust for domination.

The 17th-century use of Achitophel as a term for dissembling ambition draws on the Bible for a single name around
which to group the necessary and expected qualities of rebellious leaders. Bishop Hall develops some lines that seem to
recur in *Absalom and Achitophel,* however altered and adapted. We hear of the danger of great ability misemployed. The
policy of "this Machiavell of Israel" was "no less deep than
Hell itself." Achitophel is shrewd, unscrupulous, but though

gifted with powers to govern a state, he cannot command his own passions. His mad folly in killing himself when Hushai's advice prevailed over his own seems to anticipate Dryden's poem which refers to Achitophel's destruction of his own body. One of the signs that he combines great wit and madness is that he has needlessly punished a body "which he could not please" (167). *David's Troubles Remembered* (1638) makes more of his selfish opportunism and godless alliance with hell. Achitophel is eloquent, cunning, impious, disloyal —entirely bent on his own power. He is like "the counsellor of Hell":

> O subtile politician, wicked fool,
> Achitophel! taught in an atheist's school.

During the civil war both parties used the biblical story and the name Achitophel to condemn each other. The name carried any degree of hatred or contempt for one's political enemies; it was especially preferred against evil counsellors, leaving aside the ruler himself, who received exalted treatment according to the rules of decorum. Notes that recur constantly compare Achitophel and Satan, in striking against a weak defense; they deplore the misuse of great abilities and show that without piety, wisdom or genius is futile. No matter how shrewd the advice of Achitophel, it is vain before the wisdom of God, a note well adapted in Dryden's poem, which demolishes the conspiracy the moment the king, the Godlike, chooses to speak. The conspiracy is bound to fall by entanglement in its own plots and devices, and the counsel of every Achitophel becomes folly. At the Restoration, the name Achitophel signifies the king's enemy. The name stands for treachery, and is used as a term of reproach for the Puritans. Any political disturbance might demand reference to the biblical traitor, and when the disaffection of Monmouth declared itself, condemnation in terms of Achitophel and his influence became inevitable.

Use of Achitophel being made to order for Dryden's assignment in 1681, he can draw on other characters with similar

traits to support the sense given by the poem that here is someone presented as he must be. Achitophel's traits are seen in
many poems and plays before 1681, in Dryden's own work, in
various "characters," and in the view inevitably taken of
Cromwell after the Restoration. Then, too, any view of political falsity was bound to draw on the long tradition against
Machiavelli.

In 1660 *Astraea Redux* presents a punishment for too great
cleverness; it destroys itself as later in *Absalom and Achitophel:*

> Thus Sforza, curs'd with a too fertile brain,
> Lost by his wiles the power his wit did gain.   (201–2)

In dedicating *The Assignation* (1672) to Sir Charles Sedley,
Dryden anticipates Achitophel's advice to Absalom to use the
king for his own ends: for " 'tis an usual trick in courts, when
one designs the ruin of his enemy, to disguise his malice with
some concernement of the king's: and to revenge his own
cause, with pretence of vindicating the honour of his master."
This holds in the poem when the enemy is in fact one's master,
the king, whose cause one may betray through a pretense to
serve it. From such a work as *The State of Innocence* (1674)
we might expect more of the devil's traits to anticipate the
qualities of Achitophel, since the Satanic analogy is so clear.
But in some ways *Absalom and Achitophel* seems more deliberately Miltonic than *The State of Innocence* itself. This work
presents the devil as subtle, false, and full of hatred, but the
temptation scene is a vision presented to Eve while she is
asleep, with no suggestions of royalty or imperial grandeur as
in *Paradise Lost,* IX. But in Act IV the devil assumes a reptile
and then a human shape, in which he speaks to Eve directly
in royal terms of "sovereign" and "empress." He tells Eve that
eating the apple changed him to human form: "God-like, and
next to thee, I fair became." Thus images of royalty shade into
divinity, as in *Absalom and Achitophel.* If Eve eats, she will
become Godlike, and so will Monmouth if he consents to become king. Lucifer also argues that Heaven must have intend-

ed men to take the blessings at hand, as Monmouth is clearly intended for royal power. Eve's response is not like Absalom's, however. She says nothing of God's goodness or patience, as the youth does of his father's clemency and justice.

The conflict in *All for Love* being more clearly political as between Antony and Octavius, we are not surprised when Antony finds selfishness inseparable from falsity. Reflecting to Dollabella on a message from Caesar,

> ... yet he
> Is full of deep dissembling; knows no honour
> Divided from his int'rest.   (Act III)

As we near 1681 *The Spanish Friar* seems at times a preliminary exercise before the poem. The Queen's fear to try a new love (III, 2) uses the image of dangerous ice; but here the ice is not slippery, only too thin to bear a boy's weight, whereas the wild ambition of Achitophel (198–99) loves to slide on Fortune's ice and not to seek the firm land of Virtue. The play as a whole develops the theme of reward for villainy, and one thinks of Achitophel, whose temptation of Absalom has to offer a great reward in return for a mortal offense. As Lorenzo says, "no man will be a rogue for nothing," so the Queen reflects when Bertram offers to commit murder to secure a throne for the Queen's lover:

> How eloquent is mischief to persuade!
> Few are so wicked as to take delight
> In crimes unprofitable, nor do I.   (III, 3)

Later when the Queen defends herself from Bertram's true charge that she had ordered the murder of the old king, she implies that any attack on a prince must proceed from selfish motives. A counsellor to save himself will lay miscarriages upon his prince, with no sense of honor or patriotism.

> But centered on himself; and uses his master
> As guardians do their wards, with shows of care,
> But with intent to sell the publick safety,
> And pocket up his prince.   (IV, 2)

The poem shows Achitophel doing just this: he complains of the king's incompetence to go on and urges that his person be seized on grounds of protecting it but really to ensure the elevation of Absalom.

By 1681 ideas of political falsity and scheming ambition, being well concentrated in "Achitophel," transfer themselves readily to Shaftesbury, so that the biblical name, the qualities it represents, and Shaftesbury himself are finally indistinguishable. In *Hudibras,* III (1678) Butler's portrait of the intriguing politician makes of Shaftesbury almost a caricature of Janus-faced intrigue:

> So politick, as if one eye
> Upon the other were a spy.

He has watched the constant changes of government, and has profited from each one in turn, raising himself by whatever rope-ladders he could find:

> Would strive to raise himself upon
> The public ruin and his own.

He turns out more lucky than clever, and being adept at deeds of darkness he foresaw the way things were going simply in the line of his own crimes. Butler sees him as totally selfish, cynical, and unscrupulous, a time-serving hypocrite who would

> . . . to the utmost do his best
> To save himself and hang the rest.

The resulting impression is of someone far less an intellect than Shaftesbury-Achitophel, on the whole more contemptible than dangerous and sinister.

The year 1681 itself offers some remarkable parallels with *Absalom and Achitophel,* to show again the immediacy and availability of Dryden's materials. *The Waking Vision: or, Reality in a Fancy* sees a poet suddenly encountering a murmuring rout. He beholds a crowd with an old man in the lead,

known too well by "that false trayterous name Achitophel."
The "bold" leader, the "snake-like Achitophel" reminds them
of the Good Old Cause, urges them to let '81 be like '41. He
recommends as a plan of action that they pretend to relieve
the nation of troubles, terrify the people with a return of Popery, and denounce the king as an arbitrary tyrant. Now Absalom steps forward and declares that as the king's son he will
be king and will redress their grievances; the rout hails him
as a liberator. The poet now returns from his vision to reality
and sends the king a letter urging on him what, in effect, Dryden shows him doing in the poem, that he suppress his enemies
and act like a king.

Thomas D'Urfey's pindaric poem *The Progress of Honesty*
comes even nearer to the actual men and events of 1681. A
venerable old father utters to his wicked and rebellious son a
kind of Juvenalian lament over the state of the world. After a
charge against the corruption of the court, the old man gives
contrasting pictures of the forces of good and evil. In his allegory James II is Resolution, the rebels are Discord and
Treason, and Monmouth is Marcian. Religion becomes a
cloak for villainy, the vulgar believe all they hear, and the
young Marcian is misled into ambition for a crown he can
never attain. Various elements on the rebel and loyal sides
lead to the usual portrait of Achitophel-Shaftesbury. He is
made old in order to seem wise and shrewd and formidable.
He is a sly fellow with the eyes of Argus, seeing a hundred
ways, but his body is diseased and useless. Ambition and pride
dominate him behind a pretense of meekness and humility,
and his lechery has now passed into a form of zeal that complains loudly against the wrongs in the state. After condemning the ungrateful vulgar who resemble the Israelites of old,
the poem ends with an apostrophe to loyalty.

These thinly disguised fictions enlarge the stock of common
materials and inspiration ready for Dryden's use. But the
standard anti-Puritan dislike of Cromwell, having drawn upon
the same notions of what a rebel leader has to be, is almost
enough to serve as a model for the false Achitophel. In suc-

ceeding years Richard Flecknoe had given two views of Cromwell quite different in tone. His "The Idea" of Cromwell in
1659 is still respectful, but in *Heroick Portraits* (1660), Cromwell is "a great dissembler" whose power and resolution have
to be admitted while the nation feels ashamed to see "how they
were fooled by him." Cowley's "A Discourse . . . Concerning
. . . Oliver Cromwell" (1661) contains some remarkable anticipations of Dryden's Achitophel, seeing in Cromwell's life a
record of artifice, hypocrisy, ambition, broken faith, and usurpation. An interpolated poem cries out a curse on the man.

> Who of his nation loves to be the first,
> Though at the rate of being worst.

Much is made of Cromwell's religious pretense, so extreme as
to become ridiculous; he attained his ends by "falsehoods and
perjuries even diabolical." He got his way because men believed him to be "rather a well-meaning and deluded bigot,
than a crafty and malicious imposter." Cowley uses the standard medical and architectural images to good effect; Cromwell
further misemploys the virtues of energy and diligence, which
become vices in the cause of evil. The same is true of his courage, which Cowley deplores repeatedly in the terms "bold"
or "boldness." Finally, like Achitophel, Cromwell can only
leave the results of his labor to a son: ". . . Where's now the
fruit of all that blood and calamity which his ambition has
cost the world? Where is it? Why, his son . . . has the whole
crop."

Clarendon, too, sees in Cromwell the mythical traits of a
rebel leader—falsity and ambition joined with sagacity and
resolution. He discards Machiavelli's supposed advocacy of
injustice and so illuminates his analysis of Cromwell. Machiavelli does not favor injustice, but he says clearly that if men
have wicked designs they must have no scruple about doing
anything impious. He seems to advise—if you attempt to get
power wickedly, don't lose it by not being wicked enough.
Cromwell saw the truth of this. Although he was "the greatest
dissembler living" he always made "his hypocrisy of singular

use and benefit to him, and never did anything . . . but what was necessary to his design."

This technique resembles the practice of Shaftesbury-Achitophel, who is inevitably compared to Machiavelli. In Mulgrave's *Essay upon Satyr* (1680) Shaftesbury is called "our little Matchiavel" whose weak body is overworked by the search for power of his hard mind. Again, *Grimalkin, or The Rebel Cat* (1681) becomes the devious and unscrupulous politician Shaftesbury; the cat lives by surprise and stealth in the dark, and nowhere has this "little Matchiavel" been more active than in late operations against the lion. The cat-Machiavelli analogy is pursued through the standard complaints against the generous king, the effort to stir up discontent, deception of the unthinking brutes under the guise of liberty, and their credulity that takes "all shews for realities," so that they accept an illegitimate son of the lion instead of the rightful successor.

With this wealth of associations making for suspicion and mistrust, Dryden can be sure of meeting his readers' expectations when he begins his great portrait of "the false Achitophel." Such a man is bound to be false, to be "first" among the various elements given a chance to show their discontent through the opening made by the Popish Plot. In a few deft lines (142–49) the narrator speaks of those thought to be wise, the vain, the envious of power, the once great but now rejected, who in their hardened impenitence function to set up the devil-hell implication for rebel leaders. Then, too, the king's fatal mercy has rehabilitated some of his own enemies, raised them to high office while leaving them ungrateful. If Achitophel is the first of these, he is bound to be false, as he must be false being called Achitophel. He is close, crooked, an uncertain friend, a pretended patriot, a traitor, a criminal skulking behind the laws, a hypocrite pleasing by careful artifice and flattery, an impious seducer of mistaken men, a contriver of designs, a smooth pretender of love and duty. But a gifted deceiver requires victims to be deceived, and the age of Dryden, finding the world so readily divisible into fools and knaves, sees the fool an easy prey to the designs of selfish ambition. Achitophel pretends to champion the popular cause, but only fills the general ear with jealousies and fears. His first and necessary victim is the multitude whom he in fact despises while using them as tools. Describing their joyful welcome to the king, he sees them "Cov'ring the beach, and black'ning all the strand" (272), as if they were ugly, crawling things. His contempt underlines their folly in accepting the role to which he has sentenced them.

The multitude is necessary to Achitophel, but his other chief victim, Absalom, is even more so. Both of Achitophel's speeches of 230–302 and 376–476 are addressed to Absalom, and they show the conspirator's falsity so clearly that they seem to stand in apposition to the first epithet applied to Achitophel—false. They are based on Absalom's dubious title to the throne as suggested in 222–27, which nevertheless he must be made to think stronger than it is, or at least more desirable. Like Satan in *Paradise Lost,* Achitophel confuses his young victim by glowing images of royalty, adding biblical allusions to create the belief that his name has become a household word among a people longing to accept his kingship. Absalom would be a fool not to seize the ripened fruit now made ready to his hand by the favor of Heaven and of fortune. His father is old; Absalom is young and should behave as the king had done when he was a young prince. By pretending that their cases are the same, Achitophel adroitly begs the question. Like Hotspur, he pictures the opposition as weak, the rebellious design as invincible, but out of calculating falsity rather than impetuous generosity of spirit. He omits what might give pause, or hastens over possible dangers like foreign aid to the king, as if they would be more handicap than assistance to David. The rapid, specious, rushing arguments are subtly ambiguous, or would be to anyone who, unlike Absalom, is soberly estimating right and wrong, possible success or failure. The crafty leader has estranged "all sorts of men" from kingly rule and from David, filling them with the usual abstractions and phrases that make an impressive sound when cried aloud, as if they were something good not now enjoyed, something to be had only by means of a new champion of what is now supposed to be missing, a new king of royal blood to replace the king who is opposed because he is simply a king. "What may not Israel hope?" indeed; but "what must Israel fear" does not emerge.

The first temptation speech draws to an end (299–302), with Achitophel's supreme falsity, the "big lie" which comes after long preparation by flattery, confusion, rapidity, speciosity; Absalom is in a softened mood to accept the notion of kingship for himself on terms that are completely ruinous to the kind of power he desires, the "solid power" just referred to in 298. Achitophel obscures Absalom's real status as king. He needs Absalom now, since he has to offer someone with royal blood to replace David; but the artful one needs Absalom far less than his victim would need Achitophel after becoming king. Just as he will use the mob that he despises, so will Achitophel use Absalom to get real power; for it is clear that Absalom would become king only through a sentiment that abhors kings (290), a sentiment deliberately fostered by Achitophel as he himself says. Achitophel abhors kings in fact, and desires power for himself which he can obtain only if he persuades Absalom to be king in name only. He must persuade Absalom that this form of kingship by popular will is better than a genuine royal right; he solves this dilemma by the specious reasoning which Absalom is too befuddled to expose. A limited command may be "nobler," but it is by no means able to ensure "solid power" except to someone like Achitophel, who would not be king but who would in fact rule. The "successive title, long and dark" means to A. W. Verrall the dubious nature of such claims to the throne as Absalom has. We might better see it as a real title, which would have to be established from "mouldy rolls" of actual historical records; this is less to be desired than "a limited command" from all the people, since for Absalom there can be no pretense that he really has such a genuine title from the long past. Verrall implies that Absalom is to make no claim to any title of king-

ship other than popular choice; that is, the reason for his can-
didacy is not at all that he is the king's son. But Achitophel
would never have come near him were he not a son of the king.
His kingship therefore would clearly rest on a flimsy basis, at
the mercy of the ingenious scoundrel now luring him on his
suicidal course. Achitophel's real motive is to get a king who
has power only from the people; that is, a weak and dependent
king. Absalom has to be persuaded to be this kind of king, by
flattery and deception. Achitophel as Shaftesbury here may
well have thought on a high constitutional level anticipating
later English policy. Seen as the traditional rebel leader, necessarily false in the myth, he is a scheming hypocrite, betraying a victim for the sake of his own power.

The following passage, leading to Absalom's reply (303–12),
gives the excuse for the young man already offered in the prose
preface "To the Reader"; the better the man, the more easily
he is perverted by ill counsel, especially when baited by fame
and glory. But this love of fame is not quite like the Miltonic
"last infirmity of noble mind." It is hard to escape a note of
irony in these lines, based on reasoning so clearly fallacious.
The foolish multitude is deceived as part of its weakness, but
Absalom as part of his nobility and strength. Absalom is too
nobly gifted with Heavenly fire and is therefore an easy mark
for the false Achitophel, as if there were a necessary connection
between his being noble and being a fool. Absalom's being
fooled is part of the necessary portrait of Achitophel, but the
fact that he is taken in does not prove that he has an excellent
nature; he may have been deceived because he wished to believe these things for his own selfish reasons. Absalom then
believes Achitophel because like all tempters Achitophel suggests things that are already there or acceptance of which has
been prepared for by desire. Achitophel reasons only as well
as he needs to here and elsewhere. The whole passage, at any
rate, seems to Ian Jack a case of special pleading. If it is so,
Dryden must know that it is, unless we think him less in command of the poem than our reading implies. But let us assume
that the narrator of the poem accepts the facile, unexamined

platitude and is not offering a piece of fallacious reasoning as one more sign of the unscrupulous villainy of Achitophel. Absalom is then excused in a classical fallacy: The most excellent natures are the soonest perverted by ill counsels. Absalom has been perverted by ill counsels. Therefore he has an excellent nature. If we change the last two members of the syllogism, then we must question the major premise: Absalom has an excellent nature, therefore he is soon perverted by ill counsel. It all depends on what in the excellence it is that makes one easily perverted. In turn, if one is excellent, ought one to be so easily soothed by flattery or blinded by ambition? And if ambition is excused in Absalom, why is it condemned in Achitophel?

Let us take this so uncertain passage, then, as a necessary part of the narrator's function, which as far as Dryden is concerned allows him to present Absalom with an unresolved ambiguity. If the prose preface shows Dryden speaking directly to us, he admits that "the violent" on one side could see Absalom as too hardly drawn, and that in fact he has deliberately committed the fault of overindulgence. And remembering from the title page that this is a "poem," we can ask whether the defense of Absalom's surrender to temptation on the ground of his superior virtue is not a deliberately unresolved paradox. But if we are not sure how much of a scoundrel Absalom is, we cannot doubt the extent of Achitophel's falsity, especially after his second speech. He begins by appealing to the eternal goodness and wisdom of God Who clearly intends the virtue of Absalom for the kingly role. This is medieval reasoning indeed, so hilariously ridiculed by Boccaccio in exposing the effort of weak sinners to get the support of God's intention for something they are going to do anyway. There follows an admission that the king is mild and generous to a fault, which is contradicted by 387–88:

> But when should people strive their bonds to break,
> If not when kings are negligent or weak?

Having just admitted that the people have no bonds because

the king is so "negligent and weak," he now asks that they break their "bonds" since the king is so good to them. Meanwhile Parliament will keep reducing his power by withholding money until he grants more concessions, Achitophel himself will foment new plots, perhaps start a costly war, and gradually alienate what friends the king has left. He will, Iago-like, discredit the rightful heir through his own virtues, force him to sell his birthright for the mess of pottage that his poverty will demand, until finally the king in his desperation will "pass your doubtful title into law." This seems to contradict his first urging to rely on popular appeal rather than on any form of title in the accepted sense.

But should these grand predictions fail, Absalom is justified once more if the people choose to make him king. Here follow the standard arguments, partly reviewed later in the essay on innovation. People can make their own kings, they can alter the right of succession as they have done in the recent past; Absalom can always rely on "the public good" as a slogan to justify anything. He must not give in further to his father's love and kindness, one of the many admissions that Achitophel makes of the king's goodness, showing that Absalom has really no cause whatever for complaint and that his attempt against his father is in fact an inexcusable ingratitude. But then (429–40), it seems that Absalom's father does not really love him at all, because if he did, he would make Absalom his heir instead of leaving him things worthless or meaningless. Now the young man is warned as to the legal heir, who is jealous of his popularity and wise enough to see through Absalom's disguise, as if it had all along been understood that their joint operation was in reality a fraud, known just as clearly to Absalom as to Achitophel. The rightful heir is like a lion who lies in ambush for his enemies, the hunters; at the last the lion will suddenly spring up and rend his enemies "with a lordly rage." Absalom's case now seems desperate; the easy conquest becomes a matter of life and death. He must defend himself quickly and violently with armed rebellion if need be, leaving the people no time to stop and consider: "For then rebellion may be thought a crime" (460)—not only may be, but is certain to be thought criminal in the last degree. If Absalom is willing to accept this advice, he stands convicted of the worst offense possible in the conservative myth: he would risk civil war to achieve his own ambitions.

Achitophel now offers typical advice, as modern times have seen it carried out in unscrupulous drives for power. One first creates the trouble which then has to be corrected, allowing the malcontent to say that he desires power in order to secure peace and order, now so clearly troubled. In *Tyrannick Love* (II, 2) Placidius observes to Maximin,

> Those ills by malcontents are often wrought,
> That by their Prince their duty may be bought.

Now Absalom is to take up arms, pretending to secure the king's person from the "plots" of "seeming friends, and secret foes" (466)—that is, from the very persons offering to protect the king. Then, too, the king may wish to be seized by force, since love for his son may exceed fear of his brother, or it may combine with this fear to make him willing to give way at the very moment of greatest reluctance. Once they have seized the king, the malcontents have in effect the law in their own possession, and their cause has prevailed.

This last advice we are told, best suited Absalom's "mild nature." If he merely seized the king's person, no further violence would be necessary. After all (479–80), Absalom is not cruel or proud. His life is "unblamed" except for ambition. He is innocent, then, except of the worst thing he could be guilty of. All of the narrator's excuses for Absalom cannot remove this one unforgivable offense. But Absalom has been softened and prepared for his deadly commitment so that the extent to which he is the victim of Achitophel becomes in turn part of the whole masterly presentation of the great political scoundrel. Absalom has grown so compliant that in his second speech Achitophel can say almost anything, however vague, contradictory, or unsound—his victim is already won over to any course. Achitophel does this while at the same time

admitting that Absalom's revolt is not really justified, that he
has no real case, human or political, against his father. The
young "prince" does not see, or chooses not to see, the tissue
of contradictions he has accepted. He seems a fool, an ingrate,
a classically selfish public enemy—as indeed he must be all
these things before Achitophel can work on him so successfully.

And what again must Achitophel be? The mythical Achitophel, that is? First and always he is false, he is intellectually
gifted, yet he too is something of a fool. His intellect is suggested in the famed portrait by "sagacious," "great wits," his
"discerning eyes" in Israel's courts, but more by what he
manages to accomplish as malcontent leader, tempter, and
deceiver. Yet the case against him in the poem seems deliberately weakened or balanced by the famous interpolated passage of 186–91, where the character seems entirely to become
Shaftesbury, who is given his due and ceases to be the mythical-
poetic creation whose qualities go with his kind. As a judge
Achitophel is discerning, honest, incorruptible, efficient, con-
scientious, and fair. Such high praise amid the terms of an indictment at times so violent has been variously explained.
Dryden wishes to seem impartial so as to get agreement for his
real, over-all aim to discredit the malcontents; praise of the
villain is part of the rhetoric of persuasion then. The Horatian
tone brings the satire within acceptable lines. Legouis sees
this praise added to the poem's second edition for literary
effect, to complete the portrait, "L'enrichir par le renforce-
ment d'un contraste déjà esquisse." The passage is supposed
to show that Achitophel is not wholly evil, that he is a man
with many virtues overcome by a turbulent nature—as if this
indeed were not the whole point, that his nature is in fact
dangerously turbulent. We might make more of this high
praise of Achitophel if it did not come in the poem *after* the
worst has already been said of him, after he has in fact been
demolished as a national leader in a way that no praise could
possibly offset.

A certain amount of praise is sometimes called for as part

of satiric convention, as Mulgrave says in *An Essay upon Satire* (1675):

> Though satire nicely writ, no humour stings
> But those who merit praise in other things . . .

Praise underlines the thing to be deplored. Pope on Atticus shows how effective in satiric portraiture is praise that will be, or already has been offset by clear exposure of faults. We might expect then some praise of Achitophel even if Shaftesbury had not been such a fine judge, and to be sure there has been great praise of Achitophel's talents, which are shown to be inseparable from grave faults leading to actual madness. To praise so as to deplore is a device in a work much relied on by Dryden, Davila's *History of the Civil Wars in France* (1678). Here we read of the wisdom and talent of De Caligny with regret; "what a pity it is" that such superior gifts were not on the right side. Here again the rebel leader had to be false, ambitious, and selfish, as well as gifted and superior, a possible instrument of good employed for "base ends." Misuse of talent, the betrayal of a chance to do good, shows what Achitophel might have been had he not suffered from the invariable combination in all dangerous politicians. His ambition makes him misuse talent which, as in his work as a judge, might have become a public asset instead of a danger. Thus the narrator sighs "O, had he been content to serve the crown," 192, and utters the mythical regret that gifted men are led into rebellion instead of obedience.

The portrait of a wicked man who is gifted, who is in fact a good man when he is not misusing his great talents, when he is not being wicked, that is, suggests finally that this man is also a fool. His wisdom turns to folly indeed, in his restless, impatient, daring temper, and in the madness to which his great wit is allied when he so unreasonably overtaxes his weak body.

After the praise of so excellent a judge, the portrait of Achitophel uses one of the sententiae to return to what had been said of him earlier—that he was a reckless gambler:

But wild ambition loves to slide, not stand,
And fortune's ice prefers to virtue's land.   (198–99)

If Achitophel is a gambler prone to taking foolish chances, he is also foolish in wasting resources, both his own and the public's. Achitophel as Shaftesbury here draws on the many contemporary allusions to the Statesman's puny figure, the contrast between his strong mind and weak body. In the poem a triplet gives added attention and emphasis (156–58), as the fiery soul frets the pigmy body to decay. The "tenement of clay" uses a common reference to the human body, and carries in the passage as a whole a number of suggestions. Achitophel might seem Godless in behaving as if his body were not the perishable house of his spirit. This frail vessel has foolishly been strained by a great wit, for what end but to leave the result of his toil to a most inadequate heir, his "lump" of a son. The passage (169–72) drives at Achitophel as Shaftesbury through his son, and using echoes of Chaucer, Milton and Donne, makes Achitophel seem foolish, vain, and dangerous. The son is a lump lacking wisdom because of his father's "huddled notions" and is like the "anarchy," the Shape that had no shape, of Paradise Lost which is bound to prevail if Achitophel rises to actual power.

Achitophel's bodily weakness illustrates at once his folly and his too great intellectual force, long established as a danger in the myth, a form of energy hard to control. Achitophel's body was too weak to sustain the constant intellectual and emotional effort brought on by his ambition and his gambling instinct. The weakness of his body is only one more reason why he should have controlled his imagination, his ambition, and his intellect. He is thus a fool in not controlling himself better, and so the famous lines on the alliance of great wit and madness, adapted from Seneca and Burton's Anatomy, deplore his folly. If he is so unreasonable as to ignore his own health, how much greater the danger of his folly, if he were responsible for the health and care of the state?

Temptation

Finally, in considering the means taken by Dryden to discredit Achitophel-Shaftesbury, we might reexamine some of the Miltonic echoes so effectively employed. The speeches of Achitophel and Absalom's responses draw upon the temptation scenes in both *Paradise Lost* and *Paradise Regained*. A glance at these, the second especially, will remind us of the limitations, intended or otherwise, which comparison with Milton will place upon Dryden's characters. Arthur W. Hoffman in his Yale dissertation "Some Aspects of Dryden's Imagery" (1951) finds the Miltonic echoes more numerous and more explicit than is common, with Satan resembling Achitophel and Absalom becoming Christ as Messiah. However, the resemblance to Christ works in the end to discredit Absalom, he admits, since Absalom is a false Christ set up by Satan and accepted by a deluded populace, whereas Christ is rejected by men and is really the son of God. Absalom's yielding to temptation shows that he is not the true son of God; he reverts to the status of Adam who fell and lost Paradise. If this is so, does not the comparison of Achitophel to Satan work in two ways against the former; as he is like Satan and as he is unlike the greatest of all tempters and deceivers?

Milton's temptation scenes in *Paradise Regained* are far more complex than it suited Dryden's purposes to follow. They show Satan infinitely more brilliant and crafty than Achitophel; *Paradise Lost* shows Eve as easy to conquer as Absalom. In response to temptation Absalom does not invoke Scripture as Christ does to answer the devil. He is not outraged at being tempted to such sordid actions; he does not lose his temper as Christ does, does not rebuke Achitophel for insulting his father. Christ simply uses the resources available to any human being in resisting evil and remaining true to what is good: that is, faith, wisdom, piety. After a brief and half-hearted adherence to these in his first response to Achitophel, Absalom is an easy prey and never again offers the least resistance. The physical setting of desert and mountain is important for Christ's temptation also; this is irrelevant for Absalom, since where he is tempted is not mentioned—he could fall anywhere, the state of his mind being constantly what it is. The greatness, elevation, perfection of Christ are constantly insisted on in *Paradise Regained* and Satan himself is greatly impressed by his antagonist. This is not true of Achitophel save where he flatters Absalom to suit his purposes. We get a sense of Satan's increasing desperation as the difficulty of weakening the defenses of Christ increases; but Achitophel has very little trouble in overcoming Absalom. He is bound to succeed, just as Satan was bound to succeed in *Paradise Lost* and bound to fail in *Paradise Regained;* both Eve and Absalom desire the things by which their selfishness and ambition are tempted, and Christ continues to remain above what Satan offers. When Christ is offered fame and glory, he draws a contrast between the many and the few so much observed in the myth of Dryden's poem. He rejects the praise of "a miscellaneous rabble" and admires only the few intelligent and wise, who can never raise a man's glory. Absalom makes no such reply, but on the contrary he tries to appeal to the very weaknesses of the multitude rejected by Christ. Christ's humility and submission make him accept the pain and labor that must precede his triumph; Absalom thinks mainly of his own grievances and "rights," never of the price that would have to be paid for his rise to power. When world power is offered to Christ, not merely a single nation's throne, he has the added strain of hunger and thirst from which to resist temptation, while Absalom is a spoiled darling, much indulged in every way but one, with no excuse for his weakness.

If Absalom is less than a true Messiah and suffers by comparison with Christ, so is Achitophel less than Satan. Achitophel is wicked enough to remind us of Satan, but as we continue the comparison that the poem invites, Achitophel suffers in another way. The degree to which he recalls Satan discredits him as a public leader as compared with David: he is to David as Satan is to God. But we see that Achitophel is not what a truly great scoundrel should be; he cannot match the genius of Satan. We admire Satan for what destroys him—ambition, energy, defiance—whereas Achitophel's ambition never thrills us. He is never admirable through his faults but only for his motive as a judge which his Satanic quality denies. Milton never explicitly regrets that Satan was not loyal.

We are studying to bring Dryden's poem into higher esteem, but this should not mislead us into thinking that the good surpasses or equals the best. Satan is an imaginative creation of enormous range, revealed on a much larger scale by many-sided speech and action. His speeches to the other fallen angels, to Eve, to Christ and alone to himself allow for revelation of character in depth, whereas by comparison Achitophel's frame of reference is narrow and particular; he addresses only the single object of his temptation. Dryden's poem expressly invites a comparison which should go only so far, and should derive from Milton's Satan only the standard mythical qualities that he has in common with all evil counselors, tempters and politicians. If we go beyond these familiar traits into the real depths of Milton's creation, we will bring out limitations of Dryden which are not to the purpose; nevertheless such comparison will help to discredit Achitophel-Shaftesbury from another side and so will sustain the purpose of the portrait as far as it goes in the poem. When Mr. Hoffman says that the action of the Achitophel portrait is the action of Satan's emergence from Hell for his attack on mankind, he obliges us to recall that Satan's difficulties are much greater than Achitophel's, whose task is so much easier against his weak, too-willing antagonist that he has little chance to display a comparable genius in overcoming him. Even before Satan gets Eve alone by herself, as Achitophel does Absalom, in order to make the flatteries and speciosities of the temptation more effective, he has had to display his enormous versatility, not to speak of the total exhaustion of his resources in his approach to Christ in *Paradise Regained*.

No sooner does Satan break "the horrid silence" than he begins to display his pride, ambition, envy, guile, malice, re-

bellious and unrepenting defiance, bitter ironic humor, cruelty, hatred and hypocrisy. Although he seems inwardly hurt, re-
morseful and despairing, he shows only a Promethean energy
and belligerence, an optimism that refuses to accept defeat, to
believe that Heaven is lost so long as Satan can imagine,
scheme or talk. He is the supreme ruler in his kingdom who
does all his own leading, and exercises his own power, boldly
undertakes himself the long journey to earth "with difficulty
and labour hard" pursuing his way, "and swims or sinks, or
wades, or creeps, or flyes" until at last he beholds the world
"with mischievous revenge." His feelings are confused as he
lights upon the earth, wonder and envy, bitter grief, fear and
despair afflict him; like Absalom he seems to admit the goodness and justice of the God-king he rebels against, and wishes
too that he had been born to an inferior station and so have
avoided ambition. The repentance and pardon opened by
Dryden's David to Absalom will never be Satan's, however,
since he cannot submit and evil remains his good. Beholding
our first parents, he feels a measure of love and pity, as later
on he admires the beauty and virtue of Christ. These passing
moods do not contain, however, the essential malice and envy
of Satan, so that when at last his opportunity comes to ruin
the happiness of mankind, he brings to the successful temptation of Eve the full power of evil, and displays in attacking
Christ unsuccessfully an even more impressive energy and
ability.

Greatly as Satan has feared and respected his opponent in
Paradise Regained, he seems to have underestimated the de-
termination of Christ to resist. Unlike Absalom Christ fights
back, tries to answer the arguments of Satan, forcing him to
display more energy, versatility and adaptability than Achitophel is called upon to show. If these two are measured by the
quality of their antagonists, the degree of difficulty faced
throughout, Satan becomes the more compelling figure. Satan
has made a powerful assault upon the whole range of the defenses of human nature; even in his last defeat, he seems
greater than Achitophel in victory that has come too easily.

Thus Achitophel-Shaftesbury does not follow Machiavelli's advice to make sure, when seeking power by wicked means, to be wicked enough. He has Satan's qualities then only up to a point, and these might have come to him through associations familiar in Dryden's myth. When compared explicitly to Milton's Satan, Achitophel is not Satanic enough. He lacks the "desperate agility of Satan," in Louis Martz' happy phrase. He fails by not being shameless, defiant, resourceful, malignant, subtle, adaptable enough. He does not grasp the realities of human life and human nature, does not understand his enemies clearly enough to invite comparison with Satan except to his great disadvantage. Dryden does not allow the ambiguity of Milton's Satan, even of his God, to intrude. If Achitophel is never attractive in his faults, neither does God ever seem alien or threatening through David-Charles-the Law. As Dryden is never of the Devil's party with or without knowing it, so Dryden's reader is never allied against order by the enormously compelling energy of Satanic ambition and defiance. From both sides then of his Satanic possibilities, Achitophel must be rejected.

The Minor Portraits

The other three developed portraits of malcontent leaders may depend more on the persons to whom they refer than does the mythical figure of Achitophel. Yet Zimri-Buckingham (543–68), Shimei-Bethel (583–629), and Corah-Oates (630–81) also tend to draw heavily on what has gone before them.

So far we have not distinguished sharply between "portraits" and "characters," since Dryden's creations are clearly both. A portrait in theory describes an individual with some comment on his appearance; a character is of a type or kind of person. The regular Theophrastan formula gives each one an appropriate title, the first line stating a certain quality in human nature. The second sentence refers to the man himself, and the rest of the character gives examples of his behavior. English character writers used this formula but gradually be-

came more particular and familiar toward recognizable types
from the English scene, more journalistic and topical. This
moves into actual situations, especially from contemporary
politics, until general types combine with persons then alive.
As Nichol Smith has shown, a character is not any one person's
life, and when biography develops, the 17th-century character
declines. The civil war in England had brought the character
into public controversy, where it became a useful weapon.
In Butler the character is transformed into political or religious satire, resembling more the subject of an essay or an
argument, than a person or kind of person.

So we watch again how Dryden takes up and applies the literary devices and materials available to his hand. In *Absalom
and Achitophel* we tend to speak of "portraits" as if Dryden's
people were only men living in his time. The portraits are
more complex than this, combining what the historical figures
in fact were, what the biblical parallel called for insofar as it
suited Dryden to use it, and what they had to be in the larger
mythical meaning of the poem. Thus by combining several
portraits, we get a general "character" as established in the
conservative myth. If we join the four main satiric portraits
to one of Absalom, to one of the multitude assembled from
several passages, and to one of the miscellaneous elements in
the conspiracy to suggest the common denominator of rebellion, we get a total of seven "portraits," so to speak, from
which we could write a "character" of let us say, *The Restless
Malcontent.*

On the other side, the individuals are not so sharply defined; yet if we enlarge the term "portrait," we might assemble
some four of five units representing certain virtues to be
praised. It is said of Pope's *Epistle to Dr. Arbuthnot* that one
should add another portrait to those specifically outlined in
the poem—that of the author himself. This is less true of *Absalom and Achitophel.* The "I" or "me" references hardly
seem to distinguish Dryden himself and do not develop any
special characteristics. If there is a "portrait" of Dryden, it
is derived from the poem's content and meaning; Dryden is

one who believes the ideas set forth in the essay on innovation
and the rest of the poem's doctrines expressed in the sententiae, through the satire and the poem's entire rhetoric. Since
these are his beliefs, he must be the kind of man who believes
these things to be so—a classical conservative. Thus if we
count Charles-David as one portrait; Barzillai as one and his
dead son as another; Jotham and the other loyalists as one
combining similar qualities of high birth, wealth, and learning; and "Dryden" himself, the voice of the poet-sage, as one,
we have a total of five. From these we derive the "character"
of *A True Loyalist* to set over against *The Restless Malcontent*. Taken together, the two groups so unified follow the
lines of 17th-century character writing—they denounce men
who pursue their own selfish ends like that first individualist,
the devil, and uphold men of conformity, moderation, and
decorum. The central opposition of the conservative myth
moves into the clash between two combined forces in *Absalom
and Achitophel*.

Dryden's people emerge with telling effect, more remarkable in that the presentation is not dramatic throughout. Only
five speeches are made, by three persons in all: Achitophel utters about half of all that is said in the poem directly, with
Absalom and the king dividing the rest, and even Absalom's
"progress" speech is by Achitophel, since it is just what the
"devil" would have Absalom say. Other "portraits," as we
have used the term, are descriptive and analytical of certain
characteristics, less the actions than the qualities or passions
of the men that make them what they are. The method covers
a great deal of important ground, especially within the range
of our assembled unit, *The Restless Malcontent*. This takes
in ambitious politicians, wasteful nobility, scheming tradesmen, and Popish Plot fanatics. It includes no one from the
Church of England clergy, although there is some implied
denigration of the church, 535–40; the Anglican clergy supported the king up to James II, so they come with three high
names into the loyal few and help make up our "portrait" of
the *True Loyalist*. The four principal malcontents are divided

equally between commoners and noblemen. Shimei and Corah, being the commoners, are seen with a kind of contemptuous disdain from above, a tone not proper for Achitophel
and Zimri. Mr. Ian Jack suggests that commoners must not
seem as dangerous as noblemen; they are condemned outright,
with nothing in them to deplore. Since these particular commoners are also religious nonconformists, they deserve the
hostile irony that charges their exposure.

The noblemen are offered with a sense of waste, of something regrettably lost. Achitophel is not specifically a "prince
of the land" as Zimri is, but we know that he is in high place,
near the king's throne. Zimri seems the more general portrait,
a kind of smaller character of *The Inconstant Man* in the
Theophrastan formula. Taken from the Bible (Numbers and
Kings), the name Zimri held many unpleasant associations of
restlessness, sexual intrigue, and treasonable conspiracy. Dryden of course knew what a brilliant performance the portrait
was, but his pleasure in it as expressed in the *Discourse Concerning Satire* (1692) suggests that he found it more pleasant
than damning when applied to the second Duke of Buckingham. If we persist in thinking that Dryden always knew what
he was about, we must see Zimri the dangerous malcontent as
far more odious than Zimri-Buckingham was supposed to be.
His unstable, fragmentary nature recalls Horace's Tigellius,
and Horace's other themes of lack of restraint, addiction to
needless luxury, discontent, fickleness, and illusion all come
within the range of Zimri's variety. Juvenal, as Van Doren
remarks, had "invented the chain of scornful epithets," and
especially anticipates Zimri in the Greek parasite of his third
satire, "the hungry Greek" of Dryden's own translation. Zimri
also shares the standard themes in Juvenal of extravagant living, lack of integrity, fickleness again, and seems in fact to
partake of the character of all bad men in Satire XIII. Although
he is not an actual criminal, Zimri's inconstant, shifty nature
is seen in the fine "mobilis et varia est ferme natura malorum"
—though we remember that Virgil says much the same thing
about women. In the actual character of a politely accom-

plished libertine Zimri reminds us of Fabius Valens in Tacitus' *History* 3. The historian's fine aristocratic aloofness would certainly have agreed with the scorn implied in showing Zimri as fiddler and buffoon, 550. In condemning Nero for playing the harp and singing in public, Tacitus remarks, *Annals* 14, that in 200 years not a single Roman citizen of rank or family had so degraded himself as to enlist in a troop of comedians.

Zimri seemed to have little control over himself, his own impulses or passions. Such a man was unacceptable as a public leader in the Renaissance when thinkers held that reason had to control passion and that a man who could not govern himself should not be allowed to govern others. Achitophel and Zimri both could not properly conduct their own lives, and certainly had no credit to lead the nation. Joseph Hall's characters of "The Malcontent" and "The Unconstant" both find their happiness in change, and the latter suggests Zimri in asking of books and fashions not "how good" but "how new." He is in possibility "anything or everything; nothing in present substance"—anything, that is, "rather than himself." The lines on Buckingham in Mulgrave's *Essay upon Satire* (84–102) and the character of Buckingham by Burnet show how common were the Zimri traits of a witty but careless and unstable man. Burnet makes a great deal of Buckingham's influence on the young Charles II, whom he corrupted by bad example in Paris, underlining once again the danger of prodigal or voluptuous persons in stations of power. Not wishing to reflect on the king, his hero in the poem, Dryden avoids all mention of any corrupt influence on Charles. He cuts down Zimri in other ways by a remarkable concentration of language, and shows him as a fool, perhaps not so wicked as other malcontents. But for satire a fool might be worse than a knave, and for a public leader it was fatal to persist in opinions that were always wrong, to be so many different things while the moon turned only once. The term "fiddler" had long associations of contemptuous ridicule, continued by Francis Osborne, who advises his son that fiddling was something no gentleman would think of doing himself; in *Hudi-bras* (I, 2) it suggests one who stirs up trouble as well, but the tone of contempt is central and continues into Chester-field's advice to his son, like Osborne's before him. If Zimri now is "fiddler, statesman, and buffoon," what kind of states-man must he be who is a statesman only between being a fid-dler and a buffoon?

As Coleridge says, the Zimri and Achitophel portraits pro-gress and evolve, every line counting toward the last verse. This skill in adapting means to ends marks the exposure of Zimri in its bare twenty-six lines, drawing a picture of variety, extremity, instability, and folly, of unresolved contradictions becoming mere ridiculous futility at last. Zimri's instability is additionally contemptible in resembling the multitude, and the revolving moon makes us think of the giddy Jews again, likewise governed by the moon, 216. The "blest mad-man" of 553 is then not far to seek from these lunatic influ-ences and similarities—in his ten thousand freakish thoughts, in hourly search for what is new, in contradictory pursuit of opposites, in the violent rushing to all extremes, in the indis-criminate throwing away of his inheritance, in silly jokes that lost him all credit, and in the sin that the conservative myth would never forgive—the making of disturbing factions and parties that went beyond his control. Zimri could not pass the test of "The True Englishman" (1686):

> He only merits a true English name,
> Who always says, and does, and is the same . . .

Zimri is totally devoid of the third element between extremes, and he lacks any sense of order by which to control his energy. As he seems not to have any real talent, he seems not to be really dishonest, being wicked only in will, 567. He resembles Dante's trimmer, who simply lacked the character to get into hell itself, swaying forever back and forth in the mere vesti-bule of damnation. As Zimri could not really achieve hell, he could not lead his own faction, which had to rely on a proper devil and his instrument. After all, it takes a certain amount of talent to be wicked, like Achitophel or his superior, Satan; it demands character of a sort that might do good in the world if properly used. Zimri simply does not show the qualities of a gifted scoundrel; he cannot lead any enterprise, even one that is wrong; he is merely futile.

To get the effect of something below the dignity of verse (570) the verse itself seems not to rest until it has finished with Zimri in the fine last couplet with its classical use of alliteration, balance and antithesis, and rhyme that seems to conclude something that has been proved once and for all:

> Thus, wicked but in will, of means bereft,
> He left not faction, but of that was left.   (567–68)

The double rhymes that would be out of place in high epic passages or "manly satire" are used (551–52, 557–58) to lower the key for ridicule of Zimri's excesses and contradictions. As with Achitophel, Dryden achieves "a pliable instrument of satire," a tone of casual conversation as if these were the things one would naturally, inevitably say when observing such individuals. A series of loosely appositive modifiers imply predication, but after a complete sentence at the outset seem to avoid subjects or verbs. From 545 to 555 neither Zimri's own name nor any pronoun for him is used, but the nouns, participles, epithets are allowed to accumulate upon their victim's luckless head. Zimri is casually demolished with aid of the moon and madness, and in keeping with the poem's myth becomes totally unreliable.

The transition from Zimri to Shimei (569–82) has little of fresh note save 577–78, which suggest the narrator's personal involvement with some of the rebels. He will not name these, out of scorn in some cases, but more because they are his friends or seem worthier than their associations. The rest of the passage concludes the poem's summary of the great accumulation of odds and ends on the rebel side. It would be tedious and undignified to go on rehearsing the names of lords, wits, warriors, Puritan sympathizers—ordinarily harmless individuals of no special note. The following references to Hastings, Grey or Essex, Howard, and Sir William Jones, with the multitude thrown in, are not developed. Using the names of Balaam, Caleb, Nadab, the rascal rabble without sanction from earth or Heaven, and "bull-fac'd Jonas" with its rare touch of personal appearance, the passage makes points already made or implied as to dullness, volubility, lechery, hypocrisy, and illegality.

We suddenly meet the wretch Shimei, whose portrait begins with a most skillful opening rhyme, 583–84, that impales him on his own curse. Preceding reference to Shimei in the 17th century invariably dwells upon his biblical curse against David, and as we should expect of character writing, Shimei is somewhat anticipated in exposures of the greedy merchant bent on nothing but his own gain. Joseph Hall's commentary makes Shimei a violent, cursing, insolent hypocrite uttering blasphemies against the king, God's anointed. Other comments on the biblical story before and after the civil war expose Shimei as the malicious railer, insolent defamer of the king, one who must needs be cursing where God has blest, a creature of malice, violence, and hatred inspired by Satan. The more worldly side of Shimei that enables him to get and keep money is remarkably summarized in Machiavel's *Advice to His Son* (1681). The passing reminder of Machiavelli's supposed unscrupulous cunning is relevant, and maxims given are such as might govern anyone so monstrously selfish as the profane rebel of Dryden's poem. The son of Machiavelli is instructed in pretense and concealment, along with shrewd dealing, caution, wise sparing, saving, and hoarding of money. The general lesson is that one should get and keep money for oneself; as Satan had told Christ in *Paradise Regained,* no one is effective unless he is rich.

If these and other lines are anticipated, there is little before Dryden of the brilliant use of means toward ends by which his verse exploits the satiric possibilities of the couplet for anticlimax and the clash of opposites. Pope was indeed lucky to have Dryden precede him. Shimei prepares for Atticus in the balance, hesitation, and surprise, in revealing something

to be condemned through the construction of lines and couplets that set up the anticlimaxes showing the man as odious
after leading us to hope that he is better than we have thought.
But in Shimei there is little to deplore, no sense of something
potentially valuable being lost, unless it is the misapplying of
so much shrewdness and calculation. After the opening curse,
Shimei's zeal, wisdom, and piety are only the visible side of
what in fact becomes hatred, cunning, and blasphemy. Not
only his character but his public career defeats expectation;
his holding high and responsible office suggests care of the
general good, loyalty, and obedience, but in fact Shimei's impiety means an equal degree of disobedience; a selfless public
servant is shown to be a scheming, avaricious hypocrite. The
success of pious hatred, of cheating or trading and praying, of
promising to uphold justice while actually betraying it to the
sons of Belial shows what is possible for one who delights in
profane insults to God and the king. The passage in 599–603,
containing the triplet which carries over the cursing rebel of
the Old Testament into the person of Christ in the New, has
been read as blasphemy on Dryden's part. But the very beauty
and tenderness of Christ's promise always to be in the midst
of two or three gathered together in his name reflects by its
skilled anticlimax once more on the crude impiety of Shimei.
The incongruous association of Christ with Shimei has the
effect of further discrediting one who is not in the least
Christlike, of suggesting the hypocrisy of pretended Christian
feeling such as he ought to be capable of, as distinguished
from the reality in Christ's own behavior. The similarity to
Christ, then, is like all other mention of virtue in Shimei's
portrait—it shows the opposite in his own evil.

Unlike Achitophel, who was an incorruptible magistrate,
Shimei has used his office to pervert the aims of law and justice he has sworn to uphold, 610–11. Shimei's energy seems
also misused, and the puritanical severity he feels against any
wasted time turns out to lead only into abuse of the king as
a possible danger to the only thing that Shimei really cares
about—making money by trade. As religious dissent among

the Whigs shows them dangerous to the conservative myth, so also their frequent origin from the trading or commercial classes becomes through Shimei a means of accusing those against the king of pursuing private gain at the expense of the common welfare. In *Annus Mirabilis,* trade was essential to the future greatness of England; now it seems dangerous as emphasized by Samuel Parker's *Discourse of Ecclesiastical Politie* (1670). He warns against enriching the dissenters "whilst their heads are distemper'd with religious lunacies; for it only puts weapons into the hands of madmen, whereby they may assault their governors . . . wealth does but only pamper and encourage their presumption, and tempt them to a greater boldness and insolence against authority." But there might rather be something of Juvenal's harsh view of trade as necessarily demanding selfish materialism, of wealth as always contaminated by the means required to obtain it.

These general considerations against dissenting tradesmen have suggested that our reading of Shimei gains nothing from knowing that he is supposed to represent the Whig sheriff Slingsby Bethel. Contemporary references denounce Bethel for disloyalty, and in spite of some evidence that he was privately generous, he is unmercifully ridiculed for stinginess in *The Poor Prisoners Lamentation for the Loss of S—— B——* (1681). Bethel is again ironically compared with Christ, here by means of the miracle of loaves and fishes. At his table, out of the tail of a red herring and two sprats, he produced shoals of fish, all the way from shrimp to the Great Leviathan. Bethel is also charged with zeal for reform, his loyalty and hospitality "shall survive the reforming the church and government." Bethel's actual belief in the value of trade is set forth in two works of his own. *The World's Mistake in Oliver Cromwell* (1668) attacks the Protector fiercely as a dishonest and unjust oppressor, who damaged England severely after the nation had grown rich by trade. From his entrance, England's trade began to decline, contrary to the interest of the kingdom. Other comment of the time shows that Bethel was not alone in decrying the loss of trade supposed to have followed from Cromwell's policy. His larger work, *The Interest of Princes and States* (1680), suffices to document the couplet 614–15:

> His bus'ness was, by writing, to persuade
> That kings were useless, and a clog to trade.

The work is variously interesting for its hard anti-intellectualism, and even for its use of the expression "sons of Belial" the presence of which in Dryden's portrait may owe something to Bethel's obvious irritation with it as applied to nonconformists like himself: "I suppose the new philosophy of poverty, and the transplantation of all non-conformists, called the sons of Belial . . . will have but few disciples." The phrase recurs again, with obvious annoyance, and the work as a whole makes commercial prosperity a function of religious freedom, seeming to justify the portrayal of Shimei as making impiety and greed, if not also rebellion, inseparable. Trade being essential to the national interest, the king should "advance and promote trade, by removing all obstructions and giving it all manner of encouragement." Bethel now offers a long series of measures for the king to take, Number 14 of which says that "imposing upon conscience in matters of religion, is a mischief unto trade, transcending all others whatsoever." He pleads for entire liberty for nonconformists, removal of all religious impositions as being "the true interest of king and kingdom, in that it is absolutely and indispensably necessary, for raising the value of land . . . and advancing the trade and wealth of the kingdom."

Shimei as Bethel then quite properly favors the prosperity of trade and the freedom to dissent. His personal abstemiousness is not a virtue but only another function of his avarice, not justifiable "by writing" (614) or otherwise. The entire passage (616–29) on his frugality and parsimony reinforces the contrast between his holding back from anything that will cost him money or advantage and the violence of his flaming hatred against God and king. From seeming formidable as a threat to order, he grows cheap and mean, with something pinched and meager in all ways except impiety and rebellion, the religious dissent that leads to faction and disorder. He shows at last the invariable selfishness of all dangerous men. In 1644 Richard Vines preached a sermon, *The Impostures of Seducing Teachers Discovered*, that sought the common trait among all "false teachers." Using much of the imagery of trade, the sermon finds these men making merchandise of people and "negotiating their own ends." For "men in seeking themselves, may drive several trades; one is for credit, another for his palate, another for his purse . . . but this in the general will hold good, seducers are selfseekers." In these terms Shimei stands condemned in the myth, as are the false, the ambitious, the unstable, and all others who would go their own way apart from the common good. His virtues of industry and frugality are turned into the pitch of rebellion and avarice, of self-seeking materialism.

The last of the rebel portraits follows directly on the exposure of Shimei. Ironically the narrator will not include the usual Homeric list of heroes, for it would exhaust even the voluble liars of his day to rehearse them all. But in a Virgilian line, 632, he is determined that Corah shall not find refuge in oblivion. This is different from Pope's generous rescue of his dunces from the obscurity for which their invincible blockheadism had otherwise prepared them. To let Corah be forgotten seems too good or kind a fate, although he too is clearly destined, in the nothingness of his mind and character, to be forgotten. But this would let him escape the contempt that his monumental impudence and falsity have earned. Let Corah then come under examination, let him stand erect now to be seen for what he is—the most odious and despicable in a vast crowd of fools and scoundrels. Corah seems to be the last in a descending scale, the most informal of the main portraits, the only one directly addressed by the narrator in the second person. This direct discourse continues for only four lines (632–35), and its familiarity is a move to lower the tone, to insult Corah by speaking to him in a way different from the others. Achitophel uses direct discourse to Absalom, but the narrator does not. Likewise the narrator's use of the personal pronoun for himself, 668, is unique in the poem: "Were I myself in witness Corah's place." Line 832, "By me (so Heav'n will have it) always mourned" is from Virgil's *Aeneid,* and passes as literary adornment in an elegy. In these and other ways Corah is shown as insignificant and contemptible, save in the danger of which he is the inadequate cause. Achitophel is much the most formidable of the leaders, with Zimri more subject to ridicule in his futility. Shimei's personal stinginess is enough to show him small and mean, making use as it does of one of the standard objects of ridicule, enjoyed to this day in Scottish jokes and the self-abasement of radio comedians. But Corah's lines are the most disrespectful and abusive in the poem, seemingly directed more at an actual contemporary than the other portraits, including more specific details of personal appearance than any other, and bringing him down to the commonest possible level.

It may not be fanciful to see in this descending scale of estimation from Achitophel to Corah an increasing contempt for the whole rebellion which begins as an impressive danger from very able men, but ends by being simply ridiculous if it must rely on such half clowns as this. We learn (636) that Corah's birth has been low, a further descent from the high station of Achitophel and the princehood at least of Zimri. The details of his appearance are specific and are joined, after Dryden's custom, to the general qualities behind them, in this case ironically:

> Sunk were his eyes, his voice was harsh and loud,
> Sure signs he neither choleric was nor proud;
> His long chin prov'd his wit; his saintlike grace
> A church vermilion, and a Moses' face.   (646–49)

Sunken eyes and long chin have Chaucer's vividness, and the red shiny face makes us think of the Summoner and Monk. We wonder how, when Corah as Oates was the toast of London, his face could have appeared on ladies' fans. The portrait takes on the qualities of farce if we accept the hierarchy of

genres kept by Dryden between poetry and painting. Epic
would then equal historic painting, comedy genre painting,
and farce would resemble the grotesque. The description of
Corah, like that of Shadwell's bulky figure in *Mac Flecknoe*
and *Absalom and Achitophel*, II, draws a farcical parallel. He
is low and ugly like his character. The higher genres show
more ideal forms as in the beauty of Absalom and take on
epic, Miltonic tones. By contrast Corah gets a farcical literary
treatment parallel to his grotesque painting treatment.

Again, all reference to Corah's talents are sarcastic, except
his talent for lies; but this too does not come of great mental
power, unlike the falsity of Achitophel. His "monumental
brass" recalls the brazen serpent of Moses that saved Israel, as
Corah would save its modern counterpart by the fantastic impudence of his lies. "Brass" here might also expose its victim's brainless head as suggested in the "Epilogue" to John
Crowne's *The Ambitious Statesman* (1679):

> 'T is strange fond Nature often takes great pains,
> To build brass foreheads to defend no brains.

The sarcasm grows more bitter with reference to Corah's low
birth, out of which to be sure, "prodigious," that is, monstrous actions have come; the measure of Corah's nobility is
in the means he has taken to achieve it, the deed whereby he
has ennobled all his blood, 641. At the martyrdom of St.
Stephen after testimony by false witnesses, or at the execution
of Stephen College in the Popish Plot frenzy, no one inquired
into the ancestry of those whose lies sent innocent men to
their death. Corah, in fact, was in his way highly placed, given
the opportunities of the twisted world of false values in which
he lives. The biblical Levites were a royal guard exclusively
assigned to the Tabernacle and became a learned caste. Corah's world made him one of these gentlemen of God; only
in a world so false, in times so perverted could such a monster,
that is, seem a nobleman.

After the revelations of Corah's appearance, we learn of his
principal talent—a "prodigious" memory indeed, as the term

is used in 638. His memory achieved such miracles of report-
ing that they are not merely lies; after all, a lie has to be the
result of human wit, and since Corah had none, he was reduced to invoking supernatural aid. He became prophetic,
saw visions, was so carried away in spirit as to win a learned
doctor's degree. The biblical reference again is to the Levites
of Numbers 3, witnesses and prophets in the Lord. The contemporary allusion is to Titus Oates with his dual pretense of
acting as a witness in the Plot and of being under divine guidance or special Providence. The lines are a bitter attack on
the falsity of Corah, both as witness and inspired prophet. But
Corah's judgment seems an even more remarkable talent than
his memory. It was equally suited to the times and the opportunities they offered, and Corah obtained such credence as
made it extremely dangerous to challenge his recollection, or
his judgment as having less than biblical sanction. In fact, the
narrator feels that if he were Corah and found himself affront-
ed by certain doubts as to his veracity, he would summon his
miraculous memory once more to the aid of his judgment and
recall what had somehow been forgotten so far—that his ac-
cuser was in fact one of the original plotters, 668–71. Corah's
memory as a thing to "whet" (670), by any sort of challenge,
becomes a ghastly reminder of the whetted, sharpened executioner's axe that Corah's lies had so often caused to sever innocent heads; it suggests too, how deep, how passionate sometimes is the bitterness lying beneath the poem's surface of iron-
ical contempt.

  To his memory and judgment Corah adds religious zeal,
which like that of Shimei has the contradictory result of in-
spiring animus against the king and allowing Corah such latitude and privilege that he might piously make capital for his
own purposes of murder itself. But in the end his allies in
"evidence" (678) will share Corah's insoluble dilemma in ex-
tricating himself from the predicament to which his falsehood
has reduced him—even though they are "the best" he could
get for the usual alternatives. They bear the common title of
"witness" (681), and as the word is used five times in the por-

trait of Corah it can mean only falsehood. All those who share "witness" as a name in common, are involved in the damnation to which it has always led.

But all that Corah may summon to his aid will be in vain. His low-born impudence, his false pretense of public service, the enormous lies brought forth by his memory and judgment, the cynical exploitation of religious sanction for his own odious purposes—all must avail him nothing. He is redeemed by nothing, offers nothing to deplore, is totally wrong by every assumption that underlies the poem that has denied him escape into oblivion. How far is the distance we have come, how great the descent from the powerful mind and evil shrewdness of Achitophel to this wretched ugly quack! Yet the last word on Corah and his kind is the same as the first on Achitophel. All are false, and threaten the stability of the mythical order by selfish pursuit of their own ends.

CHAPTER 8

The Plot and the Malcontents

If such were the leaders, the nature of their following and the means taken to secure them must necessarily follow. We must now move into the contemporary reference of Dryden's poem more exclusively, and in the process we become involved in the Tory line with emphasis on civil war. In the 1680's the trump card of Toryism is the fear of civil war, endlessly insisted upon in the propaganda of such hirelings as Roger L'Estrange and coming to dominate the heavy political satire to which the London theater had turned. The Catholic issue and its "Plot" now had subsided, and of the three parties—Catholics, Whigs, and Tories—the first had been ruined by the lies of Oates so thoroughly that James II in the end could not revive the Catholic forces. Dryden's poem shows the temporary defeat of the Whigs as well, since they had relied so heavily on the fabrications of the Plot. As this had given Shaftesbury his opportunity, now Shaftesbury's Exclusion "plot" gives the Tories their text whereon to preach the threat of another civil war, which Shaftesbury and his followers seemed willing to risk in order to get rid of the future James II. Since both parties hated Catholicism, however, the Tories had to supply churchmen with something to be afraid of; otherwise the old fear of Catholicism might return and give new life to the Whig cause, always based on fear of Rome and thus aided by Oates and his Plot. The danger had to be made real, immediate, and threatening, and if leaders of the Exclu-

sion party were convicted of treason, this would prove the
need for vigilance.

As a convinced Tory and as a professional writer assigned
to a given task, Dryden would make *Absalom and Achitophel*
whatever the historical situation demanded. If it demanded
that a threat of civil war be shown, he was ready to expose the
danger. Yet the terms in which he writes throughout are taken
from established ingredients of the conservative myth: the
civil war that is now threatening England will emerge with
the same elements, causes, and motives as civil war has shown
since the beginning of literary attempts to chronicle or describe it. In order to have civil war there must be falsity, ambition, and selfishness once more, and we shall find Dryden, so
much influenced by Renaissance political views, interpreting
civil war too as the worst affliction that the body politic can
endure. Indeed the whole attitude of mind to which we give
the name "conservatism" arises from the issue of civil war.
Fear of this upheaval dominates late 17th-century England,
and Dryden's view of it continues what Roman writers had
said after the disruption of life in the first century B.C., what
English and French writers of the Renaissance had said of the
civil wars in their own countries, and what Clarendon and
others had said of the most recent civil war in England. Dryden has then the response to the Roman, French, and English
civil wars to draw upon, and in so doing he provides Burke
and others with their inevitable response a century later to the
French Revolution, also a civil war and so interpreted in England. The fear of change that cannot be controlled before
bursting into violence is essential to the myth as interpreted
by Dryden. The fear of something worse than anything now
to be endured, however bad, is in fact the fear of civil war
which is worse than the evils it tries to cure.

The Roman civil war between Caesar and Pompey as re-
counted by Lucan and Plutarch makes less of deceit than of
ambition and self-interest as causes. The danger of incendiary
eloquence, also noted by Tacitus in his *Annals,* was seen by
Plutarch as threatening to stir up the multitude. He reflects

too, in the life of Pompey, on the pass to which Rome had been brought by private ambition, and on the blindness and madness of men overcome by passion. Lucan establishes for perpetual use afterward the standard literary figures of fury and madness at the very outset of his *Pharsalia:* "Quis furor, o cives, quae tanta licentia ferri." In reviewing causes, he finds the triumvirs blinded by ambition, "cupidine caeci" and later, in Book II, all the main participants are shown to have their own motives.

We must admit some danger in pushing the analogy between the Roman conflict and the possible English civil war that Dryden fears. There was no established kingship in Rome to which Caesar and Pompey had no right to aspire. Neither tries to get for himself what has already been declared as belonging to another man by law, as in England. Lucan makes less then of notions of falsity and more of the personal desire for power, or the mad folly of civil war because of its cost in suffering and bloodshed. In Rome both parties are wrongly in pursuit of supreme power; in England only one is wrong and the other right. In Rome one might be neutral between Caesar and Pompey; in Dryden's England neutrality was as bad as outright attack on the established order. But even in Rome, despite these differences, there was something to correspond to the rightful order of England—namely, the defense of law and the prevention of personal tyranny. As Lucan suggests, 283–84, the noble Brutus must therefore be the enemy of whoever wins between Caesar and Pompey, and Brutus does in fact help to kill Caesar at last. Whoever wins will be a tyrant, therefore one who violates the lawful Roman order, therefore one who must die.

In preparing to write *The Duke of Guise* in 1660, Dryden used a work on the 16th-century French civil wars in which he later found a close parallel to the operations of the king's enemies in England. In his brilliantly scathing "Epistle to the Whigs" prefacing *The Medal,* he tells them: "Anyone who reads Davila may trace your practices all along. There were the same pretenses for reformation and loyalty, the same as-

persions of the king, and the same grounds of a rebellion."
Davila's *History of the Civil Wars in France* was available in
translation (1678), so that the example of two civil wars, the
recent English one and the more remote French one, were
constantly in mind as warnings. Dryden is certainly right to
draw attention to Davila as a discredit to the Whigs, since he
makes the French civil wars a classical study in the development of the conservative myth by which Dryden himself
hoped to expose the rebels of his time through analogy and
association. Both the Huguenots and the Catholic League are
shown with standard characteristics. The Huguenots are composed of miscellaneous elements, including leaders of noble
families and unsettled or desperate persons, inspired by conscience in some cases, by the love of change in others. They
also use religion to disguise faction and to advance private
ambition or passion. Davila uses a medical figure for the Hu-
guenot plotters who bring on a distemper that is curable not
by lenitives but only by violent purgation. Admiral de Coligny
turned out also to be overwise or subtle; what a pity, as with
Achitophel, that he had to be ruined when he had such impressive ability. The Catholic League is more fully developed
and remarkably anticipates the malcontents of Dryden's poem.
The usual references to the multitude in general, to noble
eminent persons dissatisfied at lack of preferment, to middle-
class townsmen and other simple men of good intentions
genuinely afraid for religion—these might have given Dryden
much of his text. The League makes use of popular, eloquent
men to make everything plausible and entice general support,
and it contains a Zimri-like man in the witty but unstable
Guillaume Sieur de Fervaques. Anticipation of Absalom appears both in the Duke of Guise and in his necessary instrument, Charles Cardinal of Bourbon. The use of charm, easy
access, and graceful behavior to attract popular sympathy suggests the beauty and appeal of Absalom. The Duke of Guise
chooses the Cardinal, since he must have a man of royal blood
with some pretense of right to the throne. His man also is
easy to control; he is a brother of the King of Navarre, a known

enemy of the Huguenots, and as the eldest prince of the blood he could pretend that the crown was rightfully his. The clever and subtle Guise easily deceives this weakling. Again, when Guise returns from splendid victories over the Germans, Paris is alive with pamphlets and discourses against the king, while the city resounds with praise of the Duke who is celebrated in verse and prose as a new David, the second Moses. Finally in 1590, the papal legate Cardinal Gaetano is urged to procure that under a single good and pious king the people may live in peace after so many dangers and calamities.

Dryden's obligations to Montaigne are clear and freely acknowledged. The interest of both men in established law, order, and justice is partly due to the unsettled history of their countries throughout their lives. Even a glance at the violence and bloodshed in 16th-century France suggests that Montaigne was influenced by seeing what it costs mankind to live amid disorder, instability, and violence. If he is the wisest of Frenchmen to Sainte-Beuve, his wisdom lay deep in the search for principles of order in a disordered world. If his hatred of confusion then derives partly from the French civil wars, Montaigne's essays take their place in the long development of the conservative myth and are naturally familiar to all men of cultivation in the age of Dryden. Such men would learn from Montaigne that it is dangerous for individuals to go their own way. He denounces those who follow their personal advantage, and wish to prescribe their own duty. Private judgment is unstable, and if allowed to fix their own duty, men will devour each other. All arrogance or self-assertion, too much talking and contending, too much spirit, mind, or vivacity, too much learning—all end in trouble and in diversity of opinion. Subtlety, curiosity, and knowledge breed malice, whereas society is best preserved by humble obedience and honesty. As goodness is the best quality in a ruler, so is observance of the law best in a subject. Let every man obey the rules of the place where he lives, keep to the worn path, and stay within the common forms without novelty. As for the multitude of mankind in the mass, they are the classical many-headed monster, the vulgar sort unable to judge save by outward appearance, inclined to fly from one extreme to its opposite.

As we should expect, Montaigne uses the standard terms of control in showing how great a danger is freedom. Men need rule, the bridle, bonds, fetters, order, and decorum. Since change in a law will not make a profit as great as the harm done in changing it, Montaigne falls naturally into the medical figure: the cure is worse than the disease, and he sees no point in curing one evil by introducing a greater in its place. In public affairs, therefore, almost any established course is better than change. This follows in turn from the order in the universe, which being unified cannot be changed without loss. Montaigne has given the architectural figure so often encountered one of its clearest expressions. God is the architect of the vast world-frame, which is held together much as any established order must be. Indeed a settled public policy is like a building of many parts so joined together that if one part is displaced, the entire structure must be shaken. The conservative myth then always insists that change will do more harm than good. The architectural figure shows why. It supposes that the public order is a unified whole, with one part built upon another. To change anything, one has to disturb other things built upon it. One cannot remove a bad part without harming another part which is perfectly all right as it is. Therefore one does not remove, cut out, knock down, or destroy anything that is wrong; one merely repairs it, with a patch or buttress, as Dryden says, 802. One simply adds on to the structure something that will enable it to survive well enough, without really changing anything in the original fabric. It is the architectural unity of the political order, then, that makes change impossible without doing more harm than good. The building figure became indispensable in the myth, until Burke himself had no choice but to employ it.

In 1595, not long after the death of Montaigne, Samuel Daniel composed a long verse treatment of the English internal wars of the 14th and 15th centuries, including the strug-

gle between Richard II and Bolingbroke, and Jack Cade's
rebellion. Daniel too reads the world by its need for order:

> Order, how much predominant art thou!
> That if but only thou pretended art,
> How soon deceiv'd mortality doth bow,
> To follow thine as still the better part? (II, stanza 95)

Daniel finds some unrest inevitable in a vigorous state, yet the
expected gains of revolt are never realized "But gain of sorrow,
only change of woe," mere aggravation of "thine own afflic-
tions store." Medical images and the standard figures of fire
describe civil war; the rebels kindle "each other's fire" and
raise "the smoke of innovations." As Bolingbroke rises against
Richard II, fiery, burning portents, comets, and meteors are
seen in the sky, and "red fiery dragons." The rising sun for
Bolingbroke and the setting sun for poor Richard II keep to
the accepted figures for kingship. Fishing in troubled streams,
gambling with innovations as "the hazard of a bad exchange"
and "fair baits" are used, the baits as usual "pretence of common good, the king's ill course." Daniel makes less of religious
pretense as a prelude to revolt than of the political claims for
public benefit, but the motives of individual men are selfishness and desire for private gain. The multitude receives the
classical epithets of "many-headed monster," "th'altering vulgar, apt for changes still," the "unconceiving vulgar sort";
under Jack Cade "of base and vulgar birth" we hear of the
"disordered rage" of the "wayward multitude." The increase
in rebellious strength under Cade reminds us of the formidable size of Dryden's malcontents; the occasion stirs up restless elements, their size grows rapidly, and later on when
York is bold to make his move, his noble followers increase
in number and spite.

Yet Dryden's "loyal few" are also on hand supporting Henry
VI when Warwick "Shakes the whole frame, whereon the
state did stand." They follow in the wake of Richard II, who
has a "sweet aspect" and "mild access," but like Charles-David

he was too kind and generous, so clement that demands on himself were increased—a virtue "Destroying far more love, than it begets." Yet he commands the fidelity of a few men, true even to affliction, "The better few, whom passion made not blind," and as Richard confers with his "small remaining troop" Daniel mentions six of them by name, including Carlisle and Scroop. Similarly when Jack Cade rises, a small element, "the better sort" again, "rather will like their wounds than such a cure."

These antecedents from Rome through France and Renaissance England might have provided Dryden with mythical ingredients enough for his purposes. But in his own lifetime the Puritan rebellion had made the nature of civil war unmistakable, and in 1681 its memory was certain to act as a warning lest the tensions caused by the Popish Plot and Exclusion Bill should break out into violence. The great Clarendon had shown the falsity of rebel elements, especially in 1640 when they pretended only to reform the worst enormities "and dissembled all purposes of removing foundations." He anticipates the cry of Charles-David against petitioners when he exposes both their excess and fraud in the 1640's. He suggests that petitions may become a means to civil war and that they easily lend themselves to the fraud that must precede any revolt. The lessons of that most unhappy time are told in a letter from the Anabaptist William Howard to Charles II in 1656. Clarendon prints the letter, an eloquent summary of mythical teachings. By now it is clear even to fools that political cries of liberty, religion, and reform "are but deceitful baits, by which the easily deluded multitude are tempted to a greedy pursuit of their own ruin." As for Cromwell, Howard had once been deceived, but sees him now "under the painted pretences of sanctity" for what he is, "a prodigious piece of deformity," reminding us of the "Prodigious actions" of Corah. Now God has revealed Cromwell until none is so blind "who does not plainly read treachery, tyranny, perfidiousness, dissimulation, atheism, hypocrisy, and all manner of villainy" written on his heart.

An unfinished poem found in manuscript was published in 1679, twelve years after the death of its author Abraham Cowley. *A Poem on the Late Civil War* contains the expected multiple associations of zeal, pretense, the influence of Hell, the curse of too much wit, the sense of violent natural energies out of control. In "Of Liberty" Cowley had likened the Roman civil war under Caesar to "setting his country on fire." His view of the English upheaval cries out against petitions that stir up "the many-headed rout," against the inevitable lies and deceit of rebel leaders, yet in praise of the loyal few who stand firm against so many. Along with these mythical terms, Cowley hands on for Dryden's use an extended medical figure near the very center of *Absalom and Achitophel's* lesson: those who had fomented civil war were hard put to it to find maladies in the state;

> And then with desperate boldness they endeavor,
> The ague to cure by bringing in a feavor:
> The way is sure to expel some ill no doubt,
> The plague we know, drives all diseases out.
> What strange wild fears did every morning breed,
> Till a strange fancy makes us sick indeed?
> And cowardice did valours place supply,
> Like those that kill themselves for fear to die!

Tory propaganda poems never allowed the analogy with the 1640's to lapse; '81 was redolent of '41, and in such a "loyal song" as "The Downfall of the Good Old Cause" men are warned in this refrain: "Charles the first they murdered / And so they would the other." To make capital of the "martyrdom" of Charles I was evidently not part of Dryden's assignment, but it was sufficiently remarked by other Tory spokesmen. One of Dryden's points in defense of the loyal few, however, achieves support in *Character of a Rebellion* (1681). Dryden's line 873, "And never rebel was to arts a friend," suggests the remark of this Character that in the late civil war colleges and universities were nearly ruined, and would be again under a commonwealth. Some Judas would cry out to let them be sold on behalf of the commonwealth: "Thus it was, and thus it would be again, if they had power." As for the enemies of established government, they are known by law and experience. The law condemns dissenters, sectaries, and Papists as public enemies, and experience shows that in fact dissenters did overthrow the government and kill Charles I. And this they did under the same pretenses as now: of loyalty and duty.

As we near the time of Dryden's composition, the materials of his poem seem almost forced upon him, so much has the myth established itself as an inevitable way of looking at things, the only interpretation of human affairs possible for men of sense and moderation. Indeed the poems and plays before 1681 had already touched on most of the ideas given their classical expression in *Absalom and Achitophel,* and the sea of Tory literature surrounding the poem might have provided a source for Dryden even without a long mythical history back to Rome. The poems written at or near the Restoration make much of the political deception whereby leaders hungry for their own power mislead the multitude. The heroic plays expose the impiety of rebels, the untrustworthiness of "priests of all religions," the folly of too great clemency in the king, the role of pretended religion before revolt, the dangers of freedom of conscience, the hypocrisy and false patriotism of factious leaders, the greater threat from rebellious change than from tyranny, the making things worse by any effort to correct unbalanced power, and the ease with which ambitious men deceive the foolish multitude for their own selfish interest. Mr. Lewis Chase has observed that in the heroic plays no one is ever ambitious except a villain. Such men always pretend to help the king and reform the state, but as Torrismond in *The Spanish Friar* (1681) says, "that's a stale cheat" used by Lucifer, "the first reformer of the skies."

But Dryden's prose dedication of *All for Love* to the Earl of Danby (1677) seems to offer almost a deliberate summary of the main ideas of *Absalom and Achitophel.* Dryden, dividing

himself into two parts that agree like lines of a couplet, declares his abhorrence of the republican, commonwealth system: "Both my nature, as I am an Englishman, and my reason,
as I am a man, have bred in me a loathing to that specious
name of a republic." It offers only the mock appearance of
liberty, since all who are not part of the government are
slaves, "and slaves of a viler note than such as are subjects
to an absolute dominion. . . . If I must serve, the number of
my masters, who were born my equals, would but add to the
ignominy of my bondage." Yet there are "malcontents among
us" who try to persuade people that they would be happier for
a change. These of course, are descended from the devil, "their
old forefather," who tried to seduce men to rebellion by offering them greater freedom. These malcontents cannot be interested in public good, but only in their private benefit, since
a man who changes party often "changes but for himself, and
takes the people for tools to work his fortune." But experience
shows that those who first trouble the waters don't do the
fishing, as those who began the late civil war were crushed by
their own instrument; and so the paradox of selfishness recurs,
and he who loves his life wrongly shall lose it. Since all insur-
rections are founded on pretense of reform, it follows that
"every remonstrance of private men, has the seed of treason
in it; and discourses which are couched in ambiguous terms,
are therefore the more dangerous" as being seditious without
being illegal.

Dryden here states the case against the petitions that
Charles-David was to denounce, 986. Petitions must by definition be a step toward rebellion and must proceed from bad
faith. The petitions had already been forbidden by a proclamation of December 12, 1679, yet the petitions calling on the
king to summon Parliament went on under the guidance of
Shaftesbury-Achitophel, and bombarded the king from all
over the nation. A counter flood of addresses abhorred the petitions, so that the division of "abhorrers" and petitioners
followed the lines of Tory and Whig. The abhorrers assumed,
as the myth in which they believed demanded, that private

men remonstrating in this way must be ill-disposed and must be using the petitions as a cover for some deeper design or plot—must be enemies of order and loyalty.

Throughout the Tory literature surrounding Dryden, as Godfrey Davies has shown, three main themes were repeated: the danger of civil war, the inherence of sedition in dissent, and the benevolence of the king. The smear words go on as before, now concentrated and assured more than ever, as the Whig cause declines and the Tories get the upper hand. The cry is against novelty, sedition, dissent, ambition, self-interest, imposture, and the known father of these and all lies—the devil. To expose deception in the late 17th century, one almost had to draw on the serpent-devil-falsehood connections of the Old Testament, as seen for example in a work like *Naboth's Vineyard* (1679). In turn, all self-seeking, headstrong, ambitious individuals were bound to clash with the laws of a reasonably organized society, aimed at curbing their energy. In moving against order, such men once more proceeded in a standard way. As Dryden was to ask in his *Vindication of the Duke of Guise* (1683), "Have not all rebels always sung the same song?" The Tory indictment then, drawing like Dryden on the conservative myth as well as contributing to round out its doctrine, found the same steps to rebellion as the Old Testament had shown in the troubles of King David. Flattery of the people, promises of redress, charges against the government, religious guile on the part of leaders bent on their own power—such are the necessary means to the offense beyond forgiveness.

One of the compulsions of the conservative myth is to show why deviations from itself, from what is so right and sensible, can occur. They occur because of wicked leaders and because of their victims. The leaders are false deceivers, they are mistaken in their ambition and self-will, or at best are men who misdirect their energy and ability. Their victims are the multitude, foolish and unstable, or misguided individuals like Absalom, resentful of some grievance about which nothing can be done save at a price too high for any single person to demand. In Absalom's case the price was disruption of the social order, betrayal of his father, rebellion against the king. Still he would not have rebelled save for Achitophel, whose shadow lurks behind everything to be deplored by the age of Dryden, back to the distrust of rhetoric and eloquence. Men are, to be sure, always inclined to see the opposition as wicked; we have to see the other side as knaves against transparently honest men like ourselves. Then too, we do not blame the nature of things when a hoped-for change fails to bring the good results expected; we feel cheated or deceived, and denounce someone's falsity for misleading us, not thinking to blame our own illusions as the instrument of deception, even though the conservative myth is always there to warn us against them. Falsity in any event there must be, practiced by us on ourselves or by someone else out to advance himself. Hobbes and other enemies of the arts of persuasion see Achitophel therefore in such means of deception as rhetoric, eloquence, and figurative language, used by men to persuade others of things not to their interest, but to the selfish ends of the persuader.

We come then inevitably to the word "plot," which like the word "design" was used for many purposes and after 1678 was indispensable to both sides in the raging political conflict. The atmosphere of intrigue had carried into the Restoration generally, and *Hudibras* makes a good deal of fun of the need for seeing Machiavellian plots, deep designs, "false alarms of Plots" on every hand. The whole idea of "plot" is so much in the air of Dryden's world that it seems necessary to ask, when anything bad happens, whether there were not some scheme, some double-dealing falsity behind it. In *Annus Mirabilis,* after the fire of London, Charles II tells his stricken people that the catastrophe was an immediate chastisement from the hand of God, and not the result of a plot—as if it would have to be one or the other. In *The Spanish Friar* (IV, 2) the attempt to involve Bertram with the mob makes Raymond say dryly, "So now we have a plot behind the plot." And in *Absalom and Achitophel,* "plot" moves in and out of the poem—there are sixteen uses of the word, with no hint that the narrator is exaggerating.

The size and scope of the conspiracy is never explained in the poem; it is only stated, its true nature only hinted at in 108–17, showing how the multitude had swallowed it all, just as it was. Actually it seems to have been less the rebellion of Monmouth and Shaftesbury that attracted the people than the fantastic tales of Oates and his Popish Plot. The populace were indignant, obsessed by the Plot, and ready to believe anything said against the allegedly guilty ones, including even the queen herself. Without clearly defining the term, Dryden uses the "plot" as a binding element in making transitions from one part of his view of the conspiracy to another. In this way he suggests how much the attempted Whig revolution really owed to the Popish Plot, or any plot, to keep itself going. Nothing but plot unified or held it together, apart from Achitophel's "arts" or "successful arts," 402, 289. Certainly the use made of "plot" in the first 750 lines of the poem suggests that Dryden saw how the attempted rebellion would have collapsed, perhaps never have been tried at all, without the continued influence of the Plot to keep the discontented elements aroused. References to the Plot give a form of continuity to the poem, as the Plot itself gave coherence to the king's enemies.

The poem's first notice of plots, 82–84, establishes their contemporary, and accepts their mythical importance:

> The Good Old Cause reviv'd, a plot requires:
> Plots, true or false, are necessary things,
> To raise up commonwealths, and ruin kings.

When the narrator comes to "that Plot, the nation's curse," 108, it is not clear from what it is supposed to begin. "Hence," as referring to lines 104–7, may mean that the Plot began from the operations of the Catholic clergy against the existing legal restraints upon Catholics, in which they had the sympathy of the Anglican clergy, priests of all religions being the same, 99. The Plot becomes the nation's curse, made to seem worse than it was, both sides going to extremes and swearing that it was true, swearing to death that it was false. The multitude as befits the animal-like nature of the crowd, believed in the Plot without discriminating between what might have been its grain of truth and its heavier mixture of lies. Succeeding ages will no doubt remain in the same dilemma of extremes.

At 134 the Plot has failed for want of common sense, but the line serves as transition into the Plot's consequences, suggested by images of disease, heat, overflowing, and boiling. After portraying "several Factions" and their prime mover, Achitophel, the narrator uses (208) the "wished occasion of the Plot" to get back from the analysis of Achitophel to the consequences of the Plot, arousing the people. The passage has contemporary reference to Shaftesbury, who seemed with the Whigs to be in retreat before Oates appeared. The Popish Plot gave Shaftesbury a new chance, but there is no real evidence that he had connived with Oates to begin with, since Oates had exonerated James II and had even implied that James was to be a victim of the Plot. Since James was the Whigs' real target, Oates was hardly under Shaftesbury's rule at first. Yet Oates was the great stroke of luck Shaftesbury needed and "wish'd," as the narrator says; he went on to make the most of it. Although it would have made Achitophel seem more "false," the poem does not imply that Shaftesbury first set on Oates. The poem therefore stays within the known facts, and within the needs of the myth.

At 275 Achitophel is describing the king's decline, "Betray'd by one poor plot to public scorn"; capital letters are not used for this plot, as apparently for the Popish Plot. If this is the same Plot as before, however, it is well used here to increase the sense of the king's being weakened by it; to build up a show of strength for the king's enemies, since so much of their strength did in fact come from the Plot. At 393 Achitophel will ply the king with "new plots" added to the Popish Plot, except that the new ones may represent genuine intrigue. This keeps to the notion of the Plot or "plots" as a danger to the king at any time, and essential to his foes. At line 466, Achitophel shows that the king's life must seem to be threatened, exposed "to plots, from seeming friends, and secret foes," leaving him no security in any quarter. Again "plot" is an instrument of policy; here it means a pretended threat against the king to justify one of the measures against him, a real "plot." This is to take up arms on pretense of securing the king's protection against any "plot" there might be, except the one now being carried out to seize his person. At 490 "popularly prosecute the Plot" is a transition from Absalom to the other malcontents. The Plot is used to rally and unite all sorts of discordant elements, and in the poem's structure to move from its particular exploiters to the more general elements attracted by it.

Lines 517–18, where the London rabble see an Ethnic plot begun and will not be surpassed in plotting by Jebusites, are less clear in function. They could mean the tendency of the Popish Plot to develop offshoots from the original stock of lies. Such a thing as the Meal Tub Plot would show the infinite possibilities once the Plot era was under way. Some forged papers exposing Catholic treasons were hidden in the bottom of a meal tub by the maid of Mrs. Collier, an accomplice of Thomas Dangerfield. Coming in 1679, the Meal Tub was supposed to confirm all the suspicions aroused by the Popish Plot. It was sometimes called the "Presbyterian Plot," as being a scheme of the Papists to blame the Presbyterians for what was only another of their own "plots." In any case it seemed to confirm the Popish Plot itself, and inspired many of the petitions so annoying to the king. In time this Meal Tub Plot, being an even more grotesque fabrication than its original model, became a synonym for any sham plot. If 517 refers to it, the reference functions to show the constant need of the king's foes to rely on "plots" to bolster their cause.

For over 100 lines now there is no mention of "plot" or the Plot. At Corah, we hear that the rest of the rebels are best forgot. To speak of them "Would tire a well-breathed witness of the Plot," 631. Use of the Plot here recalls how reliant all

these elements are upon it. Who then should tell what the rest
of these people were? One of the Plot's witnesses certainly,
whose lies had already been of so much profit to the malcontents. The reference to the mnemonic power of Oates (651)
and his incredible "plots" suggests that by now everyone
knows the Plot for the tissue of lies that it always was. And
its fatal, capricious consequences are again implied in the narrator's reference to himself (670–71), suggesting in "whet"
the tragic losses and sacrifice of life caused by the brazen falsehoods of Corah. The narrator says that anyone trying to discredit him, were he in Corah's place, would whet his memory
"To make him an appendix of my plot." He would whet
memory indeed, like a sharp knife or executioner's axe, so
much used with dreadful effect as a result of Oates' "memory,"
which kept supplying new evidence not brought up before
because he had momentarily "forgotten" it, and now "remembered" it.

The poem is now ready to turn from wrong to right. Lines
751–52 are placed strategically:

> Thus in a pageant show a plot is made,
> And peace itself is war in masquerade.

The "plot" here refers to Absalom's own intention to make
capital of his great popular success, just reported in the poem.
The lines precede the verse essay on innovation, and they bind
the poem's lesson against change with one of the main reasons
for distrusting it: namely, the means usually taken to achieve
it. Just before the king speaks (921–22), we return to the
function of the Popish Plot as necessary to the king's enemies,
seen now by the loyal few as improved "by hireling witnesses"
—that is, liars. The lines converging on the king are heavily
concentrated, and 929–30 are used to draw two motives together: the king's enemies and the use they have made of the
Plot:

> That false Achitophel's pernicious hate
> Had turn'd the Plot to ruin Church and State:

Here Plot is both the Popish one and Achitophel's own plot which had grown out of it or had used it. The Popish Plot itself was supposed or intended to ruin Church and State; now Achitophel has actually turned it toward their ruin.

The king himself cries (985–86) to be free of "plots and treasons"; he has reason enough to be preserved from "plots," but now it seems to him that the petitioners are a worse pest than the fraud which had united his foes for so long. The king's final remark on the Plot (1012–17) shows once more its importance to his enemies: The witnesses will swear against each other, "Till viper-like their mother Plot they tear." By its own nature the Plot will destroy itself; it is the mother, in that the entire revolt against the king was born from and sustained by the Popish Plot. When the witnesses turn against each other, the king may say that "on my foes, my foes shall do me right." The king is right, as it is the need of the poem to show that he is right. Therefore Dryden has used the Plot in the poem's meaning and structure as transitional tissue, a binding, recurring theme.

Finally, who are the king's enemies, "the malcontents of all the Israelites," assembled by political intrigue, religious bias, ambition and popular fear aroused for special ends? The king's enemies are great in number and variety like those in the Bible who followed Absalom, a mixture of the deceived, the lovers of novelty, the ambitious, the fishers in troubled waters. While the poem's rhetoric demands that the malcontents be made to seem a vast, threatening danger, there was certainly a point in the history of Monmouth-Absalom's fortunes when he seems to have rallied a formidable number of the restless, the zealous and ambitious to his cause. On his return to England in 1679 without leave, he struck from his arms the bar sinister showing his irregular descent; Dryden was to expose the futility of this gesture in the brilliant opening lines of *Absalom and Achitophel*. On being ordered out of London by the king, Monmouth made his great popular progress through the country in August, 1680. Crowds of 20,000 met him, and every stop on his way seemed eager to outdo all the rest in enthusiastic reception. Most of the largest assemblies were at pretended amusements like races or athletic contests, like the Cavalier gatherings under Cromwell that made him issue a proclamation forbidding horse races for eight months. Having the London mob on his side as well, Shaftesbury-Achitophel had arranged these demonstrations for Monmouth to extend his appeal and to show the size and strength of his party until its cause must appear irresistible and opposition simply useless or foolish. The lower classes seemed especially taken in, as required by their mythical weakness.

If the "better sort" were less carried away, they had ample outlet for their dislike of the king through such a group as The Green Ribbon Club, almost as influential in its heyday as the Jacobin Club a century later in France. Sir John Pollock's analysis of this club might stand as a prose summary of Dryden's review of the malcontents, 491–542. It contained nearly every Whig of any note among its members of all classes and characters. It included scoundrels and statesmen, "pious enthusiasts and tired profligates, the remains of the Cromwellian party, the forerunners of the Revolution, poets, aldermen, country gentlemen, assassins, bound together by a common league of animosity against Charles II and his government." With all of these and the "Solymean rout" and mass enthusiasm for Monmouth, Shaftesbury could boast that his party greatly outnumbered the king's. The 1681 elections returned a large majority of Exclusionists, so that although Dryden is writing after the triumph of Charles II against the 1681 Parliament, he makes effective rhetorical use of what had at one time seemed the overwhelmingly greater force on the rebel side.

His account of the opposition is deliberately heterogeneous and formless, shading into images of animals, beasts of prey, or monstrous growths in pack, herd, and hydra. The uncertain allegiance on both sides in the civil war is implied here for the vast, amorphous wrong side which could be anything or everything from anywhere in society. This will stand effectively against the loyal few, about whom there is no question, who need merely to be listed to declare what they are and always will be. In addition to the main passage summarizing the malcontents, the poem makes a number of vague references implying great extent or variety in the conspiracy beyond the poet's present scope or power to delineate. This device suggests endless stretches of popular enmity to the king, a mass of formless disunited ingredients. In 142–49 three couplets begin with "some" and in 211 we hear of "list'ning crowds," in 289 of "all sorts of men" misled by Achitophel. Various uncertain suggestions of many adherents come in with "others," "all the haranguers," the "titles and names" too tedious for rehearsal, "the rest who better are forgot," "friends of every sort," "powerful engines," and "a numerous faction," 919. The actual malcontents of 491–542 begin somewhat astonishingly with "the best." In the myth as it grows from Rome onward, there is seldom a hint that civil war may come of honest and sincere men rising against evils greater than the revolt which is required to correct them; the myth has to say that any tyranny is better than civil war. Now in order to seem impartial with a cool Horatian fairness, the poet admits that the best of the malcontents were only mistaken patriots, some of them being in fact princes. But after this concession, the expected ingredients follow with individuals selfishly interested in their own good; the money savers, preachers of economy; the rabble rousers, eloquent demagogues, and others swayed by political theory against kingship; the London rabble as a separate political force; Presbyterian clergymen and their followers, mostly tradesmen who wished to see the country dominated by priests and parliament —these elements made the loudest disturbance.

Then follow the holy Puritans, victims of destructive enthusiasm, "the ultra-Protestants" as Oliver Elton called them, fanatical members of sects imagining themselves inspired. *Hudibras* had been fierce in ridiculing the factions of dreaming saints and true blue Protestants, showing them as selfish frauds bent on their own advantage. Here at 529–30 the "dreaming saints" are a "host" as of a heavenly group of angels or blessed, blessed in their own estimation that is, making the word "host" highly sarcastic and disdainful. ". . . the true old enthusiastic breed" is full of contempt, with "breed" suggesting anything but heavenly hosts in its note of a prolific mass of animals. Then comes a great "herd" of mindless but voluble persons, who had no reason for whatever they believed and took unexamined the Anglican and Calvinistic notions that came their way. Here is another example of Dryden's economy in using a good line of his own more than once: *Annus Mirabilis,* 548, has "And thinks too little what they found too much." Referring to the prejudice of those who held a religious view just because it was English, the passage in *Absalom and Achitophel* (533–40) recalls the only half-line of the poem (87), where the superior historical claim of the Catholics seems also to denigrate the Anglicans accepting the local religion, "their father's God," 536. The half-line "And theirs the native right" has poetic precedent in Virgil, Cowley, Oldham, and Marvell, and as used it is striking and final, something having to be admitted as undebatable, with nothing to be said further, nothing to be added by rhyme or completed couplet statement. Now in "far more numerous was the herd of such," herd is directly disdainful with no ambiguity as in "host." As Halifax says, the world being fools and knaves, "those few who have sense or honesty sneak up and down single, but never go in herds."

Finally below all these, 541–42,

> . . . a whole Hydra more
> Remains, of sprouting heads too long to score.

The malcontents may number among their best a few mistaken men of honor, but in the end they are to be dismissed in a common image of monstrous, proliferating evil. This being true, when the poem turns to the essay on innovation its lesson cannot be other than the inevitable one, that change is always discredited in its result by the means taken to achieve it. More than a century and a half later Thomas Carlyle was to denounce the democratic process as necessarily leading away from the truth, as Dryden shows the makeup of rebellion as necessarily producing change for the worse. To adapt Carlyle's powerful words, no matter what "overwhelming majorities and jubilant unanimities and universalities" vote for rebellion, 752–810 of Dryden's poem answer simply, as the narrator has maintained throughout: the thing is not so, it is otherwise than so, and "the whole of Adam's posterity" to the contrary notwithstanding, it never can be so. The greater the magnitude and talent of the malcontents then, the better for the poem's lesson. Yet in detail now and then, the narrator's contempt lessens our sense of a thing immensely dangerous and impressive in its scope and power. Here again if we distinguish between Dryden and the poem's narrator, the latter may be carried away by his prejudice and find himself too scornful from time to time. Dryden's line in the poem is best served by a most impressive construction of the wrong side, showing at last that no matter what its magnitude and resources, it must fail before the nature of things and the king's power.

CHAPTER 9

The Essay on Innovation

A common objection holds that *Absalom and Achitophel* changes character at line 752, and from having been a satire exposing falsity it now becomes a different kind of poem. We must see the poem as a whole, however, as we must see *The Essay on Man* in larger terms than as a mass of brilliant and familiar quotations. If we take a fresh look at lines 752 ff., the poem should appear a greater artistic success as the interdependence of its parts reveals itself. The essay on innovation concentrates the aim to discredit rebellion and to recommend obedience. The poem has kept to public affairs, and has used the conservative myth to unify its action and the narrator's commentary. While it is easily divisible into a number of small parts, these are kept to an aim that carries us straight into lines 752–810. The rational progression so grateful to an Augustan mind proceeds here from particular to general. What follows 810 as to the king and the loyal few applies affirmatively from good example what has for so long emerged from bad example. The essay on innovation then looks both ways toward good and evil, each of these opposites illustrating the truths summarized in the essay; this is not a detachable fragment but is integral to the poem's structure.

It seems that men are destroyed more by wishes that are fulfilled and by prayers that are answered, than by doing as best they can within things as they are. The myth declares this ancient theme as well in exposing the illusion of change

in the political and social order. Up to 752 the poem has
shown that revolt against the established order is only an attractive fraud—alluring, but a fraud nonetheless, based on
deception of ourselves, on deception by someone else who
may himself be deceived like Monmouth-Absalom, or on deception by an unprincipled knave bent on satisfying his own
ambition. If this is the way all revolt must go, the essay on
innovation declares what must be thought as a result. The
desire of change attaches itself to what is always wrong. No
amount of argument will alter this, no theoretical defense can
justify it, and to argue back and forth will only leave us suspended, inconclusive.

The familiar dualism of Dryden's age allows royal government to function in two ways: by social contract subject to
popular will, or by unquestioned royal sovereignty. There
are objections on both sides. Royal sovereignty leaves the
people defenseless against tyranny, while popular control
makes a slave of the king and destroys the security of property
and public order. The device of setting up opposing views
so that neither seems acceptable leads to taking things as
they are. The reader is left no choice but to go on in the prevailing order, especially when the controlling images used
by the poet show that change is certain to be for the worse.

The essay on innovation, then, does not establish any coherent theory of politics, but it continues the poetic reliance
on order. It declares for the king in his mythical role, as having the qualities that a king is supposed to have. "The gallantries" or other faults of David-Charles are then irrelevant,
save as they have given a chance to declare against illegitimacy
as demanded by the myth. The reasons for going on with the
existing scheme of things are poetic reasons, offered in place
of a fully developed rational argument as to the right political
system. Wearisome theorizing disappears before the myth:
Why change? There is nothing in it.

The essay seems to divide itself into three parts, 753–58,
759–94, 795–810. The third section ends by returning to the
medical figure of 756. The opening cry "O foolish Israel," is

a text for what follows; the essay shows wherein their being foolish consists. There are two ways of looking at the political question. "What shall we think?" (759) introduces a review of possible attitudes. Is the right to rule given properly without limits or question to a king? The narrator does not remind his audience that as Englishmen they quite willingly gave "their native sway" (760) to Charles II in unquestionable terms. Clarendon had included the proclamation of Charles as king, which acknowledged him as "lineally, justly and lawfully next heir of the blood royal of this realm" and therefore "undoubted king; and thereunto we do most humbly and faithfully submit and oblige ourselves, our heirs and posterity forever." The question will not be answered by referring to what the English have in fact done; it will simply be left where it was in favor of the myth. The further question now is, if a king has power only on trust, this must have been clear when kings were first made. But the contrary was in fact clear, and the first agreement had power to bind all posterity, just as God has permitted the sin of Adam to affect all subsequent human beings. The right of kings to rule governs every man permanently whether he actually consented to it or not. Otherwise the people command the king and not he the people, "kings are subjects, and all subjects kings" as objected in John Crowne's *The Miseries of Civil War*. The rights of property cease, and the Renaissance theory demanding that men be enabled to enjoy their own possessions is denied; no one is then secure "of private right," 779.

The essay now turns to observe that popular government is as much subject to error as rule by the few. A king may be faultless, yet condemned by the "common cry," 783. The rout is fickle with no real standard to rely on. Parliaments are also unreliable, susceptible to losing their minds. If they are free to do as they please, not only kings but government itself will be left to the chaos of nature. At this point the essay abandons discussion of the proper seat of power. It has constructed a dilemma between royal and popular control which it cannot resolve. It falls with relief into the conservative myth. Even if a king does obtain power from the people, the narrator says, it remains imprudent to change the established order because the change will always be for the worse. Innovation is fatal, and the architectural image for something established that must not give way in essentials follows, with the religious sanction of something sacred in "our ark," 804. To do more than change a few details, to alter the existing order as such, is necessarily the work of selfish rebels trying to get control of church and state for ignoble ends. ". . . rebels who base ends pursue" does not mean only a certain kind of rebels, as distinguished from those who pursue good ends. It summarizes all rebels, for by definition rebels pursue base ends. Rebellion must proceed from base motives and has always done so; it could not exist alongside motives of genuine patriotism, although patriotism is one of the excuses of a rebel for his behavior.

The mythical dread of change here recalls some features of metaphysical optimism which held that removing a given evil in the world brings on a worse evil by its absence. The optimist tells the individual not to confuse his view of the world as a single part of a general harmony with the view that commands the whole. The order in the world being maintained by certain laws, things are not referred to the individual self but to the general order. Individual assertion is dangerous for metaphysical optimism then, as for the essay on innovation, which avoids the religious note of the optimist. The narrator relies on the medical figure, and does not say that we will make things worse if we try to improve the works of God. He involves all rebels pursuing their base ends in a paradox from which there is no escape: they must ruin everything by trying to change anything. The last couplet (809–10) returns to the question in 755–56:

> Did ever men forsake their present ease,
> In midst of health imagine a disease

and the answer is yes, men have been such fools as to mistake their own health for illness, and in turn to aggravate their real political troubles by trying to cure them through fundamental change.

Before looking further into the poem's controlling images as illustrated in the essay on innovation, we must be sure that such details of a poem's art or manner are in harmony with the poet's intention and with the needs of the particular genre he is using. The medical and architectural images invite our study then since they are integral to the myth which it is the poem's destiny to express; they are proper to satire, which must expose error, disease, and must offer a positive ideal, the established order resembling a building in this case. The medical image derives especially from satire, its nature and demands; the architectural suggests conservation itself, and *Absalom and Achitophel* fuses them together in a rare adaptation of means to ends. The effect of the poem is to embrace the conservative myth while giving it a classical expression.

Again the images must be so used as to sustain the idea of order, and they are in fact able to support the centrality of order by showing both danger and stability. Medicine stands for what must be solved or dealt with—architecture for what is to be sustained, strengthened, and preserved, but never fundamentally changed. These figures have the added virtue of being familiar and so able to carry just those associations and implications which the poem needs. They become central to the poem's message and its rhetoric. They show Dryden's artistic skill in using their commonplaceness to work toward the unity of the poem.

The common remarks as to Dryden's imagery are useful here; as Ian Jack shows, Dryden keeps his idiom close to the subject and avoids a great wealth of witty images that are more ingenious than appropriate where they occur. Unlike Shelley's practice in *Prometheus Unbound*, "the operations of the human mind" nourish *Absalom and Achitophel* less than physical structures, bodily actions, or effects. Much that goes beyond this seems drawn from the ordinary, expected poetical counter of the day. For example, the opening lines of *Religio Laici* draw on a common usage in late 17th-century sermons, with reason equaling the moon, revelation the sun. The analogy between a political leader and the pilot of a ship used for Achitophel, the "daring pilot in extremity" (159) has a long history besides many contemporary uses. Plutarch makes effective use of the comparison in the life of Caesar; Rome without a government is like a ship without a pilot, and it was sad to behold the city given up by her pilots and left to run upon any rock in her way. The pilot figure for a skillful governor who guides the ship of state safely to port recalls the function of prudence or wisdom in artistic criticism. Prudence and reason are not only the curb or bridle upon an artist; they act also as a ship's rudder, an anchor, or a sober pilot.

Plutarch uses another set of figures that depend on fire, and in time comparisons based on heat, flame, combustion of various degrees or stages passed into the common stock of available figures. The use of fire to suggest uncontrolled energy or force may have owed something to the doctrine that fire preceded other elements out of which the universe was made. Lucan 2.8–9 refers to the fire giving way to the creator's effort to establish order out of chaos. Fire was thus early associated with disorder. Plutarch uses fire for anger, for rebellion, and Tacitus speaks of the flames of discord, burning impatience, flaming ardor. As the conservative myth develops, fire and related images become standard and we hear constantly of the fire of rebellion, the firebrands of sedition, incendiary or inflammatory factions, the tinder and sparks that become unquenchable flames, party feeling and zeal.

The many uses of fire and its kindred meanings in *Absalom and Achitophel* keep to the associations of destructive force or energy uncontrolled. The disastrous London fire of 1665 did much to make such uses inevitable in a poem written to idealize order. Like the plague and the general omnipresence of disease that invited the medical figures of speech, the immediate experience of uncontrolled fire intensifies fear of the heat of rebellion. Dryden's passages on the fire of London in

Annus Mirabilis (stanzas 212–59) show powerfully the destructive force of energy out of control, how the fire begins weakly and obscurely, then gradually asserting itself and aided by the wind it becomes a "wanton fury," a "dire contagion" and even a hydra that lifts up a hundred heads. The prodigious, ominous force rises in the mean dwellings of the poor and sweeps on to devour palaces and temples; in this it resembles rebellion which begins among the humble and spreads throughout church and state. But as fire can be an image of rebellion, it can seem in fact a punishment for treason and revolt. The poem being written to unite king and people and not to recall past offenses, this note of punishment is not stressed as it was later on in *Britannia Rediviva* (1688). The fire is used rather to idealize the king still more, and in stanzas 240–43 Charles II is shown as brave and wise in fighting the fire, as he is similarly noble in opposing rebellion in *Absalom and Achitophel*. In 1665 he fights fire and offers generous bounty; in 1681 he shames rebellion by his clement, forbearing paternalism both to his subjects and to his son.

The first hint of the poem's use of the fire comparison shows in the delightful opening passage, when at line 8 the monarch of Israel "His vigorous warmth did variously impart." At the outset, "warmth" suggests energy "promiscuously" used. Monmouth-Absalom is himself the result of energy out of control, born outside the law; so also is rebellion in any form throughout the poem. With few exceptions from this point to the end of the poem's analysis of the evil side, the associations of warmth or fire are used to condemn or to warn against danger. Lines 37–38 do in fact seem to excuse Absalom's behavior as a very young man, joining the medical and heat images as already tried in *The Conquest of Granada*, Part II, where Boabdelin's jealousy boiled over:

> Some warm excesses which the law forbore,
> Were construed youth that purg'd by boiling o'er.

Later the restless energy of the Jews is implied in their "melting" down the idol that is the king, whom they had set up, 65–

66; we hear that "these were random bolts," 67. Bolts of light-
ning are the prime example in nature of free energy with immense destructive power. The Jebusite Gods are "burnt like
common wood" (97), but this has less hint of danger than 98,
"this set the heathen priesthood in a flame." The burning
zeal of religious fanatics is always dangerous, especially when
they are priests, much distrusted throughout the poem.

The Plot and its consequences invite the comparison, in
tone like a Homeric simile, of 136–41: "For as when raging
fevers boil the blood." The sense of something heated to the
point of overflowing describes the factions fermented by the
Plot, that "work up to foam." Heat is joined to ferment, a
related suggestion of surging force. Again, Achitophel himself, 156, destroys his body by uncontrolled energy, the assertion of "a fiery soul." Lines 307–8 seem to excuse Absalom,
while they permit him to exercise what is a danger in others,
the fire of ambition. Desire of power is a glory in God,

> . . . and when men aspire
> 'T is but a spark too much of heavenly fire.

The medical and fire images join again at 333–34:

> If David's rule Jerusalem displease,
> The Dog-star heats their brains to this disease.

The uncontrolled nature of the multitude emerges in 459,
the advice to

> Leave the warm people no considering time;

this is allied to 489, "To head the faction while their zeal was
hot"—that is, before their zeal comes under sober control.
"Hot Levites headed these" refers to the old enemies, the
zealous priests who are "hot" with uncontrolled zeal. So also
is the heat of Shimei a danger in one sense, 621: "Cool was
his kitchen, tho' his brains were hot." This frugality was
necessary to the Jews:

> For towns once burnt such magistrates require
> As dare not tempt God's providence by fire.   (624–25)

The reference to the fire of 1665 and to the civil war suggests that the couplet is literal: London must not wage civil war again so as to invite the wrath of God; it does indeed require a cool magistrate.

The last direct use of fire (684–85) concerns the ambition of Absalom and so stays within the danger to be feared:

> Impatient of high hopes, urg'd with renown,
> And fir'd with near possession of a crown.

The poem now abandons all use of warmth or fire comparisons in the section devoted to the king and his followers. Many of its implications are carried by references to madness or anger. The essay on innovation makes no use of fire, and the loyal few clearly have no faults to demand its use. On the contrary, as Amiel shows, when chief of parliament he guarded reason and "their passion cooled," 903. The final proverb listed in *Ludus Literarum* (1674) utters this wholesome warning: "Who follows truth too close at the heels, she may chance dash out his teeth." This note of caution governs the immense variety of medical images that lie everywhere on the surface, especially in satire. In the cure of disease, beware lest the means of cure only make things worse. Medical terms for comparison rest on the analogy going back to ancient times between the functions of the human body and other activities—especially political. The state resembles the body, the family, the solar system, a machine, a beehive, a ship, or a building. From these possibilities Dryden settles upon two for the controlling images in *Absalom and Achitophel:* the body and a building. These figures are common in the work of his predecessors and contemporaries, and are traceable from Aristotle, Plutarch, Virgil, and the Romans, through Dante and the Renaissance.

Medical imagery might suggest itself to Dryden's age through a general view of sorrowing human affairs, or from simply observing how much actual bodily suffering mankind then endured. If Thomas Browne is typical in seeing the world not as an inn but a hospital, we should expect a sense of illness, misery, and death, with poets conveying in their

images an acceptance of gloomy reality as it is. Anyone responding to the pervasive influences to see things as they are,
would have to take note of the vast amount of physical misery
then endured in the world. The wounds and sores left from
intermittent warfare, the results of diseases almost unretarded
must have made the flesh and its illness seem inseparable. The
practice of medicine, quack or honest, could do little but let
blood, or prescribe emetics and cathartics—the purges that
are constantly referred to. Witness the ghastly death-bed torments of Charles II himself, for added horrors. So much physical suffering, curable by little beyond old nostrums and su-
perstitions, helps to account for general reference to the body
and to provide all literary forms with a common stock of images drawn from its concerns.

The neoclassical ideal of pleasure and instruction also invites the figure of medicine. In religion the sinner is ill and
must be improved by moral precepts; in politics, the rebel or
malcontent is diseased or causes disease in the state, to be
cured by purging; in literature, the ideal of instruction may
be realized, as Horace said, by giving the honey of pleasure
to make palatable the medicine of improvement, always being
careful, as Milton warns, not to insert poisonous principles in
sweet pills. If, as Rapin says, poetry must render pleasant that
which is wholesome, it must rid itself of formal defects, such
as loquacity, which John Spencer describes as "the fistula of
the mind." The higher forms of epic and tragedy, we are
assured by Rymer and Le Bossu, must be capable of acting like
skillful physicians, not only purging, curing, and improving
mankind, but observing for general edification the order,
harmony, and beauty of the works of Providence. As for satire,
everything expected of it seems naturally to have turned on
its medical function. Satire always had found analogy its most
obvious method, and Ben Jonson, whose figures in *Timber*
rely heavily on the physical side of life, compares the corrective writer to a physician who has to use sharp medicines or
corrosives; what is lawful in curing the body is equally good
for cure of the mind.

Human vice and folly may take a great variety of forms, just as the number of possible bodily diseases is endless. But there is no mischief more miserable or shameful, Charron says, than the commotion brought on by turbulent and tumultuous spirits whose vain conceit and opinionative zeal disturbs the public peace. Discontent that leads to sedition or rebellion usually comes of supposed or imaginary wrongs, and the results in actual experience are endlessly compared to plague, ulcer, fever, dire contagion, headache, dizziness, dropsy, inner rottenness and putrefaction, ague, itching scabs, or windy stomachs that hinder proper bodily functions. The whole analogy is drawn together by a writer against the Puritan rebellion who describes the diseased Parliament of 1648. He wishes to make his last will "insomuch that I am desperately sick," poisoned throughout the body. His title page, like so many others in the 17th century, summarizes his message: *The Last Will and Testament of that monstrous, bloody, tyrannical, cruel and abominable Parliament dissembled at Westminister, May 15, 1648. Being desperately sick in every part of its ungodly members. . . .*

Rebellion we are told is certainly the worst of diseases in society, and violent means are needed to cure it. Yet most other human complaints will only grow worse from attempts to remedy them. In fact, rebellion itself shows this, in that it comes of discontent over something supposed to be wrong in public affairs which should become better after rebellion has succeeded in changing the abuse. But experience shows that the effort to cure by rebellious change only brings on worse forms of the many diseases already complained of. Leaders of change and reform either fail to see this, or they conceal it from their deluded followers. They make the future seem attractive and hopeful, instead of admitting that anything good will come only from medicine that is bitter and unpleasant to taste, and will in the end offer little reward but itself, like personal health, virtue, or controlled behavior. Halifax sees that even the best remedies are melancholy to contemplate, and Glanvill allows the physician to relieve one disease by causing another that is only less desperate. Even the effort to improve literary expression away from the obscurity of too many words too figuratively used, may result in a worse obscurity from too few words too narrow in meaning. Anyone who thinks too much about what is wrong is like Butler's character "A Medicine-Taker"; he tampers with his health until he has finally spoiled it. And let the ignorant reformer, who cannot shave his father's beard without cutting his throat, realize that the phlebotomy, laxative, or emetic called for in order to get rid of trouble is likely to make him wish that he had left the general condition as it was. As we should expect of a father on one hand, and of someone writing in the "Advice" genre on the other, Francis Osborne shares the traditional caution. In 1656, when Cromwell had long since replaced the king, Osborne offers this *Advice to a Son:* "Contract not the common distemper, incident to vulgar brains, who still imagine more ease from some *untried government,* than that they lie under. . . . If happy for the present, 'tis no better than madness to endeavour a change; if but indifferently well, folly."

The myth discredits the enemy by some strange process of reasoning. In Dryden's *Tyrannick Love* (1669), IV, 1, Maximin complains, "You forbid me change (the sick man's ease)." If the sick man is he who most desires change, the desire of change in a nation is a sign of illness; the move to rebellion turns out to be worse, however, than the illness which inspires it. A sick organism desires change; England desires change; therefore England is sick. Whether by this or whatever process of reasoning, the myth found the medical image indispensable. The political body's disease must be left untreated, since the cure will be worse still. Once the comparison of political trouble with bodily disease became one of the commonplaces of Renaissance thought, anyone could be made to see the dangers of radical cure. So Dryden profits from a notion having become axiomatic and lets it work for him in the poem. The attempt to cure human illness was in fact likely to make it worse in the 17th century; therefore the myth could use this particular excuse for not changing things because the analogy between the body politic and human, contained just enough truth to enforce conviction—cure really is worse than disease.

The inconsistent response to cure in the myth shows in Dryden too, as he defines his own role in the poem. As a cure, rebellion is worse than any disease; as a disease, rebellion demands whatever cure will remove it, always with the hope to be sure, that surgery of radical violence will not be required. The last paragraph of Dryden's "To The Reader" of *Absalom and Achitophel* applies the medical figure to a satirist who may amend "vices by correction," just as a physician cures disease by prescribed remedies. The satirist may apply harsh remedies too, but these are only to avoid extreme surgery. The "hot, distempered state" now needs only an "act of oblivion" to do the work of an opiate "in a raging fever." That is, once the following poem has shown everyone what is wrong and how the king proposes to correct it, the best course is to forget the entire upheaval, forgive all, and go on as if nothing had happened. Dryden here invokes the familiar role of the satiric poet as a public benefactor, virtuous on the side of virtue, aiming to do good and avoid evil. The medical figure then, when used on his side to defend satire, becomes a wholesome and necessary means of making things better. But in the hands of social and political reformers it is a means of making things worse. On one side the thing to be cured is rebellion in any form, and Dryden is the doctor-poet-satirist who prescribes for the disease. On the other hand, the disease is largely imagined, or less than a reformer thinks, so that the effort at cure is a mistake. The satiric poet-doctor is defensible, the reformer-innovator-projector-doctor is wrong since he will only make things worse. The poet may cure rebellion, since he diagnoses and prescribes for the ailment justly, this being his assignment from above, his role in the nature of things, just as it is Dryden's assignment in particular from King

Charles II. The same attempt is not to be made by the reformer, however, since he will be wrong in diagnosis and
ruinous in attempted cure.

The medical figure occurs first, save for "purg'd" (38), in
the transitional passage from the Plot to its consequences, "as
when raging fevers boil the blood," 136. The passage concentrates against the Plot the dangerous associations of violent
anger, illness, and fire, becoming the means whereby calm
waters rise into a threatening flood, or physical balance is dangerously upset, the established order threatened. At 163 the
comparison of great wits and madness keeps to the danger of
disease, here mental disease likely to become violent at any
moment. Association with mental illness continues in 333–36:

> If David's rule Jerusalem displease,
> The Dog-star heats their brains to this disease.
> Why then should I, encouraging the bad,
> Turn rebel and run popularly mad?

Here discontent with the king's rule shares the diseased nature
of all rebellious sentiments, and Absalom, not yet wholly
tempted, sees himself insane if he becomes an outright popular rebel. This sense of rebellion as inseparable from madness
or at best illusion continues into the key passages of the essay
on innovation, as line 756, "In midst of health imagine a
disease." When reformers think the state is ill, they either
imagine it or exaggerate it, unlike the entirely justified poet-
satirist. Again at 786–89:

> Nor only crowds, but Sanhedrins may be
> Infected with this public lunacy,
> And share the madness of rebellious times,
> To murther monarchs for imagin'd crimes.

The infection, the disease, the delusion or imagined grievance, the murder of Charles I, the moon-giddiness of the multitude are all blended together in this concentrated passage
clearly gathering its numerous suggestions from throughout
the myth and the poem itself. These are technically bound

into inseparable unity by an alliteration on five uses of the
letter *m*. No madness enters the last two lines of the poem's
moral lesson, 809–10:

> The tamp'ring world is subject to this curse,
> To physic their disease into a worse.

This suggests at least illusion, a form of self-deception or
folly, but in 813 the trouble has passed into outright madness,
to emphasize the mythical delusion and falsity essential to
rebellion: "Friends he has few, so high the madness grows,"
which anticipates the "pretended frights" of 919. Of course,
if it is madness that afflicts the nation, it must not touch the
friends who are "few," but only the many as always. Finally,
923–26 show the loyal few reviewing the actual state of the
nation, and explaining it to the king himself:

> These ills they saw, and, as their duty bound,
> They shewed the king the danger of the wound:
> That no concession from the throne would please,
> But lenitives fomented the disease. . . .

In its last use here in the poem, the medical figure gathers
together three of its useful implications. Lenitives are now
futile even when applied by the king, who, of course, would
always prefer lenitives to more violent cures like radical
surgery. These lenitives would in turn apply to what the
poet-satirist sees as the real disease, not the imagined one of
the popular madmen. Disease when seen as grievances by the
rebels is mostly imaginary or exaggerated by their leaders'
falsity. When seen by the poet-satirist, disease shades into
madness and becomes either the rebellion itself, which cannot
be cured by lenitives, or whatever degree of real grievance or
social evil there actually is, which is usually cured by lenitives
but which becomes worse through radical cure. Now in the
case of the threatened rebellion, disease is madness, or a
wound that demands drastic treatment to avoid disaster.

If the medical image in all its variety suggests the disharmony or pain to be avoided and the danger of too radical

cure, the architectural, building figures carry just the right persuasion toward something carefully planned as a whole. We get a strong sense of controlling things within forms already laid down. Architecture becomes a familiar symbol of harmony and order, from the idea of God as the first architect of the world's foundations through the intricate balance of man's body, and the strength of human institutions in church and state. A building has an air of permanence, something solidly established on a deep foundation; it seems intended to remain where and what it is, with changes or repairs touching only details. As a literary figure, a building is simple, and clear to any understanding. It easily makes an instructive point and avoids anything metaphysical or obscure, thus being in harmony with neoclassical ideals of style and the conservative dislike of abstraction or intellectualism. Both Fairfax and Glanvill use it to recommend experimental science, which will ensure that men live sensibly in settled, well-built houses instead of mere castles in the air. As for religion, the whole structure of divinity may be shown as a complex edifice, or religious belief may become the pillar that supports, the foundation that upholds, every commonwealth. Of all religious structures the Church of England, of course, combines the ideal of order, strength, and beauty and performs its function of maintaining the edifice of public welfare.

The need to rebuild London after the fire, as it created an outlet for practical science, may account for some of the many building images to convey notions of strength, order, and stability. Yet any society held to careful grades or strata suggests a building with a series of floors rising from a foundation. Further, the whole idea of political structure invites an architectural comparison. The wide use of fabric, frame, buttress, structure, wall, pillar, and foundation suggests an edifice to which political order may be compared. And the analogy applies with special force to England's own government, a noble pile that is the wonder and safeguard of Europe. Architectural comparisons abound in the fervently partisan *Poems on Affairs of State*. Marvell sees England resting on an unshakable foundation, and Halifax finds the laws of England like a composite building to make the happiness of Englishmen and the envy of their neighbors. The crown and the people are like stones in a well-built arch supporting each other, and even the Elizabethan Samuel Daniel had cried out to "look upon the wonderful architecture of this state of England. . . . Where there is no one the least pillar of majesty, but was set with most profound judgment and borne up with the just conveniency of prince and people."

What blind Samson of a people would in their strength and folly pull down such an ideal fabric, of government, law, and discipline? To pull down what is long established in religion and government is often an easy work, but it is the work of the devil and his children. Which indeed is the greater knave or fool—the one who told his neighbor "to pull an old house over his head for fear it should fall twenty years hence, or he that took the advice"? An old building may have defects that yield to new opinions or strange innovations, but "'tis neither wisdom, nor justice to pull down the frame of an ancient building, to make way for an alteration."

The customary history of Dryden's materials, from ancient Rome down through the Renaissance to his own time, gives the architectural image versatility and authority in the myth so as to make his use of it inevitable. We can be sure by now that the king himself will use the "foundation" of the government in his own utterances, and Clarendon reports that in their reply to Charles II the Commons join both medical and architectural figures. Praise follows to the king for his great wisdom in providing that "after so high a distemper, and such a universal shaking of the very foundations, great care must be had to repair the breaches . . . to provide things necessary for the strengthening of those repairs." It is no accident, as William Bohn points out in studying Dryden's criticism, that when he wishes to show the control of fancy by reason in his dedication to *The Spanish Friar,* he draws his figure from architecture, the most controlled of arts, allowing the least importance to wayward imagination.

In *Absalom and Achitophel* the architectural image is first used at 176 in the portrait of the great falsifier himself. He broke the triple bond, and so "The pillars of the public safety shook," thus fixing the connection between the support of monumental buildings and whatever is sound, orderly, and established. In 531–32 the "dreaming saints" are dangerous in using their energy,

> 'Gainst form and order they their power employ,
> Nothing to build, and all things to destroy.

Form and order here are part of whatever is built, especially anything that has been built long ago. Indeed the older the structure and the more likely it seems about to fall, the greater its symbolism of form and order which at all costs must not be radically changed. The essay on innovation rises to its climax in these lines:

> If ancient fabrics nod, and threat to fall,
> To patch the flaws, and buttress up the wall,
> Thus far 't is duty: but here fix the mark;
> For all beyond it is to touch our ark.
> To change foundations, cast the frame anew,
> Is work for rebels, who base ends pursue,
> At once divine and human laws control,
> And mend the parts by ruin of the whole.   (801–8)

The control of change, even when necessary, is here carried by the figure of an ancient fabric, strengthened by the religious note of sacrilege from the Old Testament ark. The rebel who would tear up the foundations of an old building, in order to correct some particular defect, is like the rebel who would cure disease by substituting a worse ailment for the present one. Both ruin the whole by trying to mend a part, and remain the complete mythical symbols of wickedness, folly, and madness.

If the poet-satirist cannot apply his medical analogy to anything done by the loyal few, save the implied "lenitives" of 926 that are now too little and too late, he may and does

allow the king's friends the benefit of the architectural figure
for something indispensable to established order. "To these
succeed the pillars of the laws," one of three uses of the word
"pillars" in the poem, allied to public stability, 176, and to
the king himself, 953. A suggestion at 918 makes the lawful
order a kind of fortress rather than an ancient fabric, yet the
line gives a sense of a physical structure or bulwark of good,
against which an attack is made by the wicked. The loyal few
see with grief powerful engines striving "To batter down the
lawful government." When the king becomes a public pillar,
the Old Testament tale of Samson's overthrow of the temple
on himself and his enemies adds a suicidal note to the destruction of ancient fabrics:

> Kings are the public pillars of the State,
> Born to sustain and prop the nation's weight:
> If my young Samson will pretend a call
> To shake the column, let him share the fall.   (953–56)

When in 994 the king repudiates voting that controls established power, he reminds us of 808, where parts are mended
by ruin of the whole. "Such votes as make the part exceed
the whole" once more relies on the essential construct of order,
the unit carefully assembled into a workable whole from
various elements, accumulated over a long period of time,
handed on from one generation to the next, and having in
the course of ages attained such virtue and usefulness that only
the wicked, the foolish, or the mad would think to disturb it.

CHAPTER 10

The Loyal Few

Bonamy Dobrée, in paying tribute to Dryden's portrait of Achitophel, says that "like all great satirists, Dryden created the object in destroying it." He creates the immortal example while destroying the contemporary individual. The malcontents are at once fixed as a type and destroyed as the king's enemies, but the loyal few are created only. Dryden's realism might cause us to wonder at the idealized picture he gives of the king's followers. In his dedication to *Examen Poeticum* (1693) he simply remarks that government will always have a certain number of time-servers and blockheads involved in its actions. Whatever his loyalties, he was never the victim of illusions as to what the actual conduct of England's political affairs must involve. But there are no time-servers or blockheads among the loyal few, and here Dryden serves the myth, rather than saying what he must have known would be the case.

Throughout the myth the wicked, the proud, the dull, the selfish, the ambitious, and the false have always been against the right things. A handful of the good, the sober, and the true have stood for the right, and nothing in *Absalom and Achitophel* shows Dryden's adherence to the myth so dramatically as the enormous disproportion between the malcontents in all their forms and the tiny band of men loyal to the king. In literature and criticism high quality will attract only a few, as only a few are capable of producing it. Only a few could write the great epics, poems, and plays, only a few could appreciate them, and only a few could devise or follow the laws governing them. As St. Evremond warned, among a thousand persons in the theater at any time there may be only six philosophers meditating the right response. Poetry is by and for the few; so is criticism, so is taste, so is genius in any form—so is, in fact, any quality worth having or admiring. It simply remains that there never are going to be very many persons who are right about anything. Certainly Dryden must not show his loyal few as part of the multitude, either as a literary or political body. They are not among those whose taste is bad, nor among those opposing the king. The political multitude had nobles, "princes of the land" who misled them for selfish reasons or mistaken patriotism; the loyal few would never dream of making common cause with anyone against the king.

In turn, they are cultivated in the arts, men of learning and ability. As the multitude and its leaders discredit each other by association, so must the king and his followers partake of each other's qualities, or at least the few must have traits that are no dishonor to the king. The poem must not imply that the king resents learning and ability around him; the loyal few then must possess whatever adornments are generally honored. The Royal Society statutes exclude anyone from weekly meetings save the fellows themselves and persons having the rank of Baron. It seems appropriate that the noblemen around the king should display intellect and learning, such indications being called for by their status, part of what is assumed of men in such high places, like the king's royal virtues. Yet for conspirators like Achitophel, exceptional ability becomes a means of pursuing evil ends. Dryden handles the subject here as he does similar things in the critical essays: he makes an *ad hoc* application to what he wishes to say, to support what he has in mind at the moment. His principle must be that great capacity is good or bad according to the use made of it. Intellect may give one a means of being a worse man than otherwise, as enlarging the possibilities of wickedness through greater insight and quickness or retentiveness of mind. It is dangerous in selfishly ambitious men, or it may even inspire selfish ambition by supplying an instrument for deceiving and surpassing weaker, simpler men. It is benevolent in loyal and devoted men, who will use all of their resources—human, personal, and material—for the common good.

The king's men have to be intelligent in making the right choice and must use their mind in the right cause, even though they are not so bright as to be proud, ambitious, and selfish and so misled into some special path of their own. They have learning in the established institutional sense, since no rebel is a friend of the arts (873), which are sustained in royally endowed colleges. Friendship for the Muses (877) seems dignified, and since they were used in the right cause, Jotham may show (882) "piercing wit, and pregnant thought."

In the essay "Of Custom" Montaigne remarks that lawful proceedings are heavy and dull, terms that come to mind as we read the brief summary (813–913) of the king's faithful band of worthies. Yet the shortness and dullness of this section make the inevitable triumph of what the loyal few stand for only the more impressive. They seem weak and limited; but the more limited they are, the more powerful becomes the rightness of what they stand for. They share the advantage, as well, of any party small in number, according to Anatole France in *Penguin Island*. The Pyrotists were few but they gained by simply containing fewer fools than a group of wider range; being less tempted to divide and offset each other's efforts, they cooperated harmoniously for their cause, and were more likely to gain fresh recruits than the big party that had great numbers on its side to begin with. In *Absalom and Achitophel*, moreover, the few supported the king's cause, which was certain to prevail; indeed nothing shows its power so much as the weakness of what there is to support it. The king's cause will prevail because it is right, because it has goodness and justice—that is, God—on its side. It has only to declare itself as it does in the king's speech, and the opposition evaporates—as when Charles II dissolved Parliament.

The particular group of men whose portrait is assembled under the loyal few recalls A. W. Verrall's remark: "A Parliament of loyal squires was probably Dryden's ideal." When Marvell was giving his unflattering picture of the House of Commons, he found nonetheless a small number of the right sort who seem almost a prose summary of the qualities celebrated in Dryden's poem:

> . . . there is a handful of salt, a sparkle of soul, that hath hitherto preserved this gross body from putrefaction, some gentlemen that are constant; invariable, indeed Englishmen; such as are above hopes, or fears, or dissimulation; that can neither flatter, nor betray their king or country; but being conscious of their own loyalty and integrity, proceed through good and bad report, to acquit themselves in their duty to God, their prince, and their nation; although so small a scantling in number, that men can scarce reckon of them more than a quorum.

These standard excellencies are reviewed by Dryden himself before *Absalom and Achitophel* employs them in the service of the myth. A fine couplet in *To My Lord Chancellor* (1662) connects loyalty with a small number of men. Of Charles I,

> And when his love was bounded in a few,
> That were unhappy that they might be true

we are made to feel by the force of the rhyme that truth has to be limited to a handful always: they were few so that they could be true then, reason enough for smallness of number. If we include James II among the loyal few, his idealized character in the poem (353–60, 441–42) is already present in Dryden's dedication to him of *The Conquest of Granada* (1671). Absalom admits that James has "every royal virtue," and is famous for courage, truth, loyalty, mercy, severity, and wisdom—qualities to be expected in a dedication where James is, of course, a pattern of loyalty, heroism, and honor. The dedication of *All for Love* (1677) to the Earl of Danby again

anticipates *Absalom and Achitophel,* drawing as it does on
Juvenal's picture of true and false nobility the better to denounce Rochester. Here Dryden suggests, too, why rebels are
not the friends of art. Those "Who endeavour the subversion
of governments" have their interest "to discourage poets and
historians; for the best which can happen to them is to be forgotten." But men who under kings labor to preserve their
country will "cherish the chroniclers of their actions" whose
records ensure for them the reverence of posterity. As for the
great virtue of loyalty itself, it should be absolute, and preferably inherited—like other elements of the myth, it is better
when of long standing. Danby shows this virtue ideally as
inborn and hereditary. His father was constant to the royal
cause at great personal sacrifice, and in the Restoration generally one obtained great credit if his father or family suffered
along with Charles I himself, or with Charles II in exile. Thus
the note so much emphasized for Barzillai and his kind in the
poem: the enduring of adversity for the royal cause when it
was in eclipse, which in turn displays the virtue of unselfishness against the prime evil of selfishness among the rebels.

The poem's review of the king's forces gets quickly under
way after the essay on innovation, in answer to a question as
to the relief that David can now bring. The few men who dare
to be his friends and the people's foes have stood by him in
the worst of times; merely to name them is to sound their
praises, and the first name in the short file is that of Barzillai.
The words "file" (817) and "train" (876, 938), with "faithful
band" (914), give a sense of orderly followers grouped together
behind the king in a kind of military service or acceptance of
authority. These terms, to be sure, are often applied just as
readily to followers of the wrong cause, but as used in the
poem they seem to have virtuous associations, unlike the
terms "herd," "host," or "pack" as applied to the malcontents.
The loyal file, train, or band suggests that each man is in his
place following the king, or grouped indissolubly with the
others in a true company. With Barzillai we turn to Old Testament influences, for in the story of King David, Barzillai had

been rich and old, in the last degree faithful and generous to the king, even sending his son into the king's service when he was too old himself. Dryden's own friendship with the Duke of Ormond-Barzillai does not emerge, nor does the poem hint at Charles II's failure at times to appreciate Ormond's loyalty. It is reported that Charles at one period refused even to speak to Ormond, so that the poem may seek refuge away from contemporary fact within the terms of its myth. The poet-satirist does not recall the king's failure to deserve a loyalty, which should be offered to the crown in any case.

Barzillai is first of the few, ancient, and honorable. Like most of the others except his son, he is old and ripe, as Charron would prefer. He has long opposed the rebels, has endured the heavy destiny of his master, going with him into exile, behaving with courtly dignity but without flattery or insinuation. He is wealthy and gives generously to good causes; he was once a proud father of many children, but these are now half gone, and most to be lamented is the eldest.

Here begins the elegy or funeral panegyric on the Earl of Ossory, which takes up nearly one third (831–63) of the section devoted to the king's friends. Adorned with every grace, mourned and honored by the poet, unjustly cut off in the prime of life, Barzillai's son still achieved honor as the king's subject and his father's son. Like Oldham, he ran a swift race too soon ended. The circle of his life was limited, but perfect of its kind. His warlike achievements were famous; his valor inspired others and stayed the march of tyrants. He was the scourge of the nation's enemies, but his country was unworthy of him and did not deserve to keep him for long. Since Heaven seemed to have designed the nation's ruin, it took away the young man's mind and fortune, unwilling to trust them to such a nation. His soul now rises from earth to join the angels in guarding the king. Here the poet turns to address his Muse, which must pause before the heights of immortality and tell the father it can sing no more. Indeed perhaps the Muse has not survived the young man's death, but has left only this elegy on his funeral car. Returning from Heaven, the Muse will not find another subject like this lamented youth, but will celebrate the rest of the loyal few.

It may be objected that the majestic slowness of their ponderous Toryism lies heavy on the poem's treatment of the few. One has a sense of old, long-established practices accepted mostly by old men. They are old, from old families, inheriting forms of behavior which they accept without question. They use all their resources to support the royal cause, even their sons, as now in the elegy on Ossory. The elegy is integral to the poem as part of its picture of what true loyalty to the king means, what sacrifice it will make for the right cause, through what personal anguish it will go on steadfastly loyal, with no thought of its own interests. The lament over Barzillai's son increases our sense of the smallness of the royal band; what little good and right there is now becomes even less when a fine young man dies. We think again of how much nobility has been sacrificed in the royal cause, how inevitable is the victory of good and right in the end. No matter how small in number, the loyalists are certain to prevail because they are right, because the king is theirs and he must have the final word.

The elegy has the most immediate effect of contrasting its subject with Absalom, since Ossory was all that a subject and son should be, whereas Absalom, as repeated again in 881, was David's disobedient son from whom he took away certain honors for the benefit of Adriel. Praise of Ossory also makes a contrast to Shaftesbury, who had attacked Ormond's administration of Ireland in the House of Lords in 1679. Ossory had then defended his father, and launched into a fierce exposition of Shaftesbury's behavior as a member of the Cabal. Ossory in his own right has a place in the poem, as against Monmouth by example and against Shaftesbury by public denunciation. The elegy may also be Dryden's way of paying some personal obligations, but of its literary uses we are entirely clear. The poem as a whole deliberately combines various literary genres for its total effect, and along with the notes of satire, epic, character writing and portraiture, oratory, and narrative we now see an expert use of funeral panegyric and its standard devices. Emotional exclamations, heightened pathos for the death of a young man who is made to seem younger certainly than Ossory's forty-six years, sententiae, the flight of a soul to Heaven, Virgilian echoes to elevate the tone and associations, the question as to whether the poet's life has not also ended, an effective use of the circle image as a symbol of the perfect life—all of these familiar accompaniments of poetic lamentation are blended and used to enforce the poem's myth.

The remaining fifty lines on the make-up of the few draw examples from the church, the law, and the nobility, although Amiel (901) has no great title himself. Ten lines (863–73) present three Anglican clergy of high rank. Of these we do not hear that "priests of all religions are the same" (99), as we found no Anglican clergy among the malcontents. Zadoc, the Sagan of Jerusalem, and he "of the western dome" (868), represent the union of religion and learning on behalf of the king. Together they are modest, faithful, wise, and eloquent—with heavenly but not dangerous eloquence. By teaching and example from such men the young are bred "to learning and to loyalty," as befits the dependence of the liberal arts on royal bounty.

One couplet (874–75) summarizes the lawyers and judges on David's side, "pillars" to remind us of architectural order sustained by law. Such a passage for a miscellaneous group is rare among the loyal few, unlike the long exposition of the malcontents whose numbers are swollen by formless masses from every area of society. With Adriel, Jotham, Hushai, and Amiel, the reference is specific again to unite in a group with similar qualities. These qualities are established by the term "loyal peers" (876), and the statements that follow are in apposition to "loyal peers," as the comments on Achitophel and Zimri are in apposition to "false" and "various." What we are to think of these individuals, then, is already clear from "train," "loyal," and "peers." With compact, rapid movement the poem hurries over the obvious, the informal summary of

well-known virtues that require nothing but to be named,
for "naming is to praise," 816. As Shadwell had remarked in
defending his satire, good men and men of sense can appear
only to their advantage; excellent men are known by their
excellencies and not by their faults. The loyal few are given
the qualities that adorn human nature at any time; they are
such qualities as anyone would wish to have, or would wish
others to think he has. And so the picture of an undebatable
virtue on the side of the king helps to make his victory seem
right and necessary. Jotham (882–87) is a gifted man whose
wit and eloquence are magnificently employed in a brave
defense of "the better side." Here wit is not madness nor eloquence a danger; they are good or bad according to their use,
gifts of nature that are wholesome when they serve the cause
of justice. Apart from these mythical tones, the lines pay tribute to Jotham-Halifax. On November 15, 1680, "the weight
of one brave man" (887) defeated the Exclusion Bill in the
House of Lords, when Halifax in a brilliant performance reversed the strong endorsement of the House of Commons.
The name Hushai (888–97), for the one whose advice in the
Bible had led to the suicide of Achitophel, recalls the report
of David's material needs in the old story, and celebrates
faithful friendship in distress, the sacrifice of personal wealth,
the careful use of small resources on the king's behalf. Here
the frugal man is virtuous as he uses his skill virtuously, in
contrast to Shimei, whose frugality betrays a cowardly mean-
ness of spirit. Again, the sense of David's having been poor,
in exile and dependent on the goodness of his friends, stays
with the mythical need to dramatize the weakness but rightness of the royal cause. As the narrator is about to pause (898–
913), he thinks of one more name and asks his "weary Muse"
to indulge this labor, as at 631–32 he had decided to include
Corah as the final malcontent even though a rehearsal of the
rest "would tire" a voluble witness. Amiel then is many
things that Corah is not. He is noble in ancestry and personal
worth, a great parliamentary leader, defender of the crown,
spokesman of a loyal nation, and a fit representative for all

men of sense and reason. Now he has retired from parliamentary control and sees the contrast between his own "steady skill" (909) and the rash, uncertain blundering and even "mad labor" (912) of the king's enemies.

The loyal few are now before us; less than 10 per cent of the poem has sufficed to tell who and what they are. Nearly a third of this went to Barzillai's dead son. Barzillai himself requires only 14 lines, 817–30, and Amiel 16 lines, 898–913. All the rest of what there is to help the king requires only some 38 lines. The number of loyalists, however, who are mentioned by name or otherwise identified, like "him of the western dome" (868), is almost exactly the same as the number of malcontents similarly identified. If we omit Absalom and Achitophel themselves and, to be sure, the Devil, we have 8 malcontents by name: Zimri, Corah, Balaam, Caleb, Nadab, Jonas, Shimei, and Issachar. If we omit the king and his brother, and then God, we have 9 loyalists specifically identified: Barzillai and his son, Zadoc, the Sagan of Jerusalem, him of the western dome, Adriel, Jotham, Hushai, and Amiel. Besides the "pillars of the laws" these are all David could count on—the chiefs of a pathetic band. The contrast to the malcontents is dramatic. On their side are as many mentioned by name, plus an enormous, heterogeneous crowd, most of whom are lumped together under general headings and descriptions. But the loyal few are given by name, and this is almost all, a select band indeed, so few that they are clearly known to all by name. These "dare" (814 and 915) to oppose the general madness, as their alarmed gaze surveys the results (914–32) of the violent new leadership that has followed the reasonable control of Amiel. They remind the king now of threatening danger from attack by a powerful, numerous faction that concentrates "the united fury of the land" (916) against lawful government and rightful succession to the throne.

On this spectacle of unrelieved disaster, enter the King.

CHAPTER 11

The King Speaks

The conservative myth denounces rebellion because of the means, fraud and violence, necessary to achieve it and because the results are certain to make things worse than ever. Rebellion is wrong also because of the nature of what it attacks: the king and all of the sanctions that over many centuries had clothed him with ideal virtues. As for Charles II in particular, rebellion is unjustified because he has in fact all the virtues assumed to be present in whoever is king. For Dryden's purposes, Charles-David has to be what the ideal king has always been, just as Achitophel has to be whatever the king is not, whatever the false political leader has always seemed to be. Those wishing to praise Charles I or even Cromwell drew on the traditional qualities of an ideal ruler. Now Dryden must do the same for Charles II, since it is expected. The portrait is what it is because of the myth, because of the immediate need to contrast the king with his enemies, and the need to show the closeness of the king to God as in the biblical story. Likewise, literary precedent demanded such a portrait as inherited from Rome, especially from Cicero's *De Officiis* and the doctrine of decorum, not to speak of the contemporary practice of heroic plays and French romances.

Allan Gilbert's invaluable study *Machiavelli's Prince and Its Forerunners* (1938) shows the remarkable diffusion of ideas concerning what a prince was supposed to be like. By 1700 the subject had attracted a whole library of comment instructing a king how to conduct himself. Machiavelli himself believed in the settled state, the firmly established government of Dryden's myth, to which all must be subordinate. A prince should do what is necessary to give an impression of mercy and forbearance, just as David-Charles in the poem puts off as long as possible anything like arbitrary action or the saying of unpleasant, imperious things. But in the end, as Machiavelli says, justice is higher than clemency and David must speak. The convention of giving praise to qualities that a ruler is supposed to show leads Machiavelli to require a ruler who is liberal, piteous, faithful, bold, humane, chaste, sincere, easy of access, grave, and religious. Other theorists also emphasize generosity, friendliness, ease of access. In the later Renaissance, for Shakespeare to draw upon in his histories especially, a regular genre of political literature, "the institution of a prince," described the right virtues of a governing authority. The basic scheme was the four classical virtues of prudence, fortitude, temperance, and justice, plus the Christian virtues of faith, hope, and charity. In *Macbeth* (IV, 3) through Malcolm speaking to Macduff, Shakespeare lists a round dozen of the "king-becoming graces," which Malcolm pretends not to possess:

> As justice, verity, temperance, stableness,
> Bounty, perseverance, mercy; lowliness,
> Devotion, patience, courage, fortitude.

The standard praise of James I absorbed the basic qualities, stressing as well magnanimity, liberality, and clemency, building up the picture of an unselfish, lenient, and fatherly king. James had the additional merit, according to Sir John Beaumont, of giving the best literary example to "lawless poets," for

> He knew it was the proper work of kings,
> To keep proportion, ev'n in smallest things.

A standard set of comparisons or analogies also grew up, showing resemblance between a king in his realm and the sun in Heaven, the father in his family, the shepherd among his flock, the general in his army, the schoolmaster in his school, or the captain in his ship. Dryden lets Achitophel speak in terms of the king's sun as setting while Absalom's is rising during the temptation scene, thus invoking the common saying, "more people worship the rising than the setting sun." Achitophel also draws on the current interest in astrology while tempting Absalom, 230–31:

> Auspicious prince, at whose nativity
> Some royal planet rul'd the southern sky.

This augury of a great future helps persuade Absalom that there is no real difference between himself and his father as king, for when Charles I was on his way to St. Paul's to give thanks for the birth of the future Charles II in 1630, a bright star shone in the sky at mid-day, as already seen in *Astraea Redux*, 288–91.

As the David story develops in the 17th century, the right kingly qualities settle upon the biblical king, so that when the time comes to restore Charles II, he can be compared to David as he constantly is, with the desired effect. David's virtues are then fully established as the ones Charles is supposed as king to have. The presentation of David stresses resemblance to God as father, as judge, or as supreme monarch standing against his enemies. He practices repeatedly the virtues of mercy, patience, and forgiveness and shows himself an indulgent father in the last degree affectionate and lenient. While it is true that these are part of the standard equipment for all kings, they could not apply from the tradition to David to Charles II unless he were the legitimate ruler. Only the rightful king can possess the right virtues, which do not depend on any particular person, an interesting point once more to explain why Dryden's poem begins on the note of illegitimacy. Thomas May in continuing Lucan emphasizes the

futility even of Julius Caesar, who behaves with his famous
largeness of mind to defeated enemies once he has risen to
power. But it must be in vain, for

> No virtue, bounty, grace or clemency
> Could long secure usurped soveraignty.

By 1660 Charles will be like all other kings in the tradition;
he will be like David; and all this is doubly so because he is
the rightful, legitimate ruler. His own first pronouncements
and letters or declarations on assuming the throne as reported
in Clarendon seem like a conscious effort to demonstrate that
he does in fact possess all the proper royal qualities for which
Dryden and other contemporaries now praise him. As the
portrait of Charles quickly establishes itself on inevitable
lines, that of Cromwell necessarily changes. Dryden's *Heroic
Stanzas* had even shown Cromwell as mild, combining love
and majesty, since it was a part of any ruler's equipment to
seem kindly. Flecknoe's biography of Cromwell (1659) also
clothes him with the virtues he is supposed to have, with no
hint of duplicity. But in the next year Flecknoe's *Heroic
Portraits* shows Cromwell as part lion and part fox, "whence
you may easily guess he was a great dissembler." Dryden had
praised Cromwell for establishing order, for brilliant foreign
policy, for courage, dignity, command and understanding of
men, and other qualities commonly admitted. He ignores the
vices of Cromwell and praises what he would praise in any
ruler, partly because he honestly thought such things worthy
of praise, and partly because decorum required that a ruler
have the virtues that go with his office. Once the king is restored, however, the view of Cromwell has to change. While
ruling he has to have the traits associated with his position;
when the rightful king returns, Cromwell has to revert to the
status of a rebel, and therefore he must be seen as a false dissembler. The same myth that gave him virtue now gives him
perfidy, and bestows on the incoming king, even before he
has had a full chance to show them, the established royal
virtues.

So Dryden's first poem on the king is like his best poem on
Charles II twenty years later. Like *Absalom and Achitophel*,
Astraea Redux shows Charles after a long period of suffering,
patient endurance, and seeming defeat by forces much greater
than his own, rising in triumph and revealing the same high
qualities in the process. The effect of exile on the king occurs
in a number of poems on his restoration, and Dryden too
shows that in banishment Charles developed the virtues of
patience, courage, and wise restraint; so the exile made it
seem appropriate to clothe Charles II with some of the virtues
he was supposed to have as king. The qualities arrayed on the
side of evil in *Astraea Redux* are repeated in *Absalom and
Achitophel;* associated with evil and rebellion in both poems
are madness, false leaders, the vulgar rabble, lawless liberty,
rage, sin, impious wit, wiles, and malicious arts. As to the
king's character, policy at the Restoration demanded stress on
the king's mercy and forgiveness; all testimonials mentioned
these virtues. The historical situation blends with the myth
in excluding any note of vengeful severity, and in repeating
that the king is all that justice, order, right, and law demand.
In *Astraea Redux* the king, however, lacks the full dimensions
given him in *Absalom and Achitophel*. In 1660 he will be mild
and forgiving to heal the nation's divisions, but in 1681 he
must in the end appear indignant and sternly lawful. He must,
as Dryden saw, seem as much an Old Testament figure as
Christ from the New, since the conservative myth is better
served from the less indulgent syllables of the word of God.
So the later poem shows the king more like God the father,
ruler, and lawgiver, than like Christ the healer and savior as
required in 1660.

In the panegyric *To His Sacred Majesty* (1661) Dryden enlarges on the king's achievements and virtues. His goodness,
wisdom, patience, and mercy are restoring peace and order,
and healing the wounds of rebellion. The king is like the sun
as expected, here warming away the damps and vapors of rebellion. Comparison is made to Caesar, and the king's military
prowess and his courage as savior and protector are duly re-

corded. From the title on, the poem stresses the divine analogy
as well. The king is sacred, and is like God who sent manna
down from Heaven to feed the people below. The king has
also the heavenly power of music to bring peace and harmony
out of discord. The power of David's music over the confused
mind of Saul comes to mind here, although David is not directly named, as he was for the first time in *Astraea Redux,* 79.
The association of music, harmony, and the power of creating
order was made by Cowley also, in *Davideis,* where David's
music joins the soul of man and the order of Nature. David is
thus of use to Dryden as a symbol of order through music, as
well as the father-figure and king in the Absalom story. The
coronation panegyric makes a great deal of the king's paternal
care and the divine sanction of his patriarchal authority. He
unites imperial greatness and fatherly rule, so that Dryden
combines the associations of father, king, and God even before
Charles II has the beloved figure of Absalom to call them
forth.

To My Lord Chancellor (1662) defends Clarendon vigor-
ously, and shows the poet writing in defense of the ruling
group as he was still doing twenty years later. Clarendon is
the essential instrument of the king's policy and so is an ex-
tension of the king throughout the poem. The vital influence
of the king, "the Nation's soul," is dispensed through Clarendon, and the preceding monarch as well, "our setting sun,"
had found him indispensable. The king now resembles his
father in mercy and goodness, "his fatal goodness left to fitter
times" (59), a virtue to be deplored twenty years later, when
the king's goodness is again "fatal." Along with Clarendon's
political influences, he has restored poetry to its natural function as the support of religion and government. Clarendon
revives poetry, which exists for religion and law, and so his
love of the Muses also supports his mysterious function of
diffusing the king's purposes and goodness throughout the
nation—the whole tribute carried poetically by extended use
of the sun image for light, warmth, divine power, and influence at the center of things.

Dryden's consistent homage to the king continues in *To My Honored Friend, Dr. Charleton* (1662), wherein the genius of Charles II develops just those qualities essential to the nation's well-being. The Restoration has freed England from a usurping tyranny, and it has freed science, the mind, and English culture as well. The analogy between new science and a new political order governs the poem, as Dryden argues for a limited monarchy, with the king as sacred yet with England's free-born reason untouched. As for Charles II, since he was recalled by the people from exile, he is king by election as well as by divine right, sanctioned both by God and Nature, which holds that a free-born people must choose their own king. The crown is great and powerful, the king's position unassailable.

By 1666 the lyrical devotion to Charles II inspired by his restoration had grown more sober, especially when disasters overcame the nation. Dryden writes *Annus Mirabilis*, "An Historical Poem" on the year 1666, with a view to aiding the government to avoid revolution. Like the friends of Job, the king's enemies held that suffering punishes, and they predicted a revolution coming in with signs and portents, showing God's wrath against the king and court. Using the very title of republican pamphleteers, Dryden shows that fire and plague could not display God's anger, since in the same period he had blessed the king with three naval victories. Clearly Heaven favors the king therefore, and the disasters only chastise past rebellions; now the city is loyal and the king generous and the future bright with promise of wealth and power. The expected glorification of the king repeats his generosity, his calm, peaceful control, his courage without rashness, his resemblance to God as ruler and father. During the fire he weeps over the city, he directs the general fight against the fire, a hydra with a hundred heads. He gives up in weariness at night, and his royal brother continues in his stead. The king prays at last to God (stanzas 262–70), who has aided him in past exile and distress, who knows the king's care for his people and who has taught him to be merciful. Let God now be mer-

ciful after the double scourge of plague and fire. The tone
throughout has shown Charles II as a man of exemplary piety
and unselfish devotion to duty.

Annus Mirabilis then gives the king his standard mythical
qualities and shows him as having the virtues needed in whatever crisis threatens his rule. Further, the nation's welfare,
the expansion of its wealth and power, depend on the king's
wisdom and bounty. Since he must be all these things in order
to lead the nation to success in peace and war, he is praised for
being what the general benefit requires him to be. In his
letter to the City of London, April 1660, Charles had promised
to show any favors needed to advance "the trade, wealth and
honour" of the city. He seems not to realize that promoting
wealth and trade will give the power that goes with them into
the hands of men who will move against the established order.
Mercantilism enables Shimei later on to threaten the king
with money and power, so that by 1681 such men were a danger not foreseen in *Annus Mirabilis*. The democratic energy in
trade is not implied, but the king and mercantilism are one
as he shows the way to new prosperity. The fire shows his
heroism and bounty to the people; the naval battles show his
foresight and leadership in war; his support of trade and
wealth proves that the nation's welfare is inseparable from
his royal virtues. Rebellion against such a king is unthinkable.
Like Virgil's Aeneas, Charles is "pius," valiant, wise, and
good, a father of the people, the instrument of God and the
favorite of Heaven. When the fire dies out at last (stanza 286),
the king, like God the father, opens his stores and feeds the
poor: "Thus God's anointed God's own place supplied." In
Absalom and Achitophel the king as God the father joins the
king as God the law in finally prevailing over his enemies, but
the poem's general support of Charles II is like the aim of
Annus Mirabilis. Both poems assert his royal qualities and
rally popular support to his cause. The climax of the earlier
work is the king's prayer, as the later poem rises to the king's
speech. Both show Charles in direct alliance with God, sharing
His power and relying on God's sanction to solve the problem

of the moment: in 1667 the results of plague and fire, in 1681 the threat of civil war. Both bestow on the king the expected mythical qualities that demand a corresponding loyalty and devotion.

The need for heroic qualities to be admired found an outlet or satisfaction in the heroic plays, in which art supplied the forms of dignity lacking in life as it was. David in *Absalom and Achitophel* resembles a hero in one of the plays, possessing high virtues as called for by his role, as desired by the age, and as accumulated in the poet's myth. The king and his followers are ideally virtuous yet are actual men, real and ideal fused into something to compel admiration. The long analyses of the king's enemies and the ingredients of rebellion show men as they are; the portraits of the king and the loyal few show men as they should be, and as in fact a few really are, but never more than a few. The heroic plays celebrate in various forms the virtues to be admired in the great. *Tyrannick Love* shows the greatness and finality of a monarch's power, while *The Conquest of Granada* explores the theme of clemency seen in *The State of Innocence* as well: ideally the king should be clement, yet forgiveness to rebellion may be suicidal, the "fatal mercy" of David. *Aureng-Zebe,* along with reference to clemency and the king as sun "like Heaven's eye," goes beyond the usual conflict between love and honor to distinguish between tyranny and a high ideal of kingship. Like *Absalom and Achitophel* later on, it enlarges themes from current politics into ideas of reason and the state, drawing on long tradition and experience.

Dryden's Dedication of *All for Love* in 1677 to the Earl of Danby again bestows all the right qualities on Charles II, anticipating *Absalom and Achitophel's* picture of a king just, moderate, compassionate, ruling within law and public welfare, with a soul formed by God to suit the constitution of his government, a prince of excellent character "suitable to the wishes of all good men." Thus anyone opposed to the king must be a bad man. The "Preface" to *Troilus and Cressida* invokes the rule of decorum from neoclassical theory to show that a king must have kingly virtues in a play, yet these qualities should resemble the actual king's known character. Dryden by 1681 has been celebrating just this combination in Charles II for over twenty years, making it seem as if the actual king of England was in fact what literary, political, and religious convention demanded. Just before *Absalom and Achitophel,* one of Dryden's best comedies, *The Spanish Friar,* ends on a note that praises the king's ideal virtue yet warns that he may in fact be dangerous. Torrismond tells the queen not to fear for Sancho's pity:

> Pity and he are one;
> So merciful a king did never live;
> Loth to revenge, and easy to forgive:
> But let the bold conspirator beware,
> For Heaven makes princes its peculiar care.

As the political crisis of 1680–81 nears its climax, the materials out of which Dryden will make his defense of the king's position have long since been ready to his hand. Other literature supporting the king repeats the main lines of Dryden's portrait of David. In 1680 a character of Queen Elizabeth appears entitled *A Pattern or President for Princes to Rule by, and for Subjects to Obey by,* the whole glorifying Elizabeth as possessing every quality of the ideal monarch, almost ironic it seems at times, in seeing Elizabeth as a ruler is supposed to be, not as she so often was. A recurring note as in Thomas D'Urfey's *The Progress of Honesty* (1681) glorifies the divine clemency and mercy of the king, his patience and heavenly pity for his enemies who denounce him while they profit from his too-generous policy. Indeed the king has allowed mercy to outweigh justice and this argument is taken over by Dryden along with the admonition that the king has been silent too long, that he has sacrificed his friends to appease his enemies, and that the time has come for the throne to declare its just anger after the manner of God, who by his meanest word can destroy those who murmur at the dispositions of providence.

The king himself refers to his celebrated virtue of patience in his speech on the opening of Parliament in Oxford, March 20, 1681, while in his Declaration of April 8 he characterizes the rebel leaders much as Dryden's poem will soon do—"the restless malice of ill men," some acting out of commonwealth principles, some out of anger or disappointed ambition. They try to show that the king is hostile to parliaments, but he on the contrary has dissolved the last two parliaments because they refused his moderate and conciliatory leadership, insisting on the Exclusion Act, which threatens another civil war. He will continue to uphold parliamentary government in spite of the operations of dangerous and designing men, and he will as always uphold the established order in church and state. The Declaration is a model of patience, reasonableness, and generous forbearance in the face of provocative actions by ambitious men. It was effectively answered in a *Letter from a Person of Quality to His Friend Concerning His Majesty's Late Declaration . . .;* the author laments that so gracious a king should be influenced by wicked and scheming advisers in a time threatened by popery and the rise of arbitrary power. The present church and the monarchy are in danger from Rome and France, so that the king should act more in harmony with the desires and interests of the people. Frequent dissolving of Parliament defeats the inherited right of the people, and opens the way to popery, which gains from either of two forms of tyranny: absolutism or leveling democracy. Let Parliament advise the king then, not the king advise Parliament.

Dryden's own *His Majesty's Declaration Defended* is a systematic answer to the "Person of Quality," justifying the king on every count; written in June 1681, this prose tract overlaps the poem then being composed to come out in November. The enemy is denounced, along with treachery and artifice, the folly of the multitude, the knavish pretense of patriotism, the role of angry men disobliged at court, the selfishness of ambitious individuals—the familiar outlines of what is wrong come almost automatically forward. The goodness, indulgence, and equity of the king, his love of peace, of moderation and established legal forms, the good fortune of England in its excellent governmental inheritance—these in turn expose the folly and knavery of the forces against them. Dryden likewise makes much of the Popish Plot, of the conspirators' need of this plot to keep control of the people, and their factious interest in keeping it alive as an apparent threat. He refers with feeling to Monmouth and is not ashamed to say "that I particularly honor the Duke of Monmouth"; yet his supporting faction is so diverse, it would be impossible to satisfy their conflicting interests if Monmouth came to power. The defense anticipates the multifariousness, contradiction, and disunity of the rebel cause so much insisted on in the poem, and the text makes extensive use of familiar medical and architectural figures of speech.

When we come to *Absalom and Achitophel* itself, it is fair to say that the title does not mention the poem's real subject. The poem is in fact about Charles II and his kingly office, showing that the man who is now king is really possessed of the qualities gathered in the conservative myth for the ideal king. The poem's effect is to establish the supremacy of the king and to make his triumph over the enemy seem inevitable, the natural result of his will whenever he chooses to express it. All this is true poetically or symbolically whether the king is actually mentioned or not; yet in 1031 lines at least 400 refer to the king or to his office. If we include references to the crown, kingship, kings, monarchy, divine right, or reign we will find that the poem is seldom out of focus on its royal subject. The first 16 lines have to do with David's personal life, and lines 31–42 tell as much of David as of Absalom, with their emphasis on the king's paternal indulgence. To 93 inclusive there are ten other lines referring to the king or his office. From 93 to 130, and later from 147 to 192, there are in all over 80 lines with no royal allusions. In the next 70 lines there are again some 10 that recall the king, and 262 to 296 concentrate on the weaknesses of "Old David." Absalom's whole speech (317–69), has to do with the king and his own relationship to him, to the king's brother, and the royal succession. Likewise almost all of the second temptation speech of Achitophel (381–444) concerns the king, his brother, and the justification of the villain's attitude toward them. Lines 461–76 are also largely on the king and what Absalom must do against him; thus in the first 500 lines of the poem some 230 refer directly to the king or his royal office, or bear upon it through Absalom—his ambitions, or his relationship to his father.

In the second half of the poem, the Zimri portrait excludes royal allusion, and, together with the lines connecting it with Shimei, the king does not appear from 526 to 580. Lines 503–8 refer to the throne as being too costly for frugal tradesmen, and 512 makes a distinction between David and the king, the man and his office. From 580 to Absalom's reference to his father (707–22), some dozen allusions keep the king or his office before our minds. During the essay on innovation the royal function in society is constantly explored, and in the thirty-three lines (764–96) the term "kings"—in the plural, standing for a general principle—is used seven times. The remaining lines before David's speech make frequent mention of the throne, crown, regal rights, sovereign power, prince, and king. The last 100 lines of the poem bear directly on the king and establish his control of the entire work: 932–38 introduce the Godlike David before his speech; 939–1024 contain his only utterance in his own person; 1025–31 close the poem with God's support of David and the people's acceptance of his rule. Thus after 500, 173 lines contain such allusion to the king as to keep him before our minds. Of these, 100 lines are the concluding section of the poem, and all are by the king or concerning him or his rule directly. He completely dominates the beginning and end of the poem, and only one section of the remainder (526–80) goes on for as much as fifty lines with no reminder of the king's presence.

Elsewhere the poem reflects continuous credit on the king, even in the portrait of Achitophel. If the false rebel was in fact a good judge, the king is to be praised for appointing him to the bench. Achitophel must not seem a total villain, since his appointment would then be a royal mistake. If he is good at what the king appoints him to do, he reflects honor on his master. Again the early portrait of Absalom with all the charms and graces emphasized really flatters the king, since all this is only his "youthful image in his son renewed," 32. All the good qualities of Absalom as we now see him are to be understood as also belonging to David. The poem is seldom without some tribute to the king, steadily building up his portrait so as to make the final speech the ultimate assertion of what has been accumulating all along, a summary of the king's perfections.

If Absalom's virtues are also his father's, so also the king's relationship with his son shows the qualities inseparable from David throughout the poem, qualities that also adhere to his divine counterpart. David's pleasure in his son recalls the beloved son in whom God has been well pleased. Up to his speech, David stands for God the father; as he is a human father to Absalom, so is he paternal to his subjects—patient, indulgent, merciful, affectionate, forgiving. But when he speaks, except for the passage on Absalom, he becomes God the ruler or king—entirely just, righteous, all-powerful, a stern but angry judge, implacable in determining to punish evil. The king is never far from Absalom's thoughts or words or from the center of Achitophel's temptation speeches, especially the second, 391–476. One or the other rebel protagonist refers to the king either in speaking to another or to the people, as in Absalom's progress speech (707–22), which seems to accept Achitophel's version of a weak old man now easily dethroned. The mythical, ideal portrait of the king, however, emerges in what Absalom says in reply to Achitophel's first temptation speech, 262–91. This speech makes a shrewd contrast between the old David and two youthful images—that of the young Absalom already presented (17–42) as the young king David, and that of the daring young man who responded to fortune and became king. Now he is a setting sun, the shadows lengthen, and like Satan he tumbles down from former greatness. He lacks popular support at home, foreign aid is unreliable, and all sorts of men are now estranged from him. Absalom's reply is really a hymn of praise for the king, admitting his right to govern, his many excellent qualities of goodness and justice, his clemency, mercy, and unselfish devotion to the public good, and again his mildness, a quality he has in common with God. The disease figure of 334 discredits any objection of the people against the king; Absalom admits David's generosity and favor to him as his son, and stresses again the favor of Heaven in predicting the king's final ascent among the blessed, 350. Thus the constant development of the king's portrait throughout the poem gets abundant help from his relationship to Absalom, which in turn enforces the king's similarity to God the father.

The alliance of the king and God in the poem was agreeable to all shades of belief and opinion. If "God" is a term for lawful order in the universe and in society, for whatever it is that experience and need have shown to be the right course of action, then the king rules certainly by divine right. So if God equals the order in the universe, the king stands in God's place in human affairs. As God is to universal order, so is the king to social order in the state. True, the king does not create the order over which he governs, but like God he does in fact govern. This can become more specific belief, depending on the degree of one's piety or orthodoxy. From being like God when God is thought of as a separate force directly influencing human affairs, the king may come from God or may get power from the will of God exerting personal control over mankind.

Kingship and divinity then produce a most useful relationship in Dryden's poem, since it can mean anything required by those who wish to invoke it as a sanction for royal power and established order. In *Absalom and Achitophel* it pervasively invokes the Roman question again, "What is the law?" What is it that has really to be obeyed? It is the law, whatever stands for order and control. In the family this is the father, and the poem makes much of David as a father to explain his behavior. But in the state it is the king, prince, protector, parliament—the established authority whatever its form. The

reason why David has divine sanction in the poem, then, is
that England is a monarchy, and so as king he embodies its
law and authority. The portrait of David repeatedly shows
him scrupulous as to the law, whatever it is. In turn, if the
king follows the law, so must the people follow him. The
loyal few understand this (938), "His train their maker in
their master hear." They see God the law to be obeyed in the
king. The people have not made royalty then, but in a sense
royalty has made the people and so speaks for God to them.
This contrasts with the "Adam-wits" (51), whose own hands
had made "an idol monarch," 64. They had made an idol to be
God, and as A. W. Verrall says, if the people claim to make the
king, they may just as well assert that they had made God.

The "divine" thing about David, then, is the law, but the
poem suggests his "divinity" in many other ways. He possesses
many Godlike qualities, and when so much is made of his
mercy (146), for example, the king is kept before us sympathet-
ically as resembling God even while the poem is reviewing the
opposition to his rule. But the poem begins and ends with, is
framed within, David's acting like God. At first he scatters his
maker's image over the land. David is now a creative force resembling God. At the end of the poem, he is the divinely ordained ruler asserting his imperious will from which there is
no appeal. For David as Charles II, the first ten lines show
him as he in fact was, a very faulty human being. The last
lines show him as he was supposed to be, a majestic ruler restoring divine order to his realm, like God bringing order to
the world. The poem moves from the man to the king, from
the real to the ideal, and the human to the divine order. For
the age, every great man had to seem to be what he was supposed to be or to represent, something more than human, especially the king playing a divine role on earth.

The poem's first reference to "Godlike" David is in line 14,
the last in line 1030. Within, there are some thirty references
to the divine sanction or role, to God and the king, to Heaven,
Heaven's anointed, to Godhead or the Almighty. The king is
shown to be divinely supported or favored, to share in the

qualities of God when his mildness (327–28) is a "crime" in spite of being also "God's beloved attribute." References to God and the king are numerous in the dialogue between Absalom and Achitophel. "Desire of greatness is a Godlike sin" recalls the assumed divine sanction for Absalom's hopes which is immediately picked up by Achitophel. Everyone desires God on his side, and as David has the help of God through the nature of his office, Achitophel gets God on Absalom's side by specious argument. He makes some half dozen divine allusions in trying to persuade Monmouth that God wishes him to act. Divinity is not absent from references to the multitude, to Shimei, and Corah whose "zeal to Heav'n" ironically made him despise the prince (672), reverence to whom is in fact a religious duty. At 791 kings are "the Godhead's images," and after various references in 807, 823, 838, and 869, the divine sanction is made explicit once more just before the king speaks:

> Thus from his royal throne by Heav'n inspired,
> The godlike David spoke   (936–37)

and in 997–98,

> For Gods and godlike kings their care express,
> Still to defend their servants in distress.

In 1000–1, David compares himself directly to God, when he is forced to punish individuals, perhaps here referring to the execution of Stephen College and Edward Fitzharris in 1681:

> Why am I forc'd like Heav'n against my mind,
> To make examples of another kind?

Before the last reference to "godlike David" the divine approval is expressly recorded, 1026: "He said, Th' Almighty, nodding, gave consent." The king has uttered the final word, and God has left no room for reply.

As king, David of course should and does need to speak only once. He must speak so as to leave nothing for anyone to say:

his speech should be and is the last event in a poem which now can have no further reason to continue. As in the old morality plays, the agent of God declares the lesson for mankind. In government there must be an authority beyond any appeal, whose right to speak is divine and clearly known to be final. Further, what the king says must naturally follow from what has preceded it. His words must result from the preceding action or analysis. All the rest of the poem has considered his enemies, now including his son, and the possible results of their actions; now after review of the loyalists, the king must deal with his enemies and must show that they have no chance to prevail against him. When he has done this, the poem is over, logically and artistically, poetically and mythically rounded out, with clearly related parts from beginning to end. The king's last word must be abrupt, not too long, and must not seem an anticlimax. Like the poem as a whole the king's speech will seem ready in its terms before he gives it, echoing constantly the long-established tones of the conservative myth. By now we should expect few surprises, and the speech as it is gains much of its force from the fact that it has none.

The king first declares his own virtues, not "we" but "I" possess mercy, clemency, patience, and forbearance, yet with a threat of their opposites if need be. In spite of his paternal indulgence and forgiveness, now his very right to forgive is debated. "They contend" that one was made for many; in his innocence David had supposed that this applied only to his sex life, as narrated in 3–4, but now he sees that one was made to rule. His enemies have mistaken him, imagining that he is afraid instead of courageously long-suffering. They insist on his behaving against his mild nature, so he will show them how free he is to act outside their compulsion. He will now act as a king, not as a patient object of unjustified insult. Here the architectural figure, echoing Marvell and Milton, makes an easy transition to his chief sorrow, the enmity of his own son. After 939–54, on his general relationship with his enemies, the king is a pillar supporting the structure of public welfare. He now speaks of his son (955–70), whom he warns of the consequences should he play the role of Samson to overthrow the existing fabric. This warning immediately passes into a new sign of the fatherly benevolence which the king asserts as his true nature and which he abandons for revenge with great reluctance. So Absalom may yet escape with a pardon. He is "a darling son," the "poor pitied youth," elevated as far as the kindness of his father would allow but clearly not destined for royal power. The unhappy boy has been deceived, of course—the mythical explanation for whatever challenges the existing order. False modern patriotism, a union of knavery and folly, has misled Absalom into thinking that he, not the king, should rule.

The transition from 967, "the politician's tool," is easily made to Achitophel (971–74), the "old instructor" who ironically seemed more gracious and virtuous for public effect after losing his high position than before. The more factious and troublesome, the more apparently virtuous, thus showing again the mythical need for deception.

The king now shifts (975–88) to political theory and the arguments of his enemies as to the relative strength of king and Parliament. If Parliament has the sole right to choose a future king, they must have an equal right to depose the king they now have. Their petitions are only the usual recourse of all false patriots, the voice of Jacob that would lure a precious inheritance into the vile hands of Esau. The king sees that the petitions are only a means to force him into calling Parliament into session, at which his enemies, having a majority, could impose their will upon him. But though essentially patient and forgiving, he is not deceived by the pious excuse that he will be made safe when he is out of power. Plots and treasons are evil but petitions are worse in pretending to save what they really aim to destroy. The petitioners will never be satisfied until they have what God himself can never grant them —the right to legitimate power.

Having shown that he possesses the mythical kingly virtues, and that his enemies are bent on seizing power for themselves under false pretenses, the king now has no choice but to enforce the law, and in so doing to assume the place of God in human affairs, 989–1025. For the king to invoke the law is to place his enemies outside its pale, so the remainder of his speech relies on the sanctions of God and the law. Once the law prevails, established power will not suffer control by votes which distort public values in favor of the part over the whole. The king will not allow public clamor to endanger his loyal few whom he will save as befits the divine nature of his office. He regrets that the saving function of rule is not all, but that now he is forced, in spite of his natural mildness to show that his enemies have mistaken his goodness for fear. They have asked for the law to prevail: now let them see the law face to face for what it really is—necessarily an instrument of their defeat. Their doom will be hastened by their own self-destructive nature. Once more the king blends the mythical view that all double-dealing conspirators must turn against each other, with the mutual recriminations that actually took place at the state trials. Being false to the king, the rebels must be false to each other. Their conspiracy must at last collapse into discordant wrangling and accusations one against the other. The final result is inevitable: from its own inherent unsoundness despite an outward show of original force, and from the natural superiority of lawful power, the doom of rebellion is sealed. This being in the nature of things, it must be as the king says, as God now agrees. With echoes of Virgil, Lucretius, and Dryden's own *Astraea Redux* and *Annus Mirabilis,* the poem declares a secure future for England. The nation goes back to the Restoration of 1660, and begins again under the auspices of God and the law, having learned its lesson from the immediate past. The spirit of these lines recalls the speech of Ulysses at the very end of *Troilus and Cressida* (1679):

While public good was urged for private ends,
And those thought patriots, who disturbed it most;
Then like the headstrong horses of the sun,
That light which should have cheered the world, consumed it:

Now peaceful order has resumed the reynes,
Old time looks young, and Nature seems renewed:
Then, since from homebred factions ruine springs,
Let subjects learn obedience to their kings.

We now see how useful to Dryden the mythical qualities
of kingship were, enabling him to do for the actual king what
the crisis demanded without revealing any secrets or any less
admirable traits of character. It is tempting to look at the
poem now as showing Charles II as he really was without
having to disclose the truth of his secretive, devious policy
of delay which turned in the end to sudden fury in dissolving
Parliament at the moment of its apparent triumph. We need
not emphasize the difference between what was "restored" in
1660 and Charles II himself, the man who happened to embody it at the moment. "Restoration" implies bringing back
what once was, in this case not only rule and order but the
continuity of English tradition. So even though Charles did
not always practice the things of which he was the symbol or
custodian, he stood at last by the inherited monarchical succession. He refused to get rid of his wife or his brother, standing by the order, the law, and tradition that was restored with
him.

Apart from the poem's requirements and its occasion,
Charles is shown to have all the right qualities because as
king he was supposed to have them; because the historical
situation called for them to restore order after the civil war;
because in effect he said at Breda that he would behave according to these virtues; because the literary tradition demanded them; and because he did in fact display them at
times, as in the fire and in dealing with disaffected elements
in the nation. In the poem, everyone including himself insists
on his mercy and clemency. We should expect this from the
biblical story, where David is tender and forgiving; from the
analogy to God the father, who is all merciful until he must
be just, familiar in Renaissance theory of the king as father
of the people; from the myth in general, which must see the

king as having all the right virtues so as to deserve the reverent obedience demanded of his subjects. This recalls Thomas Rymer and neoclassical decorum, wherein a king should display the qualities of great office and power, one of which is dignified generosity from above. But in the poem the king's clemency acts also to discredit his enemies. If he is clement, it must be that wicked subjects have given him reason to be so; every reference to his mercy or forgiveness implies an offense which has to be tolerated or forgiven, implies that something is wrong and demands his forbearance. The cumulative effect of this repeated clemency is to give a further sense of a long series of offenses that would have justified his use of penal power, of things that would have outraged any king but this one, who now moves against his foes only after a record of offenses long ago beyond endurance. His clemency has the threefold effect of praising the king as usually called for; of discrediting further his enemies; and of justifying finally any action he chooses to take against them.

Again, the poem uses the myth skillfully in presenting the king as ideally patient and clement but finally irresistible in declaring his power. It also reflects the actual performance of Charles II in seeming to be amiable and tender, and a "genial debauchee" until the time came to demolish his enemies. The apparent disproportion of the poem, in seeming to give little attention to the king and the loyal few at the end, corresponds to the policy of Charles II. Let the exclusionists go as far and as long and as fully as they can; let their lines and resources be developed and be given plenty of time to establish their strength until they seem overwhelming. The father image, mild and indulgent, thus supports the king's actual policy. Then as the conspiracy is about to prevail, he can demolish all in one word. Charles-David never speaks until the poem's end. After the essay on innovation has declared the principles governing the narrative, the actual power that governs by these principles may declare itself; and a declaration is all that such power needs, given its enormous sanctions in history, in the nature of things, in the moral order of the universe. If

Charles II was lenient and patient, as the poem says, it was not only to show the expected virtue of royal benevolence but the more certainly to destroy his enemies. A deadly, carefully matured aim, a shrewd and calculated delay in order to be able to strike more certainly once and for all—this in fact explains the king's "patience" and his "fury" once the poem lets him speak. The long delay before he speaks corresponds to the long delay in Charles' own policy, while the poem says nothing directly about Charles' secretiveness or the actual meaning of his tactics of delay. The plotters are allowed to assemble, make their plans, gather their forces, exploit their advantage, and do their worst. Meanwhile Charles waited—as Mr. Previté-Orton remarks, "waited till their violence discredited them, waited till the dread of another civil war should have its full effect; waited till men were ashamed of the cruel panic of the Plot; waited till the natural loyalty of the nation resented the ignominious treatment of its royal house." Then he dissolved Parliament.

If the poem seems to adhere more to the myth than to the facts about the king himself, however, we may say that it does Charles II both more and less than justice. Charles was in fact lazy and much too tolerant. But he was other things as well, of which the poem says nothing. In praising his patient fury and offering the king's last speech, the poem says nothing as to how it was that Charles could really strike against his foes. He could behave in so kingly and godlike a manner because he had protected himself by a most ungodlike action behind the arras in the queen's bedroom: he had made a secret treaty to get three and a half million francs for three years from Louis XIV of France. This is not one of the "petty sums of foreign gold" referred to in the poem, 709. Charles had enough money assured to become independent of Parliament, and could dissolve it while speaking grandly of the fury of a patient man. The patient man was patient until he was sure of having enough money so that he could afford to be furious. The poem may not reveal that Charles could be just as false in his way as Achitophel was in his, and the parade of the king's virtues, mythical qualities, has the effect of concealing his actual political adroitness while incorporating the myth with all of its effective overtones. Let us not forget that the poem says nothing of how able the king was. Only his wicked foe, or one of the loyal few could seem really gifted. The king must be all that the myth demands, even though what really saved him is never mentioned.

The poem says nothing of the fearful bloodshed, injustice, cruelty, and intrigue of the day. Although the portrait of Corah shows that a great many lies were told, we are unaware of the anguish of innocent men perjured and betrayed in the interests of political maneuvering. There is nothing like the one hint of the fearful human price paid for a sophisticated society such as Pope gives in *The Rape of the Lock,* when wretches ascend the gallows lest there be an unseemly delay in serving dinner. As for Charles II, we can only wonder how near his portrait might have come to showing him on a high level of kingship, had the poet left the security of his ready-made myth and shown the king acting as he really did act. His actual behavior might be made to seem no less ideal than the standard royal formula of clement, mild, patient, or lenient. Was Charles all these things even when, or especially when, he signed the death warrants of innocent men with tears in his eyes? They must die so that the common enemy might have its way for a time, and the rebels be allowed to discredit themselves by their violence and extremity so as to contrast with the moderation and steadiness of the king himself. Charles wept as he paid the price for established order, so precious was his duty to him. Again was he not patient and lenient on the highest divine, lawful plane, when he delayed, temporized, played for time to let the mood of the country change, to let the frenzy of the Plot subside, to let the enemy pay out enough rope to hang itself indeed? His speech in the poem is the last word then, the ritual giving effect to his myth, corresponding to the last word of his abrupt and stunning dissolution of Parliament at Oxford, a peal of thunder from on high as the poem says, that completely changed everything.

If we ask whether the actual performance of Charles in the exclusion crisis might not have served to illustrate ideal kingly virtues more dramatically than the inherited myth, we get a sense of the abstractness and aloofness of a poem which is yet knee deep in actual affairs. For his own contemporaries Dryden did not have to underline the poem's immediate application, and he could decide in favor of mythical terms because for his readers the poem would gain rather than lose in contemporary force from such materials. The poem elevates and rehabilitates Charles II in what seem to us highly artificial and conventional terms. Dryden chooses this way not because he could not succeed with a more direct handling of his problem, but because, as he expressly declared, he was writing a poem; this enabled him both to write a tract for the times and to give classical expression to the conservative outlook on human affairs.

Conclusion

Adverse criticism of *Absalom and Achitophel* usually admits that for its kind the poem is successful. If its view of human affairs seems limited, too meager, merely safe or even cowardly, the arts of persuading us to accept it are most skillfully employed. The resources of various genres combine with good effect, the assumptions and airs of satire come in without bitterness or violence, the moral clash of good and evil unfolds powerfully, and the poem's championship of the royal cause is a triumph of harmony between means and ends, of myth in union with immediate fact.

In many less obvious ways the poem gets its desired effect by skill in harmonizing means and ends. Figures of speech with long associations like those surrounding the medical and architectural images take on the force of symbols, as do common analogies which in the course of time accumulate immense rhetorical effect in making general ideas or theories seem concrete, easily understood. The poem seems inevitable, and its physical disproportion becomes itself functional in showing that what is right is so clear and simple, the poet is left with very little to say beyond obvious and undebatable truths. So also with the poetic convention or Virgilian echo "my weary Muse," 898; since it comes late in the poem, this weariness helps persuade the reader to accept the lesson before him. The Muse is "weary" from belaboring a point already accepted by the reader; it is "weary" from long service in the cause of right which ought to be espoused by everyone; it is "weary" from trying to think of more to say about something that needs only to be clearly stated to seem self-evident. If it is all so clearly right, why go on discussing it? We often hear

that Dryden is a great arguer in verse; he certainly can make
us feel that his position is the only one available to a sensible
man. But he is not a great reasoner with flawless logic clearly
pursued. His reasoning is a priori, often to the point of beg-
ging the question. Thus he argues better than he reasons, if
one of the aims of argument is to persuade the reader. In *Absalom and Achitophel* Dryden argues within the poem very
ably, supported by its assumptions, by the myth, by what he
can take for granted in the minds of his readers, by the resources of poetry and rhetoric. Indeed Dryden is nowhere
more a poet drawing on poetic inspiration and inheritance
than where he poses most as a dispassionate reasoner compelled to his results by relentless logic and experience.

Dryden not only argues speciously himself but uses false
arguments by his enemies for satiric effect. The reasoning of
Achitophel's first temptation speech is summarized so as to
expose its falseness. The "desire of power" passage (305–8) is
flatly contradictory, the desire being both a vicious weed and
heavenly fire; what is a destructive principle in fact becomes
an excess of virtue, sanctioned by heaven. The contradiction
destroys itself merely in being stated, and so discredits the
man capable of tempting another in such terms. Saintsbury
and others have shown that Dryden's arguments are ad hoc,
that especially in his criticism he thinks only of the point now
before him for proof, careless of having proved the opposite
yesterday, of probably arguing for something else tomorrow.
The position of his mature didactic poems is large and general
enough, however, to let Dryden hold a more stable line. He
gains enormously as well from his air of supporting a view
which is of course held by his audience, as indeed it must be
held by anyone able to reason at all. The assumption that
there cannot be any other opinion worth holding is allied
with an urbane, conversational manner at times, and gains
support from a further air of impartiality that is highly persuasive.

The rhetoric of assumed rightness takes for granted the
structure of society in Dryden's time. Like Molière's plays, the

poem allows no adverse criticism of the prevailing order. Its validity is assumed, and the arguments for changing it are presented only in order to show their ruinous, suicidal folly. He seems to force the audience to share his views by assuming that they already do so. In this way the audience itself might become an object of satire. If the readers of *Absalom and Achitophel* do not share the position of the poet, they must be wrong and automatically place themselves among the group or the ideas being condemned. The assumption that an audience is with him can be a telling weapon for a writer, especially if he knows or suspects that they are not, or at least fears that they may not be. The assumption condemns those who are supposed to share a view that in fact they oppose; they are then shamed into accepting or seeming to accept what is presented as right. Taking it for granted that the audience is with him is part of the satirist's superiority to what he is condemning. If the audience does not accept his view, he is superior to it as well. In dealing with Achitophel, for instance, the narrator gains by talking as if there could not be two opinions about such a person. If it is true that like Satan's, Achitophel's is "A name to all succeeding ages curst" (151), it must be largely because of what is now being said of him. The rhetoric here is effective in stating as already true of Achitophel's reputation what will be true only when the poem is through with him, assuming always that the audience agrees with what is said. Again, after the lines on the great wits and their alliance with madness, we hear a question (165–68) using the verbs "refuse" and "punish," with a subjunctive mood suspended on the auxiliary "should." The question is supposed to suspend our judgment, but it forces the judgment in fact against Achitophel by seeming to declare that he has indeed treated his old age cruelly. The reader seems allowed a free judgment, and by this seeming he is tricked into accepting the satirist's opinion. He is diverted from examining too closely the satirist's implied judgment; his mind is made up for him while seeming to be left uninfluenced. He is kept under the satirist's control throughout by making it appear that no such control is needed for those who accept what is obviously true.

The tone of familiar upper-class conversation, casual and easily allusive, is again highly persuasive; the poem sounds far less didactic in these informal terms; and when statements are made, they are easy to accept from a position of urbane familiarity. The satirist here avoids any sign of violence in treating something that was itself violent; indeed one of his chief aims must be to show how dangerously violent the enemy was. He has to treat potential violence with a tone of controlled urbanity, to seem above the possible dangers he is warning against. Restraint and aloofness go with the sense of stating things simply about which there will be no debate. The portraits unfold in easy compression, leaving out many usual verbs or connectives for appositive terms. The satirist assumes predication without making it, and so appears to assume agreement without having to argue for it in the portraits, making one clear statement after another not subject to debate. The concluding passages of the essay on innovation are then summaries of views assumed all along as true. The poem never seems to let go of us, and controls our attention as well as our response by rapid concentration of meaning. For satire it is most effective, since like the wickedness of Achitophel the object of satire is shown directly, with no need of denouncing it further. The truth of what the satirist says becomes the more unquestionable when he reports it so clearly and actively.

The satire gains further by a tone of fairness, with praise of something likewise evil, or regret over what cannot be otherwise. The poem's air of impartiality has been much exaggerated, since it conceals the fact that Dryden is not impartial at all—another means to persuade us of something about which the satirist is in deadly earnest. The satirist praises Achitophel, not to be fair, but to show that both in spite of and because of their admitted excellence, Achitophel and all men like him are highly dangerous. Any praise of virtue in satire makes the exposure of vice more telling, partly by contrast, partly by giving a sense that the complete truth is being told. The praise added to Achitophel helps sustain the movement of the poem toward a position of final, unquestionable truth. The poet will give the enemy all that is due, leaving nothing more to be explored, so that the final statement of the loyal few and the king becomes the more unanswerable. If other rebels are not so generously praised, they must have shown no extenuating virtue, else the poet would have brought it forward as with Achitophel. If praise adorns the most dangerous of all the conspirators, we can be sure that fairness and impartiality have gone as far as possible. When the king speaks at last, then, we know that everything relevant has been said of his enemies and friends; there can be no real opposition to the king remaining. This is true in theory, since he is king and so represents the only valid opinion. It is true in the poem also, where every allowance has preceded his speech. The whole dispute arises only because he has been so indulgent; he has waited for all that could possibly be said on both sides and the praise of Achitophel particularly heightens this sense of the king's absolute rightness after all the evidence is in.

The air of fairness, to be sure, is much more apparent than real, as the poet shows how wrong the enemy is by various devices, and not by reasoned argument. Until the essay on innovation, he does not allow the enemy an equal position. Only after the poem has discredited the rebels for some 750 lines is there an apparently balanced attempt to give the two opposing views. If we object that Achitophel's second speech (373-476) offers a defense of democratic principles, the answer is that this defense comes only after its speaker has emerged as false and accursed. We will not accept on its merits as argument, something said by, in fact, the devil himself.

The air of impartiality is again effective when the poem seems to deplore something that it nevertheless has no choice but to record. One of the conventions of elegy is to lament what has occurred, to say, if only something other than what now is, were in fact true. Dryden uses this early in his Hastings elegy (67), "O had he di'd of old," and *Absalom and Achito-*

phel employs the "O that," "O had," "Yet O" beginning for passages contrasting what is with something ideal or preferable. The king's speech in 957, 999, and 1003, the elegy on Ossory (838), the narrator's regret over Israel (753) and over Achitophel (192), and even Absalom himself (702) when he seems to deplore what he must do—all these in varying degrees employ the rhetoric of lament. Here again the poet influences judgment by joining "O" with a subjunctive construction. A desire seems to be expressed while shown to be futile. The king in 957 cried out for Absalom's repentance, "O that yet he would repent and live"; the very expression cancels its hope by its own despair. In 192 the narrator cries of Achitophel, "O, had he been content to serve the crown"; by the inversion and the subjunctive and the lyrical "O," he shows the futility of hoping for anything of the sort. The regret comes carefully after the devastating portrait of Achitophel's falsity, so that its location also cancels its regret just as its terms of expression do. The narrator's pious wishes are unattainable before and while he utters them, and so we are in fact not allowed to think that Achitophel will ever be anything but false—just as we are not allowed to think that Absalom will repent or that in 702 he can confine the damage wrought by the king's policy to his own ostensibly selfless person.

But the larger meanings of the poem attend on its exploration of good and evil, and the text is suffused with associations of evil on the side of the rebels. Rebellion is sickness, unrest, lack of "bounds" or control, lack of order, selfishness, falsity, the devil, hell, and evil. In contrast, loyalty is health, control, peace, order, unselfish devotion, Heaven, God, and goodness. As Courthope long ago saw, the poem's satiric moral allegory made any try for literary symmetry unworkable. An epic balance between good and evil would have required in the end an opposite emphasis, with size and power on the side of good. In *Absalom and Achitophel* there must be a vast imbalance, apparently in favor of evil. Evil is complicated, multifarious, specious, and fraudulent—hard to detect and express particularly when it aims at rebellion, as the conservative myth had so long held. The kind of evil that leads to rebellion then requires searching analysis and exploration.

In turn a complicated analysis of the rebel-evil side will suggest the formless incoherence and heterogeneity of the enemy. The many suggestions in the poem of multitude, crowd, mass, or herd are important to this end. The poet must take a long time to tell who and what these people are, since they must represent the multiple forms in which human error, stupidity, guile, selfishness, materialism, and ambition can present themselves. The calm simplicity and unity of the good needs only one kind of man, since it is the principle of order in action. Before the essay on innovation, the evil is presented at length, then the lesson to be learned from it is given; the right course of action is stated through the loyal few and the king's own speech.

When we see the poem as a conflict between good and evil, the medical and architectural figures take on new importance. The associations of disease needing cure keep with the rebels and their various forms of evil. So also the architectural notions of order, unity, stability, and useful strength remain with the good to be preserved, with the power of rightful authority. Evil is divided in its nature, as seen in the selfishness of the main portraits and of so many others who are in it only for themselves. Hence evil will end by destroying itself, and the good will prevail from its own unity and order and from the inherent flaw in evil. In addition the good has the sanction of lawful—that is, divine—authority, a sanction that can be invoked at any time an indulgent and merciful king chooses and which must prevail whenever it decides to exert itself. In spite of its enormous energy and power, evil then never has a chance to succeed—partly because of its weakness as carried by the medical images of disease, partly from the order and unified strength of the good as seen in the architectural image, and finally from the supernatural force that sustains the king's power as necessarily representing good.

When illegitimacy presents itself at the outset of the poem, the forces of good and evil are not long in arranging them-

selves. The devil is on the side of illegitimacy, God on the
side of inherited kingship and established order. Every man
may not be God or devil as Zimri is supposed to believe, but
every man in the plot is on the devil's side, and all who are
loyal are on God's side. Those in the plot partake, then, of the
devil's nature in some degree; if they are talented and misuse
their talent, the devil too is clever, and even if they are not in
themselves bad, they lend themselves to misuse and perversion. In turn, all who are loyal, on God's side, have the qualities of goodness in large measure. At 43–44 the division into
good and evil is given a heavenly sanction in the first of the
connecting *sententiae* that carry the line of the poem's didactic
lesson into its summary, the essay on innovation. Before
launching into the main body of the poem, then, the poet first
makes the distinction between good and evil:

> But life can never be sincerely blest:
> Heaven punishes the bad, and proves the best.

It is not long before "the bad" here joins the plot which so
largely controls the actual narrative. Even before the plot as
such is mentioned, the Jews and their restlessness anticipate
the plot in a reference to early signs of popular unrest:

> But these were random bolts; no form'd design,
> Nor interest made the factious crowd to join.   (67–68)

The "form'd design" or plot will come later and will discredit
those associated with it. Now the "sober" element free of
"stain," relying on past experience, displays "wise affright"
as it contemplates the "wounds" and "ugly scars" that render
the memory of civil war accursed. Sin, damnation, evil, bloodshed, ugliness all gather their implications together against
the rebels and support the wisdom and sobriety of those who
are loyal. Moderation and the king's own mildness keep the
peace, and (78) "The bad found no occasion to rebel." They
are bad because they are rebels, and while looking for an
excuse to exercise their wickedness they are held back only
by moderation and decency in others. But in the second of

the poem's sententiae, the moral lesson of the ingenious devil shows that rebellion and evil are not to be denied entirely:

> But, when to sin our byast nature leans,
> The careful devil is still at hand with means;
> And providently pimps for ill desires.   (79–81)

The devil is "provident" lest ill desire be wasted without achieving some evil result. Pimping too suggests some indulgence or satisfaction obtained outside the law, and hence evil. The mythical need of a plot then follows (82–84), to give effect to this desire for sin. In turn the plot gets support when the distinction between right and wrong is distorted. Lines 88–89 tell us,

> But when the chosen people grew more strong,
> The rightful cause at length became the wrong.

Here "chosen people" are the English; the Jebusites are the Catholics whose cause had once been right but now was wrong. They are now God's enemies (91), involved in the plot whose fabric is mostly lies, 114. They are themselves reduced to fraud to persuade others to their beliefs, especially in the sacrament, 121. This invites a reference to folly among those who are disaffected:

> So fraud was used (the sacrificers trade)
> Fools are more hard to conquer than persuade.
>
> (124–25)

Their effort to get converts brought them low indeed, as they "raked" about amid whatever waste had fallen to the ground:

> Their busie teachers mingled with the Jews
> And raked for converts even the court and stews.
>
> (126–27)

As to whether they meant to kill the king, no one knows (133) "how far the devil and Jebusites may go," thus keeping any and every disaffected element on the side of the devil in the poem.

When the poem begins to explore more fully the reasons for disaffection, the rebel cause is seen to grow (142–43), from envy, unsatisfied ambition, or defeated vanity. The devil reappears in suggestions of a Satanic revengefulness:

> Some had in courts been great and, thrown from thence,
> Like fiends were hardened in impenitence.   (144–45)

Like Satan these were ungrateful to a merciful king as well (148–49), who had raised them high in office and power.

These concentrated allusions to the devil and his special traits are well placed just before the portrait of Achitophel, the devil's agent in the poem. Having reviewed the temptation scene and the operations of the Satanic Achitophel against the seemingly passive young Absalom, we need only remind ourselves of how pervasively the language of fraud and evil clings throughout the poem to the rebel conspirators and their cause. They are discredited by multiple suggestions of wickedness, of energy out of control, of excess, of something wrong from beginning to end. Even in Absalom's reply to Achitophel, he seems doubtful in the face of something wrong that he is not sure of being able to accept, as seen in the seven questions he asks in 315–45. He begins to grow positive only when he comes to the king's only offense against him, which the poem (1–16) has already carefully shown is not an offense. His claims are flimsy, as suggested by the term "pretense" or "pretending" in 315, 362, 463, and 504; and the text never leaves Absalom far from the implications of sin, crime, madness, and rebellion, 335–36, 342, 372. The Miltonic inversion of "Him staggering" deepens the hellish quality, Absalom cannot escape "hell's dire agent," 373, who now "pours fresh forces in," 375; the attack by a military force suggests power on the side of evil, and with use of the passive voice for Absalom, as in 311–12, seems for the moment to excuse him as being misled or coerced beyond his power. The Iago-like suggestions of 403, "Turn'd all his virtues to his overthrow," reappear in 428, "his vain pretense" implying that the king's kindness is ungenuine when the poem rings with it through-

out; or in 436, "to cheat his heir," as if the king partook of the
fraud that is inseparable from the rebellion against him. The
pressure on the wickedness of Achitophel and his cause is relentless throughout, and never more so than when he tries to
drag the king to his own level.

The passages summarizing the miscellaneous elements on
the side of evil continue to associate rebellion with the standard mythical traits. The phrase "haranguers of the throng"
(509) implies the intent to mislead by eloquence, and 514
keeps the sense of betrayal alongside the civil war. Under
Cromwell the Solymaean rout were versed "In godly faction,
and in treason bold," thus using an oxymoron first and direct
evil second in "treason," which is of course "bold" and hence
evil like Achitophel, also bold, 153. Lines 523–24 have at least
three terms to condemn their subject, as we see the nation
"enslaved" by Sanhedrin and priest, their "spoils" justified by
"inspiration" implying stolen goods and the personal, uncontrolled element always to be deplored. Suggestions of pred-
atory animals are added (527–30), in terms like "pack,"
"scent," "deepest mouthed," and "breed." In 533 "numerous"
is repeated from 529, where the "host" was numerous, now
becoming a "herd," keeping the sense of mindless animals and
the always unfavorable implications of size and formlessness
in the conspiracy. Lines 535–40 refer to "mere instinct,"
"blind benefit of fate," saved "in their own despite," again
suggesting a thoughtless mass, not responsible even for such
religion as it has. In 541 "the tools" continues the meaning of
something merely used, a utensil fit only for the "base ends"
of rebels, as in 806. The hydra of sprouting heads returns to
the animal, the threatening ugly danger of energy out of
control, like the fire in *Annus Mirabilis* (993), which is also a
hydra.

After Zimri, the narrator suggests (569–70) that his account
of all the rest would be endless, underlining the magnitude of
the rebellion again. But now he must think of his dignity as
a poet, and will not be specific about those "below the dignity
of verse"—a mixture of survivals from civil war times and

current nobodies. He would be guilty of dullness, a fatal satiric word, to dwell on Balaam and Caleb with the contemptuous lewd suggestions of "well-hung" and "cold," or on Nadab with his hypocrisy of "canting." The word "scorn" (578) continues the note of contempt carried through all the lines since those on Zimri, and "bull-fac'd" Jonas suggests a sullen, fiercely dangerous animal along with the hint of his misusing a legal position to distort the law. An excellent transition is made from Jonas to Shimei, within a gradual movement from the general lot below the dignity of verse, to several particular names, to one name, Jonas, more at length, then fully to Shimei, who is of the same kind only worse, 583. The transition to Corah (630–31) is made with another suggestion of contempt toward those below the dignity of recollection; it would be too much even for a Plot witness—that is, a confirmed liar, unlike the honest narrator of the poem. The lines from Corah to Absalom's progress speech (682–97) are alive with unfavorable hints: friends of every sort, good and bad, "deluded" Absalom, at once the victim of falsity and himself a hypocrite in his concealment of joy and his bowing low to popularity, instead of reverently to his father. In 690 he "frames" all his words and looks, suggesting artifice; and the sense of a scheming calculation and cunning passes into something almost serpentine (692–93) as Absalom "glides" like a snake "unfelt" into their "secret Hearts." Their hearts are secret in being unperceived even by themselves, or containing things they would never reveal to anyone, even if they knew. Lines 694–97 suggest pity and regret for the people, and the sweetness of honey in Absalom's words implies that it conceals something bitter or unpleasant, remembering the inseparable combination in Horace.

But of all the unfavorable hints that constantly press against the conspiracy throughout its long analysis, that of a fraud with a pleasing exterior is most consistent. As Absalom begins his progress with the usual apparatus of popular appeal, he gives a royal impression when compared with the sun. The metaphor returns to the Old Testament with reference to "the promised land" (732) surveyed by the new young king. Does this mean, too, that the kingship, like the Promised Land, is something that will never be entered by one who has most desired it from afar? For some offense against God (his illegitimacy), then, Absalom will not have his dearest wish fulfilled. Yet now he is saluted and received everywhere with divine honors, as befits a true king. But at 739 this beautiful tableau becomes a fraud. Reference to "the people's eyes" and "seemed" show that it is merely on the surface a royal pageant. It is a "disguise" for the aims of false Achitophel, to whom the poem now returns as it repeats the case against the rebels. This progress of Absalom's turns out also to be part of the great villain's scheme: it is to test popular sentiment, to find out how much support he can count on before making his move. Like all such endeavors, of course (745–46), it is "colored," "a smooth pretense," and "specious." The two main lines long ago set out for all such frauds again emerge: religion and reform always cheat and always please, reminding us of the union between deceit and a pleasing exterior. Even if Absalom himself is not cheating by his lovely person, someone else is certain to be doing so—Achitophel, of course. The entire scene once and for all is exposed as a mere pageant, a masquerade proceeding as all rebellion must. It is important to see that the poem stops just before the essay on innovation to repeat its union of fraud and deception with a pleasing exterior. The poem draws together its entire case against the rebellion: it is nothing but an attractive swindle. Thirty lines (723–53) speak of Absalom's behavior and shade into the general meaning. He has charmed people by his grace and manner, and convinced them that he will improve their lot and right their wrongs. The people, the "crowd," still believe their kings oppress—still, that is, in spite of all the evidence for the goodness of David. Absalom is now a savior, a blessed Messiah, since the Jews in the New Testament could not recognize their true redeemer when he came, any more than in the Old Testament they could worship the true God instead of golden calves and idols.

Their problem remains to know their true king for what he is, and happily to accept his rule, which the last line of the poem repeats: "And willing nations knew their lawful lord." The rhetoric by means of which the poem has discredited the king's enemies has for its aim to re-establish the primacy of the king. When all has been said on the side of faction, when its many displays of number, specious attraction, and argument, interest, ambition, cleverness and intellect, knavery, falsity, credulity, and even deceived goodness, energy, and power—when all this has appeared, multiplied in every direction and summarized, what happens? Two things are encountered. The first, in the essay on innovation, is the truth in the conservative myth, maintaining distrust of novelty, refusal to cure disease by making it worse, refusal to destroy a fabric in repairing it, or to violate institutions sacred as the ark itself. Secondly, there is the king's own power, derived from God and the nature of things, and absolutely irresistible when he chooses to assert it. Against the enormous bulk of the rebellion there is an inherited set of ideas, feelings, and principles that coincide not with any individual's personal view but with the nature of things seen through long experience.

There is, of course, a grave danger in such a rhetorical device, and we have to ask whether Dryden succeeds as well as Plato, Newman, or Dostoevsky in using it. Socrates is fond of making all possible concessions to his opponents, stating their case better than they can, putting it so well that he seems caught in a position from which he cannot emerge victorious. So also Newman, who seems to give to his antagonists' view an impressive order and power, the more effectively to create the scene for his own argument. Victory is the more impressive and telling when achieved over such superbly equipped enemies. Dryden shows a poor handful around the forsaken king, standing against a mighty array. What chance have they? The chance that being right always confers. The remembrance of Dostoevsky is attractive here. Some will maintain that in *The Brothers Karamazov* Ivan is allowed to make so powerful a case against organized religion that the answer to it fails. But

perhaps there is no intellectual answer; like the unselfish loyalty of the few to David, the answer lies in virtues that are not
a function of an analytical mind like Achitophel's. These are
the virtues of simply good men: unselfishness, devotion to
ideals higher than themselves, loyalty, generosity, courage.
Thus after the case by argument is made (752–810), Dryden
the great verse debater and reasoner makes his case outside
the realm of argument, on the side of goodness and devotion,
the realm of feeling and spirit. As with Ivan, the case against
religion is intellectual: the case for it may not be.

Now the case for rebellion is that it becomes a vehicle for
so many elements in our common nature that it appears overwhelming, irresistible. Dryden does not argue for it; he merely
presents what he finds in his myth. The human tendency to
be restless, discontented, self-deceived, ambitious, and fond
of illusions as to wherein true benefit consists—all this has
an outlet through rebellion which embraces a far larger area of
human impulse and need than loyalty does. All appearance
then favors the king's enemies. There will always seem to be
an attraction from which the vast majority think they can get
something for themselves. The attractions of revolt as Dryden
sees them are as multifarious as the forms of human selfishness and illusion; yet revolt must fail, since the higher realities
are against it. The attractions of the king's side benefit none
of the loyal few. The attractions are simply that this is right,
and to mention the loyal few is to praise them automatically—
"naming is to praise," 816. They are where they belong, no
argument being needed to explain why they behave as they
do. Indeed the lack of argument is part of Dryden's rhetoric
to show that there cannot be two opinions about such men.
On the other side, an elaborate and complex series of arguments and analyses is needed by Achitophel to defend or explain the rebellion, to persuade Absalom and others to a
course of action that does not carry its own vindication.

The poem's construction supports the virtue of the king's
patience and forbearance. As Verrall says, the long summary
in 917–32—plus 933–35, giving the loyalists' view of the crisis

—is suspended in "a series of anacoluthic sentences" to post-
pone as long as possible the king's speaking. His patience
seems even more remarkable in waiting so long, in enduring
so much. We wait for the end of the sentences and so add to
the suspense and dramatize further both the king's virtues and
his message. His fairness and indulgence are tested as he waits
as long as possible before giving the last word. The enemy receives the fullest possible exploration, while the king waits.
No one says anything but the two rebel leaders, and it seems
that falsity is about to prevail. But it is only the better to
dramatize the final victory of truth. All appearances have to be
against what is right, so that reality in truth can appear stronger when it speaks. We think of the unpromising hero who wins
nonetheless, of David against Goliath indeed—of the drama
of victory snatched from overwhelming forces, victory when
the cause seems lost. But force against the king is powerful in
appearance only and lacks the power of truth that now declares
itself through the king.

Hugh Walker has repeated the standard objection to the
poem's ending. "Masterly as it is, *Absalom and Achitophel* is
yet marred by one great flaw—its end." On the contrary, the
end shows how Dryden has commanded his material throughout, how well he has adapted his means to a controlled purpose. The poem ends in the only way it can, as it must, with
the king saying just the things that must be said, in the right
manner, with complete finality. The sudden breaking off of
the poem shows the king's total command; the greatest possible structure of opposition has risen against him; yet the
moment he chooses to speak, this becomes meaningless. The
king has spoken; what else remains? To go on would falsify
the king's position, so carefully built up in the poem. If he
has spoken, then God has spoken, hence the law has spoken.
The Restoration-Roman question "What is the law?" is answered. The poem is over.

Bibliographical Notes

It seems unnecessary to draw up one more formal list of books and articles bearing on late 17th-century England; such titles are already numerous and easily found. A work of synthesis, assembly, and interpretation that starts from familiar materials must rely for its effect on the combinations and judgments offered as a whole, and the apparatus of reference may keep to bare essentials. In such a case the results of reading are more valuable than any record of the means taken or the materials used. My work in some ways resembles that of B. Rajan, *Paradise Lost and the Seventeenth Century Reader* (1947), whose references "merely suggest the extent to which the themes discussed were part of the popular heritage . . ." (p. 17), the specific source being frequently of no significance.

However, in addition to references made in the text itself, a number of quoted passages stand out in such length and importance as to invite full acknowledgment. These quotations are documented at the beginning of the notes for each chapter. For the rest, the chief sources and secondary works used are listed, with author, title, and date of publication. Ancient classical authors have been taken largely from the Loeb Classics Editions; except for occasional passages which I have translated or paraphrased myself, the Loeb translations have sufficed. The great French critics Rapin, Boileau, Le Bossu, and others have been read mainly in editions available to readers in Dryden's time. Spelling has generally been modernized.

In the study of Dryden himself the following are standard: *Essays,* ed. W. P. Ker, two volumes, 1900; for the poems to 1680, Volume 1 of *The Works of John Dryden,* ed. Edward Hooker and H. T. Swedenberg, Jr., 1956; for *Absalom and Achitophel* and other poems, the Cambridge Edition of *The Poetical Works of John Dryden,* ed. George R. Noyes, 1950; for the plays, *The Dramatic Works,* ed. Montague Summers, 6 vols. 1931–32. The 5th edition of W. D. Christie's reading of *Absalom and Achitophel,* revised by C. H. Firth, 1911, has also been of value. The "References and Abbreviations" in James Kinsley's Oxford Edition, *The Poems of John Dryden* (1958), *1*, xix–xxi, provide an excellent summary of materials essential to the study of Dryden. The fuller work of Samuel H. Monk, *John Dryden: A List of Critical Studies* . . . (1950) is indispensable for all aspects of the poet's achievement.

Introduction

QUOTATIONS

Text Page

5	John Spencer, *Things New and Old* (1658), p. 193.
6	John Webster, *Academiarum Examen* (1654), p. 15.
6	Thomas Blount, *Academy of Eloquence* (1664), p. 19.
11	Matthew Tindal, *Christianity as Old as the Creation* (1730), *1*, 186.

See also Samuel Parker, *A Discourse of Ecclesiastical Polity*, 1670.

Among the numerous commentaries on myth, these have been useful: René Wellek and Austin Warren, *Theory of Literature* (1948), chap. 15; *Myth: A Symposium,* ed. Thomas A. Sebeok, 1955; Frederick Prescott, *Poetry and Myth,* 1927; Philip Wheelwright, "Poetry, Myth and Reality," in *The Language of Poetry,* ed. Allen Tate, 1942; W. K. Wimsatt, Jr., and Cleanth Brooks, *Literary Criticism: A Short History* (1957), chap. 31; Bronislaw Malinowski, "Myth in Primitive Psychology" in *Magic, Science and Religion* . . ., ed. Robert Redfield, 1948; Jacques Ellul, "Modern Myths," *Diogènes, 23* (1958), 23–40.

See also C. S. Lewis, *Rehabilitations,* 1939; Sir John Pollock, *The Popish Plot,* new ed. 1944; and E. M. W. Tillyard, *The English Epic and Its Background,* 1954.

PART ONE

Chapter 1. The Divinity of Order

QUOTATIONS

Text Page

20–21	John Dennis, *Critical Works, 1* (1939), 335.
22	Earl of Mulgrave, "An Essay upon Poetry" (1682), in Spingarn (see below), *2*, 295.

Text Page

From 17th-century and related sources, the ideas being reviewed here are so standard that they might readily be supported by an entirely different set of references. In addition to the above quotations, Joel E. Spingarn's *Critical Essays of the Seventeenth Century* (3 vols. 1909) contain passages to which reference has been made from Davenant, Ben Jonson, Howard, Shadwell, Hobbes, Rochester, Rymer, and Henry Reynolds. For Dennis, see his *Critical Works,* ed. Edward Hooker, 2 vols. 1939–43. The collection *Poems on Affairs of State* (1697) touches on most of the important issues of Dryden's time. The text has drawn for various examples also on *The Speech of Sir Edward Turnor . . .,* 1662; Simon Patrick, *Continuation of the Friendly Debate . . .,* 1669; Thomas Blount, *The Academy of Eloquence,* 1664; Sir Thomas Pope Blount, *De Re Poetica,* 1694; Sir John Beaumont, *Bosworth Field and Other Poems,* 1629; *Ludus Literarum,* 1674; Thomas Sprat, *History of the Royal Society,* 1667; Roger L'Estrange, *A Short View . . .,* 1660; John Wilkins, *A Discourse Concerning the Gift of Prayer,* 1690; Simon Daines, *Orthopoeia Anglicana,* 1640; Thomas Yalden, *Examen Poeticum,* 1693; George Puttenham, *The Arte of English Poesie* (1589), Cambridge, 1936; James Wright, *Country Conversations,* 1694; Anthony Collins, *Discourse Concerning Ridicule and Irony,* 1729; *A Journal from Parnassus* (ca. 1688), London, 1937; John Spencer, "The Multitude Always Desirous of a Change in Government," in *Things New and Old,* 1658; Thomas Browne, "Religio Medici," in *Works, 1,* 1904; and Meric Casaubon, *Treatise of Use and Custom,* 1638.

The late 17th century has had the benefit of long study by a series of splendid and now indispensable scholars. Their work forms a common stock of material upon which any student of English neoclassicism and related areas will be certain to draw. Standard bibliographies cannot fail to list the work of R. F. Jones, Louis I. Bredvold, Edward Hooker, Basil Willey, René Bray, A. F. B. Clark, and other writers who have established the lines upon which all serious study of the period must at least begin. To these may be added the now classical articles of Felix Schelling, Ruth Wallerstein, George Williamson, Morris Croll, and Paul S. Wood. Also of special use are the comments on heroic plays and the couplet in M. E. Prior, *The Language of Tragedy*, 1947; Douglass S. Mead, *The Literary Comparison in Jacobean Prose*, 1928; T. S. Eliot, *The Sacred Wood*, 1920, and *The Music of Poetry*, 1942; William Empson, *Seven Types of Ambiguity*, 1930; Yvor Winters, *In Defense of Reason*, 1947; Arthur M. Clark, *Studies in Literary Modes*, 1946; the articles on satire and satiric theory by Mary Randolph in *Studies in Philology*, *38* (1941), 125–57, and *Philological Quarterly*, *21* (1942), 368–84; and Northrop Frye, "The Nature of Satire," *University of Toronto Quarterly*, *14* (1944), 88 ff. For a cogent discussion of the "mob" and the "few", see Ian Watt, "The Ironic Tradition in Augustan Prose . . .," *Restoration and Augustan Prose*, 1956.

Chapter 2. Danger

QUOTATIONS

Text Page

51	Tacitus, *On Oratory*, 36–41, Loeb Classics.
56	Samuel Parker, *A Free and Impartial Censure of the Platonic Philosophy* (1666), p. 76.
59	Peter Charron, *Of Wisdom* (6th ed. 1670, trans. Samson Lennard), p. 57.

Spingarn's volumes have been useful again in reviewing literary practice for this chapter. Writers like Bishop Burnet, *History of His Own Time* (6 vols. 1833) and *A Discourse of the Pastoral Care* (1692), together with Hobbes, Thomas Sprat, Henry More, John Eachard, Samuel Parker, Joseph Glanvill, Thomas Blount, Samuel Daniel, Edward Phillips, Meric Casaubon, and others already referred to are among the standard sources in discussions of this kind. Rapin, Le Bossu, Charron, and Dominic Bouhours, *The Art of Criticism* (1705) have been used for comment on language and its control. See also George Hickes, *Some Discourses upon Dr. Burnet . . .*, 1695, and *The Spirit of Enthusiasm Exorcised*, 1683; Charles Blount, *Religio Laici*, 1683; Anthony Collins, *A Discourse of Free Thinking*, 1713; Theophilus Evans, *History of Modern Enthusiasm*, 1757; Alexander Ross, "Epistle Dedicatory" to *Medicus Medicatus*, 1645, and *A View of All Religions*, 5th ed. 1673; John Smith, *Select Discourses*, 1660; George Mackenzie, *Religio Stoici*, 1665; *Heraclitus Ridens*, May 17, 1681; *The Field of Blood*, 1681; Thomas Woolston, *Hireling Priests*, 1723.

On prose style and eloquence see the articles by R. F. Jones, reprinted in his Festschrift, *The Seventeenth Century . . .*, 1951; W. F. Mitchell, *English Pulpit Oratory . . .*, 1932; Hugh Macdonald, "Another Aspect of Seventeenth-Century Prose," *Review of English Studies* (1943), 33–43. On Quintilian see Lillian Feder, "John Dryden's Use of Classical Rhetoric," *PMLA, 69* (1954), 1261.

For the rules and other features of neoclassicism see Samuel Monk, *The Sublime*, 1935; H. T. Swedenberg, Jr., "Rules and English Critics of the Epic, 1650–1800," *Studies in Philology, 35* (1938), 566–87; Anne E. Burlingame, *The Battle of the Books in Its Historical Setting*, 1920; Truman Guy Steffan, *The Social Argument against Enthusiasm*, University of Texas Studies in English (1941), 39–63; Raymond Havens, "Changing Taste in the Eighteenth Century . . . ," *PMLA, 44* (1929), 535; George Williamson, *The Donne Tradition*, 1930, and Morris Croll's review in *Modern Philology, 28* (1930), 490.

Chapter 3. The Downfall of the Good Old Cause

QUOTATIONS

Text Page

67 The "loyalty oath" is quoted from Andrew Marvell, *An Account of the Growth of Popery . . .* (1677), p. 57.

74 Samuel Parker, *An Account of the . . . Divine Dominion and Goodness, Especially as They Refer to the . . . Pre-Existence of Souls* (1666), p. 90.

77 John Spencer, *Things New and Old* (1658), p. 543.

In addition to the numerous productions of the Tory propagandist Roger L'Estrange, this chapter draws again on Henry Tubbe, Simon Patrick, Thomas Blount, George Hickes, John Dennis, Nathaniel Fairfax, and Thomas Sprat. See also Thomas Craig, *The Right of Succession,* 1603; Richard Bancroft, *Dangerous Positions . . .,* 1640; John Heydon, *Advice to a Daughter,* 1658; "Preface" to *The Indictment of Twenty-Nine Regicides,* 1660; Peter Heylyn, *Aerius Redivivus . . .,* 1672; *Massinello: or A Satyr against the Association,* 1683; James Wright, *A Compendious View of the Late Tumults and Troubles . . .,* 1685; Samuel Pordage, *The Medal Reversed,* 1682; John Partridge, *Annus Mirabilis,* 1689; Walter Moyle, *An Argument Showing That a Standing Army . . .,* 1697; John Toland, *The Art of Governing by Parties,* 1701; *Enthusiasm No Novelty . . .,* 1739.

For various Restoration problems see F. J. C. Hearnshaw, *Conservatism in England,* 1933; R. F. Jones, *Ancients and Moderns,* 1936; J. Churton Collins, *The Satires of John Dryden,* 1916; Edwin Berry Burgum, "The Neoclassical Period . . .," *Sewanee Review,* 52 (1944), 248. On the tendency of conservatism to be conscious of itself only when threatened see Karl Mannheim, *Ideology and Utopia* (1936), pp. 206–15.

Chapter 4. Dryden's Own Temper

A general discussion of Dryden's tendencies must draw on the work of George Saintsbury, W. P. Ker, Mark Van Doren, A. W. Verrall, Louis Bredvold, James M. Osborn, George Noyes, and D. Nichol Smith. Dryden's *Essays* as edited by Ker (1900), his few *Letters,* edited by Charles Ward (1942), the *Prologues and Epilogues,* edited by W. B. Gardner (1951), and the *Dramatic Works,* edited by Montague Summers (1931–32) are essential. Mr. Hugh Macdonald has dealt with the attacks suffered by Dryden, and his indispensable *Bibliography . . .* (1939) lists the principal contemporary attacks and defenses of Dryden. Besides *Towser the Second, A Bull Dog . . .* (1681) and Shadwell's *The Medal of John Bayes* (1682), see *The Friendly Vindication of Mr. Dryden from the Censure of the Rota,* 1673; *A Panegyrick on the Author of Absolom and Achitophel . . . ,* 1681; *The Tory Poets: A Satyr,* 1682; *A Satyr to His Muse. By the Author of Absalom and Achitophel,* 1682; and *The New Projector; or The Priviledged Cheat* (ca. 1660), reprinted in Benjamin Boyce, *The Polemic Character . . .,* 1955, showing how the man who had praised Cromwell and then had welcomed the King was established as a recognized object of scornful satire. See also Roswell G. Ham, "Dryden vs. Settle," *Modern Philology*, 25 (1928), 409–16, and R. Jack Smith, "Shadwell's Impact upon John Dryden," *Review of English Studies, 20* (1944), 29–44.

Tributes paid to Dryden at the time of his death in 1700 are of less interest. See, for example, *Luctus Britannici: or the Tears of the British Muses . . .,* and Daniel Kenrick, *A New Session of the Poets, Occasioned by the Death of Mr. Dryden.* The Folger Shakespeare Library is particularly rich in these and other materials indispensable to the study of 17th-century English literature. The student is happy in finding Macdonald's list of Drydeniana available to him there.

Most of the commentary on Dryden's plays used here is listed in Samuel H. Monk's *John Dryden: A List of Critical Studies . . .* (1950), pp. 25–36, including the work of Louis Bredvold, Mildred Hartsock, D. W. Jefferson, Joseph Wood Krutch, Kenneth Muir, Allardyce Nicoll, Lewis Teeter, and George W. Whiting. See also Moody E. Prior, *The Language of Tragedy,* 1947. On Dryden's criticism see Monk, pp. 37–43, especially the work of William E. Bohn, Jacob Bronowski, Prosser Hall Frye, Marvin Herrick, R. D. Jameson, Guy Montgomery, Frederick Pottle, Irving Ribner, John H. Smith, Hoyt Trowbridge, and George Williamson.

For various aspects of Dryden's language and imagery see Lester W. Cameron, "A Study of Dryden's Prose Style," diss., University of Wisconsin, 1937; Dennis Murphy, "Metaphor and Simile in Dryden's Non-Dramatic Poetry," diss., University of Iowa, 1936; George G. Loane, "Notes on the Globe 'Dryden,'" *Notes and Queries, 185* (1943), 272–81; and Reuben A. Brower's two articles as given in Monk, p. 14. See also James Russell Lowell on Dryden, *Among My Books,* 1870; Claude Lloyd, "John Dryden and the Royal Society," *PMLA,* 45 (1930), 967–76; and Bonamy Dobrée, "John Dryden," in *Variety of Ways,* 1932.

PART THREE

Chapter 5. Absalom and Achitophel: A Poem

E. E. Kellett's "John Dryden," in *Suggestions* (1923), 204, favors us with the patronizing remark about Dryden's soundness and lack of inspiration. Of more use than C. S. Lewis in *Rehabilita-*

tions (1939), once more, are the following: Ian Jack, *Augustan Satire* (1952), chap. 4; Reuben Brower, "An Allusion to Europe: Dryden and Tradition," *ELH, 19* (1952), 38–48; E. S. De Beer, *"Absalom and Achitophel:* Literary and Historical Notes," *Review of
English Studies, 17* (1941), 298–309; Bonamy Dobrée, *Restoration
Tragedy* (1929), pp. 46–47; Earl Wasserman, "Return of the En-
jambed Couplet," *ELH, 7* (1940), 247–51; Sister Mary C. Hoefling,
*A Study of the Structure of Meaning in the Sentences of the Satiric
Verse Characters of John Dryden,* 1946. See also the article by Lillian Feder, in Chapter 2 above, and John H. Smith, "Some Sources
of Dryden's Toryism," *Huntington Library Quarterly, 20* (1957),
233–43; Chester H. Cable, *"Absalom and Achitophel* as Epic Satire" in *Studies in Honor of John Wilcox* (1958), pp. 51–60; Morris
Freedman, "Dryden's Miniature Epic," *Journal of English and
Germanic Philology, 57* (1958), 211–19. See also the chapter on
Dryden in E. M. W. Tillyard, *The English Epic and Its Background* (1954), pp. 464–81, and W. K. Wimsatt, Jr., *Literary Criticism: A Short History* (1957), p. 197. *The Hebrew Iliad* (1957)
makes an interesting case for seeing the materials of Judges, Samuel, and I Kings as having epic proportions, like Homer's *Iliad;*
see the introduction by William G. Pollard, pp. 8 ff.

Chapter 6. What Is the Law?

For Coleridge's remark on Dryden see *Coleridge on the Seventeenth Century,* ed. Roberta F. Brinkley (1955), p. xxxv. The references to Charles II and his various pronouncements are taken from
Clarendon's great *History of the Rebellion,* Vol. 16. All references
to Clarendon will be to the edition of 1833. See also J. W. Allen,
English Political Thought . . ., 1, 1938.

Chapter 7. The Anatomy of Rebellion

QUOTATIONS

Text Page
   163   Bishop Hall, *Works* (1628), p. 1174.
  203–04   Francis Osborne, *Advice to a Son* (1656), pp. 43–44.

Besides those clearly mentioned in the text, the following 17th-
century materials have been used: Robert Harris, *Absalom's Funeral . . .,* 1614; Richard Vines, *The Posture of David's Spirit . . .,*
1644; Francis Osborne, *A Persuasive,* 1651; W. C., *Trade's De-*

struction Is England's Ruine . . ., 1659; A. Cowley, "A Discourse . . . Concerning . . . Oliver Cromwell," and "Of Liberty," in Vol. 2 of *English Writings*, 1905–06; William Pindar, *Sermon before the Lord Mayor*, 1677; John Caryll, *Naboth's Vinyard*, 1679; Thomas D'Urfey, "Dedication" to *Sir Barnaby Whigg*, 1681; Josias Pleydell, *Loyalty and Conformity Asserted*, 1682; *The Certain Way to Save England . . .*, 1681; *The Perfect Politician . . .*, 1681; Samuel Pordage (Elkanah Settle?), *Azaria and Hushai*, 1682; "The True Englishman," Vol. 2 of *Poems on Affairs of State*, 1697.

Extensive use has also been made of two collections of 17th-century "characters," ed. D. Nichol Smith, *Characters from . . . the Seventeenth Century*, 1918, and Richard Aldington, *A Book of Characters*, 1924; E. N. S. Thompson, "Character Books" in *Literary Bypaths of the Renaissance*, 1924; and Benjamin Boyce, *The Theophrastan Character in England to 1642*, 1947.

In addition to the work of Brown, Davies, Jones, Kaye, Wallerstein, and Wolf listed in Monk's *John Dryden: A List*, p. 23, see articles by Allardyce Nicoll, "Political Plays of the Restoration," *Modern Language Review, 16* (1921), 224–42; Merritt Y. Hughes, "Dryden as a Statist," *Philological Quarterly, 6* (1927), 335–50; Maurice Irvine, "Identification of Characters in Mulgrave's 'Essay upon Satyr,'" *Studies in Philology, 34* (1937), 533–51; and James Kinsley, "Historical Allusions in *Absalom and Achitophel*," *Review of English Studies*, new ser. 6 (1955), 291–97.

All references to the plays are to Montague Summers' edition of the *Dramatic Works*, 1931–32. A. W. Verrall's classical *Lectures on Dryden* (1914) are still indispensable. Francis S. Ronalds, *The Attempted Whig Revolution of 1678–1681* (1937), has an excellent bibliography and gives valuable historical background. For the Tory bias of Otway and his use of Shaftesbury in *Venice Preserved* see Zera S. Fink, *The Classical Republicans* (1945), pp. 144–48. For Miltonic comparisons see Elizabeth Pope, *Paradise Regained . . .*, 1947. The University of California dissertaton by Norman Oswald, "The Satires of John Dryden: A Critical Edition" (1946), has a good brief commentary and many valuable notes. For various aspects of Dryden as satirist and rhetorician see Pierre Legouis, "La Religion de Dryden avant 1682," *Revue Anglo-Americaine, 9* (1932), 526–35, and introduction to *Dryden: Poèmes Choisis* (1946), p. 21; Erich Auerbach, *Mimesis*, 1953; Kenneth Young, *John Dryden*, 1954; Raymond L. Brett, *The Third Earl of Shaftesbury,* 1951; Humbert Wolfe, *Notes on English Verse Satire,* 1929; and David Worcester, *The Art of Satire,* 1940.

Mr. Cecil Lang of Syracuse University is convinced that the word "mass" in line 113 refers to Roman Catholic ceremony.

Chapter 8. The Plot and the Malcontents

References to Plutarch are to the Modern Library Giant edition. Montaigne's favorite ideas recur throughout his *Essays;* see especially "Of Presumption," "Of Custom," "Of Experience," and *Apology for Raymond Sebond.*

Among the great many 17th-century sermons and other performances bearing on this chapter see *The Character of an Agitator,* 1647; Samuel Brunsell, *Solomon's Blessed Land,* 1660; Henry Dove, *A Sermon Preached before the Honourable House of Commons . . .,* Nov. 5, 1680; *The Character of a Fanatic in General . . .,* 1681; *The Character of a Sham-Plotter or Man Catcher.* By E. H.?, 1681; Roger L'Estrange, *Notes upon Stephen Colledge,* 1681; *The Character of a Leading Petitioner,* 1681; *The Countryman's Petition for a Parliament. . . . Mr. Barnaby Clod . . .,* ca. 1681; two *Sermons* by George Hooper: before the King, Nov. 5, 1681, and before the Lord Mayor, Oct. 30, 1681.

In addition to Clarendon for historical background see Sir John Pollock, *The Popish Plot,* new ed. 1944; F. S. Ronalds, *The Attempted Whig Revolution . . .,* 1937; the Scott-Saintsbury edition of Dryden, Vol. 9; H. C. Foxcroft, *A Character of the Trimmer,* 1946; and such articles as Godfrey Davies' "The Conclusion of Dryden's *Absalom and Achitophel,*" *Huntington Library Quarterly, 10* (1946), 69–82; George W. Whiting, "Political Satire in London Stage Plays," *Modern Philology, 28* (1930), 29–43; and James Kinsley, "The 'Three Glorious Victories' in *Annus Mirabilis,*" *Review of English Studies, 7* (1956), 30–37. In the same periodical, *17* (1941), 281–97, Joan Bennett's article, "An Aspect of the Evolution of Seventeenth Century Prose" shows vividly how the fear of deception extends from the necessary falsity of rebel leaders to distrust of rhetoric in the late 17th century. Jean Hagstrum's *The Sister Arts* (1958) has a valuable brief discussion of *Absalom and Achitophel,* seeing it as a kind of tableau picturing the Last Judgment. Ruth Wallerstein had also seen the poem as resembling a Renaissance painting.

Chapter 9. The Essay on Innovation

The poem by now is drawing together some familiar materials, endlessly repeated in the 17th century. The controlling images are seen in Butler's *Hudibras*, III, Canto 2, and in his "characters" of "A Medicine Taker" and "The Seditious Man." Sermons, pamphlets, and miscellaneous works are alive with references to foundations, fabrics, and structures, and to disease and the danger of its cure. See, for example, Thomas Pierce's sermon before Charles II, Feb. 1, 1662, *The Primitive Rule of Reformation;* John Crowne, "Epistle Dedicatory" to *The Ambitious Statesman . . .,* 1679; John Yalden, *Compendium Politicum, or The Distempers of Government,* 1680; Thomas Long, *A Sermon against Murmuring . . .,* May 29, 1680; Josias Pleydell, *Loyalty and Conformity Asserted . . .,* 1682; Francis Gifford, *The Wicked Petition,* 1681; "Preface" to *Poems on Affairs of State,* 1697; *The Character of an Ill-Court Favourite . . .,* translated from the French, 1681. Familiarity of the "ark" metaphor is suggested by the broadside poem *The Downfall of the Ark . . .,* 1661, and *A Hymne to the Ark in Newgate,* 1663.

For the King's own language see *The Letters, Speeches and Declarations of King Charles II,* ed. Arthur Bryant, 1935. On the analogy between political and natural bodies see also James E. Phillips, *The State in Shakespeare's Greek and Roman Plays,* 1940. Douglass Sargeant Mead, *The Literary Comparison in Jacobean Prose* (1926) has useful comment on typical images. On the dangers attending change see *Conservative England and the Case against Voltaire* (1950), passim.

Chapter 10. The Loyal Few

Marvell speaks of the "few" in his *An Account of the Growth of Popery . . .* (1677), p. 79. For other useful references see St. Evremond, *Works* (1728), 2, 107; John Toland, *The Art of Governing by Parties* (1701), pp. 174–75; Thomas Shadwell, "Preface to the Humorists," in Vol. 2 of Spingarn, *Critical Essays;* and John Caryll, *Naboth's Vinyard,* 1679.

See also Bonamy Dobrée, *Variety of Ways,* 1932; Thomas Carte, *The Life of James Duke of Ormond* (1851), *4,* 591–96; and Frank L. Huntley, "Dryden, Rochester, and the Eighth Satire of Juvenal," *Philological Quarterly, 18* (1939), 269–84. Z. S. Fink, *The*

Classical Republicans (1945) sees the few as leading society but responsible to the people and not to the King.

Chapter 11. The King Speaks

Reading for this chapter starts from the materials assembled by R. F. Jones in his excellent "The Originality of *Absalom and Achitophel*," *Modern Language Notes, 46* (1931), 211–18. Following his trail in the British Museum, one sees the justice of his remark, p. 215, n. 10: "The sermons and other references cited in this article . . . are only representative, and their number could easily be augmented by further investigation." In addition to many of the items already used, one finds new material in the splendid annotation of Professors Hooker and Swedenberg for Dryden's *Poems: 1649–1680,* the first volume of their edition of Dryden's *Works*. The notes especially to *Astraea Redux* and other tributes to Charles II document abundantly the celebration of the king's virtues and his resemblance to the biblical David. As examples of what might be indefinitely multiplied see Clement Barksdale, *The King's Return,* 1660; three poems under the title *Philo Carolus,* 1680; "Prologue" to John Banks' *The Unhappy Favourite . . .*, ca. 1681; and *An Apostrophe from the Loyal Party to the King's Most Sacred Majesty . . .*, 1681.

Sir John Beaumont's tribute to James is in *Bosworth Field . . .*, 1629; Thomas May's *Continuation of the Subject of Lucan's Historical Poem . . .* appeared in 1657; Halifax made an important defense of the king in *Observations upon a Late Libel, Called a Letter from a Person of Quality* (1681), as Dryden himself had done in defending the *Declaration*. See also Laurence Eachard, *The History of England . . . to . . . 1688* (1720), pp. 1007–8.

Valuable articles are by Earl Wasserman, "Dryden's Epistle to Charleton," *Journal of English and Germanic Philology, 55* (1956), 201–12, and William B. Gardner, "John Dryden's Interest in Judicial Astrology," *Studies in Philology, 47* (1950), 510 ff. See also C. W. Previté-Orton, *Political Satire in English Poetry* (1910), p. 96.

Index